# How to Access the Government's ELECTRONIC BULLETIN BOARDS

# WASHINGTON ONLINE

## How to Access the Government's ELECTRONIC BULLETIN BOARDS

BRUCE MAXWELL
bmaxwell@netcom.com

Congressional Quarterly
*Washington, D.C.*

## For Barbara

Copyright © 1995 Congressional Quarterly Inc.
1414 22nd Street, N.W.
Washington, D.C. 20037

All rights reserved. No part of this publication may be reproduced or transmitted in any form or by any means, electronic or mechanical, including photocopy, recording, or any information storage and retrieval system, without permission in writing from the publisher.

Printed in the United States of America

Cover and book design: Debra Naylor

**Library of Congress Cataloging-in-Publication Data**

Maxwell, Bruce, 1959–
   How to access the government's electronic bulletin boards / by Bruce Maxwell.
     p.   cm.
   Includes index.
   ISBN 1-56802-000-7 (pbk.)
   1. Computer bulletin boards.   2. Information services—United States.   I. Title
QA76.9.B84M39   1994
025.04—dc20                       94-37103
                                            CIP

# SUMMARY CONTENTS

Preface xv
Introduction 1
The Bulletin Boards 17

 Access to Information 19

 Environment 153

 Agriculture 39

 Ethnic Groups and Minorities 187

 Business, Trade, and Economics 51

 Government 191

 Computers 99

 Health and Medicine 209

 Criminal Justice 117

 Jobs and Employment 243

 Education 125

 Science and Technology 265

 Emergency Response and Fire Safety 133

 Transportation 285

 Energy 141

Glossary 309
Index 313

# CONTENTS

*Preface* xv

## Introduction 1

## The Bulletin Boards 17

### Access to Information 19

Gateways to Federal Bulletin Boards 20
*FedWorld* 20

Government Publications 23
*Consular Affairs Bulletin Board (CABB)* 23
*Consumer Information Center (CIC) BBS* 26
*Federal Bulletin Board* 29
*Federal Register Electronic News Delivery (FREND)* 30

Information Policy 31
*Information Infrastructure Task Force Bulletin Board* 31
*NTIA Bulletin Board* 32

Libraries 33
*Automated Library Information Exchange (ALIX)* 33
*IMA BBS* 36
*Library of Congress News Service* 37

### Agriculture 39

*Agricultural Library Forum (ALF)* 40
*Call-ERS/NASS* 44
*Hay Locator Service* 45
*NBCI BBS* 46
*National Biological Impact Assessment Program (NBIAP)* 48
*TEKTRAN (Technology Transfer Automated Retrieval System)* 49

**Business, Trade, and Economics** 51

Business 52

    *Office of Economic Conversion Information* 52
    *PTO Bulletin Board System* 54
    *SBA Online* 55

Economic Data 58

    *Census-BEA Electronic Forum* 58
    *Economic Bulletin Board (EBB)* 61
    *FED FLASH!* 66
    *Federal Reserve Economic Data (F.R.E.D.)* 67
    *KIMBERELY* 68
    *New England Electronic Economic Data Center* 70

Foreign Trade 71

    *Customs Electronic Bulletin Board (CEBB)* 71
    *Eximbank Bulletin Board* 73
    *Export License Information Status Advisor (ELISA)* 74

Government Contracts and Grants 75

    *Criteria Bulletin Board System (CBBS)* 75
    *Defense Communications Agency Acquisition Bulletin Board System (DABBS)* 76
    *ED Board* 77
    *NASA SBIR/STTR Bulletin Board* 78
    *NIH Grant Line* 79
    *On-Line Schedules System (OSS)* 81
    *Science and Technology Information System (STIS)* 82
    *VA Vendor BBS* 84

Specific Businesses and Industries 85

    *Bureau of Mines Bulletin Board Network (BOM-BBN)* 85
    *FCC Public Access Link (PAL)* 87
    *FCC-State Link* 89
    *ITC Chemicals BBS* 90
    *National Marine Fisheries Service—NW Region* 91
    *NCUA BBS* 92
    *Surety BBS* 93

Taxes and Social Security 94

    *Electronic Filing System (EFS) Bulletin Board* 94
    *Information Systems Support BBS* 95

*IRP-BBS   96*
*IRS Statistics of Income Division Bulletin Board   97*
*Magnetic Media Bulletin Board System   98*

## Computers   99

Computer Languages, Standards, and Security   100

*Ada Information Clearinghouse Bulletin Board   100*
*Ada Technical Support Bulletin Board System   102*
*Air Force CALS Test Bed BBS   103*
*Data Distribution System   104*
*NGCR BBS   105*
*NIST Computer Security BBS   106*
*NIST/NCSL Data Management Information Exchange (DMIE)   108*
*NIU-Forum Bulletin Board   109*

Shareware   110

*CNSP/CNAP Bulletin Board   110*
*HSETC BBS   111*
*Judge Advocate General's Information Network (JAGNET)   112*
*MASC Library RBBS-PC   113*
*PPCUG-RDAMIS   115*
*Small Computer Support Center   116*

## Criminal Justice   117

*National Criminal Justice Reference Service (NCJRS)   118*
*NJS BBS   121*
*SEARCH-BBS   122*

## Education   125

*FEDIX and MOLIS   126*
*NIH EDNET   129*
*OERI Bulletin Board System   131*

## Emergency Response and Fire Safety   133

*Building and Fire Research Bulletin Board System (BFRBBS)   134*
*CAMEONet   135*
*Hazardous Materials Information Exchange (HMIX)   136*
*OEPC BBS   138*
*State and Local Emergency Management Data Users Group (SALEMDUG) BBS   139*

**Energy  141**

    *Bibliographic Retrieval System (BRS)  142*
    *Commission Issuance Posting System (CIPS)  144*
    *Energy Information Administration Electronic Publishing System (EPUB)  146*
    *Fossil Energy Telenews  147*
    *Office of Statistics and Information (OSI) BBS  149*
    *Tech Specs Plus BBS  151*

**Environment  153**

General  154

    *Gulfline BBS  154*
    *OAQPS Technology Transfer Network  156*
    *Online Library System (OLS)  160*
    *Pesticide Information Network (PIN)  162*
    *Remote Access Chemical Hazards Electronic Library (RACHEL)  164*
    *Research and Development Electronic Bulletin Board  165*
    *U.S. EPA Region 10 BBS  167*

Hazardous Waste  168

    *Alternative Treatment Technology Information Center (ATTIC)  168*
    *Cleanup Information Bulletin Board (CLU-IN)  170*
    *Cleanup Standards Outreach (CSO) BBS  172*
    *INFOLINK  173*
    *Nuclear Regulatory Commission Decommissioning Rulemaking Bulletin Board  175*

Models  176

    *Applied Modeling Research Branch (AMRB) BBS  176*
    *CEAM BBS  177*
    *National Ecology Research Center (NERC) Bulletin Board System  178*

Water  179

    *Nonpoint Source Program Electronic Bulletin Board  179*
    *Technology Transfer BBS  184*
    *Wastewater Treatment Information Exchange (WTIE)  186*

**Ethnic Groups and Minorities  187**

    *INDIANet  188*
    *Minority Impact BBS  189*

**Government   191**

Ethics, Fraud, and Waste   192
   *Ethics Bulletin Board System   192*
   *Federal Deficit Reduction BBS   193*
   *GAO Watchdog   194*

Operations and Management   195
   *CASUCOM   195*
   *GAO Office of Policy's BBS   196*
   *GSA Electronic Management Information (GEMI) BBS   197*

Policies and Regulations   198
   *ACF BBS   198*
   *OCA BBS Document Exchange   199*

Press Information   200
   *HUD News and Events Bulletin Board   200*
   *PR On-line   201*

Property and Assets   203
   *Client Information Center BBS   203*
   *Federal Real Estate Sales Bulletin Board   204*
   *FMS Inside Line   205*
   *Sales Bulletin Board System   207*

**Health and Medicine   209**

General   210
   *Aeromedical Forum   210*
   *Bureau of Health Professions (BHPr) BBS   211*
   *CDRH Electronic Docket   212*
   *FDA Electronic Bulletin Board   214*
   *FDA Prime Connection   218*
   *Grateful Med BBS   221*
   *NIDR Online   222*
   *NIH Information Center   225*
   *Nutrient Data Bank Bulletin Board   227*
   *OASH BBS   229*
   *Quick Facts BBS   232*

Disabilities   233
   *ABLE INFORM BBS   233*
   *Americans with Disabilities Electronic BBS   237*

*Dial-JAN BBS* 238
*Project Enable* 239
*RSA BBS* 241

**Jobs and Employment 243**

Federal Jobs 244

*Automated Vacancy Announcement Distribution System (AVADS) BBS* 244
*BUPERS Access* 245
*Census Personnel Board* 246
*Detroit Service Center BBS* 247
*DoDIGNET* 248
*Federal Job Opportunity Board* 249
*Federal Jobline* 251
*OPM FedJobs Philly BBS* 253
*OPM Mainstreet* 255
*Washington Area Service Network (WASNET)* 257

Labor Laws and Regulations 258

*Boards of Wage and Service Contract Appeals BBS* 258
*Labor News* 259
*PayPerNet* 263

**Science and Technology 265**

Earth Science 266

*Earth Science Data Directory (ESDD)* 266
*Global Land Information System (GLIS)* 267
*Global Seismology and Geomagnetism On-line Information System* 268
*National Earthquake Information Center (NEIC) BBS* 270
*U.S. Geological Survey Bulletin Board System* 271

Space 272

*EnviroNET* 272
*JPL Info* 273
*NASA Spacelink* 274
*NOAA Environmental Information Services* 276
*NODIS* 278
*Space Environment Laboratory* 279

Technology 280

*Fleet Imaging BBS* 280

*Microcircuit Obsolescence Management (MOM) PC Board   281*
*Telephone Time for Computers   282*
*Telephone Time Service   283*

**Transportation   285**

Aviation   286

*AEE BBS   286*
*Air Transport Division BBS   287*
*Airports BBS   288*
*Aviation Rulemaking Advisory Committee (ARAC) Bulletin Board   290*
*FAA Headquarters BBS   291*
*FAA New England   294*
*FAA Pilot Examiner Section BBS   295*
*FAA Safety Data Exchange   296*
*Flight Standards BBS   297*
*ICAP BBS   299*

Highways   300

*Federal Highway Administration Electronic Bulletin Board System (FEBBS)   300*

Waterways   303

*Marine Data Computer Bulletin Board   303*
*MARlinspike BBS   304*
*Navigation Information Network (NAVINFONET)   305*
*U.S. Coast Guard Navigation Information Service (NIS) Bulletin Board   306*

**Glossary   309**

**Index   313**

# PREFACE

Until a few years ago, if you needed federal government information your options were limited. You could visit your local library, and if the library was large enough you might—or might not—find what you were looking for. Or you could call Washington and hope that after getting transferred eighteen times you might find a person who could send you the information. Or you could try to gain access to a commercial database that might contain what you wanted—for a hefty price.

Today, your options for getting federal government information have vastly expanded with the proliferation of federal government bulletin board systems (BBSs). BBSs operated by federal agencies and departments offer everything from presidential speeches to lists of federal job openings to consumer publications about how to buy a home.

BBSs are electronic libraries that you dial into with a computer and modem. You can browse through the information, read whatever you like, and download anything you need into your own computer.

Best of all is the price for accessing this information: it's free. All you pay for is the phone call—and even that's free if you live within a board's local calling area or if the board has a toll-free number. You also can save on long-distance charges if you have an Internet account, since many of the boards are accessible through the Internet.

*How to Access the Government's Electronic Bulletin Boards* provides detailed descriptions of nearly 200 federal BBSs. It describes how to reach them, how to navigate through them, what they offer, and any quirks you should know about how to use them successfully. I've spent hundreds of hours online examining every board listed in this book, so each description is written from a user's perspective.

A follow-up book, *How to Access the Federal Government on the Internet*, will describe federal government Internet sites, which are proliferating even more rapidly than federal BBSs. Congressional Quarterly Books will publish the Internet book in spring 1995.

Although the Internet's technical complexity intimidates some people, BBSs are easy to use. Most of the BBSs have menus that help you find your way around. Nearly all of them also have online help if you get stuck. Thus you need very little computer knowledge to use a federal BBS successfully. What knowledge you do need about a few technical matters is explained in the introduction. And if you ever run across an unfamiliar technical word, you can turn to the glossary at the back of this book for a quick explanation.

Federal BBSs are changing rapidly. Boards are born or die seemingly overnight, software upgrades alter the appearance and operation of boards, and new files are added and old ones deleted. I've worked hard to make this book as current as possible, but the rapid pace of change makes it inevitable that some of the information will be outdated by the time you read it.

Both Congressional Quarterly Books and I are committed to providing updated editions of this book on a regular basis. If you learn about new boards or significant changes in ones listed here, please send me a message by electronic mail. My e-mail addresses are

Internet: bmaxwell@netcom.com
CompuServe: 72634,3176
FedWorld: Bruce Maxwell

I would like to thank many people for their contributions to this book. To begin with, my thanks go to Mark Leff and, at FedWorld, to Bob Bunge and Carol Wilson. They have compiled lists of federal BBSs that were very helpful in preparing this book. I'd also like to thank all the sysops who patiently answered my questions about their BBSs.

The editors and staff at Congressional Quarterly Books have earned my heartfelt gratitude for all their help and encouragement. At CQ I would especially like to thank Jeanne Ferris, whose graciousness has helped keep me sane during the writing process, and Ann Davies, whose work on the organization and final presentation was excellent.

And saving the most important for last, I'd like to thank my wife, Barbara, whose love has made this book—and so much else in my life—possible.

Bruce Maxwell

# INTRODUCTION

This book provides all the information you need to access bulletin board systems (BBSs) operated by federal agencies and departments. The definition of BBS used here is a broad one. Most of the systems described are traditional BBSs with information you can download and messaging features, but a few are not. They're either databases or dial-up systems that provide a stream of information.

To be included in this book, a board had to meet four requirements. It had to be (1) accessible with a computer and modem; (2) available to the public; (3) accessible at no cost; and (4) operated by the federal government, funded in significant part by the federal government, or a source of large amounts of federal government information.

Certain types of federal government BBSs are not included in this book: (1) those that are closed to the public; (2) those that charge a fee for access; and (3) those that are unusable because they are so unstable.

Careful readers will notice that this book does not list any BBSs operated by federal courts. Dozens of federal circuit and district courts operate BBSs that offer copies of opinions, court calendars, court rules, and other documents. However, all of the federal courts are being forced to start charging steep fees for access to their boards. For that reason they're not listed here. Opinions of the U.S. Supreme Court are available for free on SEARCH-BBS, which is described in the Criminal Justice section of this book.

## THE HARDWARE AND SOFTWARE YOU NEED

To access a BBS, you need two pieces of hardware: a computer and a modem. You also need one piece of software: a communications program.

You can use virtually any kind of computer—an IBM, an IBM compatible, a Macintosh, an Amiga, or whatever—as long as it can connect to a modem. You don't need anything fancy.

A modem is the device that lets two computers exchange data over ordinary telephone lines. There are two major varieties of modems: internal and external. Internal modems go inside your computer, while external ones sit on your desktop.

The other factor that differentiates modems is the speed at which they transfer data. The higher the number, the speedier the modem. Modems transmit characters at about 10 percent of their baud rate. A 2400-baud modem can transmit about 240 characters per second, while a 14,400-baud modem can transmit about 1,440. Obviously, a fast modem can significantly reduce your time online and your long-distance bills.

Today, modems commonly are available at speeds ranging from 2400 to 28,800 baud. Currently, 2400-baud modems cost well under $100, while

28,800-baud models cost about $300. It makes sense to buy the fastest modem you can afford. There are two caveats, however. First, high-speed modems (defined as 9600-baud and above) are slightly less stable than 2400-baud models, leading to more connection problems. And second, most federal BBSs (and other online services) currently support modem speeds only up to 14,400 baud.

The last item you need—a communications program—is the tool that allows your computer to "talk" to another computer. Commercial communications software costs about $100. Many good shareware communications programs also exist. With shareware, you get to try the program before deciding whether to send in your fee. Fees for communications programs generally run between $25 and $50. You can find shareware programs through computer user groups or commercial services such as CompuServe and America Online. In addition, many of the government BBSs listed in this book have copies of shareware communications programs. For the Macintosh, Zterm is the favorite program. For IBM and compatible computers, ProComm is popular. Just don't confuse it with ProComm Plus, its commercial cousin.

To get the full benefit of BBSs, you will find two other pieces of software helpful: a decompression program and a file translation program. Many files on BBSs are compressed. Compression makes them smaller and quicker to download. However, you can't use the file on your computer until you've decompressed it back to its original size.

Compressed files have extensions on their names that indicate what program was used to compress them. Two of the most common extensions are ZIP and EXE. For example, a file named BBSGUIDE.ZIP has been compressed with a program called PKZIP.

Many decompression programs are available, mostly as shareware. For IBM and compatible computers, by far the most popular software is a shareware program called PKUNZIP. For Macintosh computers, the various commercial and shareware versions of StuffIt are popular.

Finally, it's useful to have a file translation program. Text and graphics files on BBSs are created with a wide variety of programs. Frequently, you'll have to translate the files so that you can read them. For example, you may use WordPerfect as your word processor. If you download a file created in WordStar, you must translate the file from WordStar into WordPerfect before you can read it.

Some word processing and graphics programs have built-in translators that allow them to read certain "foreign" files. For information about what your program can do, check your manual. However, if you're going to download many files, you should invest in a translation program. A translation program is especially important for Macintosh users, since nearly all files on government computers are created with DOS programs.

## WHAT TO DO BEFORE YOU CALL

After you hook up your computer and modem and install your communications software, you must do three things before calling a BBS:

1. Set your communications software at 8 data bits, 1 stop bit, and no parity. These are the default settings in most communications programs, and they're also the settings used by most federal government BBSs. Boards that use different settings are noted in this book. You don't need to worry about the technical meaning of these settings.

2. Choose the highest baud rate in your communications software that your modem can support. Check your modem manual for details.

3. Turn off call waiting if it has been installed on the telephone line used by your modem. Otherwise, you'll be disconnected if a call comes in while you're online with a BBS. In most areas, the easiest way to turn off call waiting is to place a prefix before the BBS number you're calling. If you have tone dialing, use the prefix *70. Thus, if you want to call telephone number 123-4567, have your software dial *70123-4567. Doing so will turn off call waiting for the duration of the call and will restore it when you hang up. If you have pulse dialing, use the prefix 1170 instead of *70. Call your local telephone company if you have any questions about turning off call waiting.

A fourth action is optional. If you like, before you call turn on the "capture" or "log" feature in your communications software. If you do, your entire online session will be saved as a text file that you can review later with your word processing software.

## WHAT HAPPENS WHEN YOU CALL A BBS

When the BBS answers, you'll hear an electronic buzz if your modem's speaker is on. If all goes well, you'll get a message that a connection has been made. What happens next varies from board to board, since each one is slightly different. Frequently, though, an opening message will welcome you to the board.

### Warning Messages

You also may get a warning message, which varies from board to board. Here's a mild version from a federal BBS:

> You have accessed a United States government computer. Mischievous use of this system is a violation of federal law and can be punished with

fines or imprisonment (Public Law 99-474). Report suspected violations to the systems manager.

A sterner version warns of fines up to $100,000 and ten years' imprisonment. The warnings can be intimidating. Don't worry about them, though, as long as you plan to use the computer properly. However, if you're a hacker who delights in harming computers, you should take them dead seriously.

If you call a federal BBS that's not listed in this book, you may get an opening message saying the board is not open to the public. All of the boards listed in this book were public when it was written, but some other federal BBSs are not. If the message says the computer is available only to certain people and you aren't one of those people, log off.

### Registering

Next, you'll be asked to register. At a minimum, registering involves providing your name, address, and telephone number. Be sure to use your real name. Some commercial BBSs allow the use of aliases or handles, but nearly all federal BBSs require real names. If you use an alias on a federal BBS, you'll probably lose your privileges on the board.

You'll also be asked to choose a password. You can use the password the next time you log on to avoid going through the registration process again. When choosing a password, make sure it isn't something obvious like your name or city. For added security, some people use passwords that include a combination of letters and numbers.

On many boards, after you provide your name, address, telephone number, and password, you'll get full access. Some boards, however, also ask for some or all of the following information:

- Whether you want graphics. If you're unsure whether your terminal supports graphics, choose "no."

- Whether you want to use color.

- What kind of computer you're using.

- How many characters your monitor can display per line. The usual answer is 80.

- How many lines of text you want displayed before you get a prompt. The usual answer is 24.

- Where you learned about the board.

- What transfer protocol you want to use when downloading files. The board will tell you which protocols it supports. If both the board and your communications software support the Zmodem protocol, choose it. Zmodem is fast and secure and supports downloads of multiple files in one batch. The second-best choose is Ymodem, and the third-best choice is Xmodem.

- Your mother's maiden name. Some boards ask this so that they can confirm your identity if you forget your password.

Once you have registered, many boards present you with the Main Menu. The Main Menu is the heart of each board. Figure 1 is the Main Menu for RBBS-PC, a popular BBS program used by many federal government boards.

Figure 1. Main Menu

| \*>>> | RBBS-PC | MAIN MENU | <<<\* |
|---|---|---|---|
| MAIL | SYSTEM | UTILITIES | ELSEWHERE |
| [E]nter Messages | [A]nswer Questions | [H]elp (or ?) | [D]oors |
| [K]ill Messages | [B]ulletins | [J]oin Conferences | [F]iles |
| [P]ersonal Mail | [C]omment to Sysop | [V]iew Conf. Mail | [G]oodbye |
| [R]ead Messages | [I]nitial Welcome | [X]pert on/off | [Q]uit |
| [S]can Messages | [O]perator Page | | [U]tilities |
| [T]opic of Msgs | [W]ho's on | \* = unavailable | [\*]Library |

Current time: 12:25 PM   Minutes remaining: 70   Security: 5

MAIN: 70 min left
MAIN command <?, A, B, C, D, E, F, G, H, I, J, K, O, P, Q, R, S, T, U, V, W, X> ? f

Federal BBSs use many types of operating software. Although these programs differ somewhat in how they look and operate, they all follow certain conventions. All require you to type a single letter (or rarely a few letters) to select an item from a menu. And all require that after entering any command, you press your Enter (or Return) key. The only exception is boards where you can elect to use Turbokeys. If you choose this option, you just have to type the command.

All BBS software packages used by federal government boards have similar features. For example, on virtually every board you'll find bulletins, files, and messages. In addition, nearly every board requires that you type **g** (for goodbye) to log off. The similarities in features and commands make it easy for you to explore new boards once you've got the general hang of BBSing.

The first time you see a Main Menu, though, the multitude of choices can be daunting. Following are brief explanations of the major areas you can access from the RBBS-PC Main Menu:

**[R]ead Messages**   Allows you to read messages written by other users of the board. As you can see, there are many other message options as well.

**[B]ulletins**   Brief text files that typically explain how to use the BBS, list upcoming conferences and meetings, and provide news updates. You can read bulletins online, and some BBSs allow you to download copies to your computer.

**[C]omment to Sysop**   Allows you to leave a message for the system operator, commonly known as the "sysop."

**[O]perator Page**   Allows you to page the sysop if you have a question while you're online. If the sysop is available, he or she will type a message that will appear on your screen, and the two of you can then type messages back and forth.

**[H]elp**   Provides information about how to use various commands on the board.

**[J]oin Conferences**   Allows you to join conferences, which offer collections of messages on a specific topic. On a few federal BBSs, conferences also have files.

**[D]oors**   A gateway to other programs available on the BBS. On federal boards, doors usually lead to searchable databases.

**[F]iles**   Written materials, graphic images, and computer programs that you can download to your computer.

**[G]oodbye**   Provides a clean break from the BBS and resets the board for the next caller. Choose this option when you want to leave the BBS.

**[U]tilities**   Allow you to change the way the BBS interacts with your computer. For example, if you're getting garbage characters from the BBS, you can go to the Utilities Menu and turn off the board's graphics.

## Other Menus

What happens when you type a letter at the Main Menu prompt? Usually, you get another menu that takes you deeper into the board. In Figure 1, the user typed **f** at the prompt and hit the Enter key. Doing that took him to the File Menu (see Figure 2).

As with the Main Menu, you simply type a letter for the function you want. You can type **d** to download a file, **l** to list the files that are available, **s** to search the files, **h** for help, and so on. In Figure 2, the user has typed **g**, the command for signing off the board.

Figure 2. File Menu

|  | *>>> RBBS-PC FILE MENU <<<* |  |  |
|---|---|---|---|
| TRANSFER | INFORMATION | UTILITIES | ELSEWHERE |
| [D]ownload file | [L]ist files | [H]elp (or ?) | [G]oodbye |
| [P]ersonal dwnld | [N]ew files | [X]pert on/off | [Q]uit |
| [*]pload file | [S]earch files | | |
| | [V]iew archives | * = unavailable | |
| Current time: 12:25 PM | | Minutes remaining: 70 | |

MAIN: 70 min left
FILE command <?, D, G, H, L, N, P, Q, S, V, X>? g

When logging onto a new board, it's usually best to begin by reading the bulletins. They frequently provide basic information about the BBS, how it operates, and what kinds of files it contains. Next, you may want to download the user's manual. Most boards have manuals that provide detailed information about how they operate. If a BBS described in this book has a manual, its file name is listed so that you can find it quickly.

Many boards also have master lists of every file they contain. It's useful to download these lists so you can examine them at your leisure without running up long-distance charges. The master file list usually includes the file name, a few words of description, the file size (so you can estimate how long it will take to download), and the date the file was created (so you can see if it's current).

Exploration is the best way to get to know a BBS. Feel free to browse and try anything that looks interesting. Don't worry about hurting the board. Harming a BBS is virtually impossible (unless you're a sophisticated computer user with a malicious intent). Most boards have advanced features that are too numerous to explain in this book. For example, if you're looking for a specific file or piece of information, many boards have sophisticated search functions that let you search all the files by keywords.

## HOW TO GET HELP

There are many ways to get help using BBSs in general or a specific BBS in particular. General help is always available from members of your local computer user group and from people on commercial services such as CompuServe and America Online. In addition, several excellent books about computer telecommunications are available at your local bookstore or library.

If you'd like to save money, three government boards have user's manuals that are excellent general introductions to BBSs. All three manuals are geared toward specific boards, but they contain lots of generic information as well. You can download them from the following boards:

- The Nonpoint Source Program Electronic Bulletin Board, which is listed in the Environment section of this book (see p. 179). The manual includes a guided tour through a sample BBS session that you can read and then try online. It also describes commands you're likely to see on most BBSs.
- The Technology Transfer BBS, which is listed in the Environment section (p. 184). The manual provides clear, detailed explanations of the major commands found on BBSs.
- The Airports BBS, which is listed in the Transportation section of this book under Aviation (p. 288). The highlight of the manual is a detailed discussion of file transfer protocols, which you use when transferring a file from a BBS to your computer.

For help in using a specific board, download the user's manual (if one is available) and read it through. Most boards also have extensive online help if a question arises while you're connected. On most boards, you can reach online help by typing h or ? at a prompt. When you do so, the board will present information about using the area you're in at the time. Some boards also allow you to page the sysop while you're online if you have a question. However, you should not abuse this privilege. Sysops of federal boards don't have time to answer basic computer questions, so you should page them only if you have a specific question about their board.

## COMMON PROBLEMS AND SOME SOLUTIONS

If you spend much time online, you're bound to experience occasional problems. Connecting to a BBS involves a lot of intricate equipment—two computers, two modems, two sets of communications software, and a telephone line—and glitches can develop anywhere. Human error—most likely by you, although BBS operators also make occasional mistakes—can cause problems too.

If you have a problem, the first thing to do is to check the settings in your communications software. To access most boards, the software should be set at 8 data bits, 1 stop bit, and no parity. Also check that the modem speed set in your software works with your modem. If you have questions, check the manual for your modem.

The following list outlines some of the most common problems you can experience when using a federal BBS and suggests solutions for each one. This list of potential problems is not exhaustive, nor is the list of suggested solutions. If you run into a problem not mentioned here, consult one of the sources of help described earlier in this introduction or your computer manuals.

**The BBS's telephone is always busy when I call.** Busy signals are fairly common on federal BBSs, since many boards have only one or two phone lines. Even boards with many lines are sometimes busy because they're so popular. Try calling back at another time, especially at night or on a weekend.

**The BBS doesn't answer when I call.** Failures to respond usually occur because either the board has ceased operating or it has temporarily crashed. "Temporary" crashes can last from a few minutes to a few weeks, depending on the extent of the problem and how much time the sysop has for repairs. If a board doesn't answer on your first call, try calling back several times over a period of a few weeks. If it still doesn't answer, you can assume it has stopped operating. To confirm this assumption, you can call the voice number listed for the board.

**The BBS answers when I call, but I can't establish a connection.** Make sure your communications software is set properly. Also check the description of the board in this book to see whether any special settings are required.

If you're using a high-speed modem (defined as 9600 baud or greater), your problem could lie there. High-speed modems can be unstable, particularly if there's noise anywhere on the telephone line. Try connecting at a lower speed, such as 2400 baud.

**I can establish a connection to the board, but I get only garbage characters.** "Garbage" can be caused by a number of things. Basically, though, either the board has crashed or the board and your computer aren't communicating properly. If you get garbage, try each of the following solutions in order until you find one that works:

1. From the Main Menu, choose the Utilities Menu (some boards call it the User Settings Menu). Turn off the board's graphics capabilities for your session.

2. Log off the BBS and try calling back at a lower modem speed, such as 2400 baud.

3. Log off and change the terminal setting in your communications software so that you emulate a VT100 terminal (don't worry about what this means technically). Then try calling again.

4. Log off, and in your communications software change your settings to 7 data bits, one stop bit, and even parity. Then try calling back.

5. Try solutions 3 and 4 in combination.

**The board looks different from its description in this book.** You may find variations from the descriptions in this book if the sysop has upgraded the BBS software, changed software packages, or overhauled the board in some other way. Use this book as a general guide to a board, not as a catalog of every feature and file.

**Sometimes in the middle of an online session, my connection suddenly goes dead.** There are two possible causes of this problem. First, most boards have time limits. If you have exceeded your time limit on the board, you will automatically be disconnected. The limits vary widely but typically run about an hour per call.

Second, your modem may have had a momentary technical problem. This happens most commonly with high-speed modems, which can be finicky. It's possible that a little noise got in the telephone line and caused your modem to burp, leading to a dropped connection. Try calling the BBS back.

**I was interrupted during an online session and had to leave for awhile. When I returned to the computer, I found that I had been disconnected from the BBS.** Most boards will automatically disconnect if you don't issue a command for a few minutes. They do this so that people who wander away from their computers won't tie up all the telephone lines.

**I'm stuck in a board and can't get where I want.** Simply press your Enter (or Return) key until you get back to a prompt.

**Something froze in either the BBS or my communications software, and the board will not respond to my commands.** Wait five minutes to see if whatever's stuck manages to unstick itself. If it doesn't, press the key that your communications software uses as a "break" key. This key varies among programs. If you still get no response, follow the procedures in your communications software for disconnecting from the board. If your communications software is frozen, follow any emergency shutdown procedures that may exist for your computer. And if that doesn't work, turn off your computer and your modem, let them rest for a couple of minutes, turn them back on, and try calling the board back. Be aware, though, that if you were saving your online session to a capture file, you'll lose it when you turn off the computer.

**The board contains files similar to what I want but not exactly what I need.** Leave a message on the board for the sysop explaining what you're looking for and asking whether it can be provided. Most sysops will do everything possible to get what you need.

A FEW GUIDELINES FOR SUCCESSFUL BBSING

Your experiences with federal BBSs can be more pleasurable and productive if you follow five simple guidelines:

**Be sure to install an anti-virus program on your computer.** Sysops of most federal BBSs carefully check files for viruses before posting them on their boards. However, it's always possible for a virus to slip through. Both commercial and shareware anti-virus programs are available for every type of computer. Many federal BBSs have copies of the most popular shareware programs available for downloading. If you want to learn more about viruses and anti-virus programs, log into the NIST Computer Security BBS that's described on p. 106.

**Always carefully read the information that scrolls on your screen from a BBS.** This information will answer many of your questions about using the board. Be especially attentive to the bottom line of each page displayed. That's where you'll see the prompt asking what you want to do next. In many cases, this prompt will ask a question and then give you various options.

**Don't abuse a federal BBS.** This guideline seems obvious, but the bad experiences of some federal BBSs make it worth repeating. A few federal boards have experienced so many problems with callers that they've shut down. Other boards now restrict access to their toll-free telephone numbers. For example, one major BBS in the Washington, D.C., area started out widely publicizing its toll-free number. Soon the bill for the toll-free line was running thousands of dollars every month. Too many of the callers were like the two kids from Kansas City who called the BBS to leave messages for each other about what videos they should watch at night. The kids had no interest in the board itself. They used it merely to send messages to each other instead of picking up the telephone and making a local call. All the abuse caused the board to stop publicizing its toll-free number.

**Don't bother sysops with basic computer questions.** Most sysops of federal boards have many other duties besides running the BBS. They simply don't have time to answer basic questions about computers or telecommunications. However, if you have a specific question about a board, most sysops are happy to help.

**Follow the proper logoff procedure when you want to disconnect from a BBS.** On most federal BBSs, logging off simply involves typing **g** at a command prompt. Some boards will ask if you're sure you want to disconnect. Type **y** for "yes." Using the proper procedure disconnects you cleanly and prepares the board for the next caller. If you disconnect by turning off your modem or using your communications software to hang up, you can cause problems for the next caller to the board.

## CONNECTING TO FEDERAL BOARDS THROUGH THE INTERNET

You can access some federal BBSs directly through the Internet. If a BBS described in this book is connected to the Internet, its Internet address is listed.

Many federal BBSs that lack Internet connections can be accessed indirectly through FedWorld's Internet connection. FedWorld (see p. 20) is a gateway to more than 100 federal government BBSs. Once you connect to FedWorld through the Internet, you can then transfer to any BBS on FedWorld's gateway. You can determine whether a BBS is included on FedWorld's gateway by looking for a FedWorld gateway number in the vital stats section of each board's description.

You can access many of the boards that have Internet connections using file transfer protocol (FTP). To log into these sites, type **anonymous** when asked for your name or login, and type your e-mail address when asked for your password.

## HOW TO USE THIS BOOK

The boards in this book have been arranged alphabetically by subject as logically as possible. However, many boards cover multiple subjects. You may find just the information you need in places that you might not think to look. Please be sure to check the index for topics of interest.

Each entry in this book lists the board's name and its mailing address. The address is included because federal government telephone numbers tend to change frequently. With the address, you should be able to track down a federal BBS even if its phone numbers have changed.

The basic connection information for each board is set off in a box. This information varies from board to board, but you will find the following whenever it is applicable:

**Data**  The telephone number to call with your communications software to connect with the board.

**Voice**  The telephone number where you can reach the sysop if you have questions.

**FedWorld gateway**  The board's number on the FedWorld gateway.

**Internet**  The board's Internet address.

**Manual**   The file name of the user's manual.

**File list**   The file name of the master list of all files.

**To access files**   Instructions for reaching the files.

**Time limit**   The board's time limit, either per call or per day.

**Available**   The hours during which the board is available. Boards are available twenty-four hours a day unless noted otherwise.

**Note**   Special instructions for accessing or using the board.

The description of each board provides details about what kinds of information are available and notes particular strengths and weaknesses. Two conventions are followed throughout the descriptions:

- Commands or other text that you must type are shown in **bold type**. You don't need to type the commands in bold type when you enter them on a BBS, however.

- File names appear in UPPERCASE letters.

In addition, one piece of shorthand is used. References made to DOS and Windows computers actually refer to computers that run DOS or Windows operating software.

# THE BULLETIN BOARDS

# ACCESS TO INFORMATION

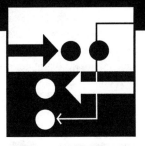

# GATEWAYS TO FEDERAL BULLETIN BOARDS

## FedWorld

National Technical Information Service
5285 Port Royal Rd.
Springfield, VA 22161

FedWorld is a marvel, a shining example of how vast quantities of federal government information can be made available to the public electronically. It offers a gateway to more than 100 other federal BBSs, documents from the White House, lists of federal job openings, images from the Hubble Space Telescope, and a whole lot more. FedWorld is by far the biggest and best federal government BBS—and its operators at the National Technical Information Service (NTIS) constantly work to expand and improve it.

One note for Internet users: if you reach FedWorld using the World Wide Web, you also can access FedWorld's gateway to dozens of federal government Internet sites. This gateway is a great starting point for exploring government resources on the Internet.

FedWorld is too extensive to describe fully. The following outline, however, will give you some of its highlights. You can reach a specific area from the Main Menu by typing the letter shown in bold type:

**VITAL STATS**
Data: 703-321-8020
Voice: 703-487-4608
Internet: ftp
  ftp.fedworld.gov *or* telnet
  fedworld.gov *or*
  http://www.fedworld.gov
Manual: FEDUSER.DOC
  (uncompressed) *or*
  FEDUSER.ZIP
  (compressed)
Time limit: 3 hours per day

**B** A catalog of NTIS products and services, telephone numbers at NTIS, information about joint venture opportunities with NTIS, a catalog of Food and Drug Administration standing orders and manuals, and a catalog of environmental studies and reports.

**D** A gateway to more than 100 federal government BBSs. Once you've typed **d** from the Main Menu to enter the gateway, type **l** to get a list of all the BBSs. To access a BBS, type **d** at the Gateway Menu and at the "Select a system #" prompt, type the number of the system you want. The only problem with the gateway is that a few of the BBSs listed are not open to the public. Most of these private boards are operated by the Defense Department. If you connect to a private board, you will receive a message saying the board is private or you will not be able to register.

**F** Hundreds of files, which are arranged in more than a dozen libraries. Here are highlights from some of the libraries:

- *Main library*   OMB Circular A-130 about federal information policy, a list of members of Congress, and an excellent list of federal government BBSs.
- *CALS*   More than 600 files relating to Computer-aided Acquisitions and Logistic Support.
- *Commerce*   The Department of Commerce telephone book.
- *Jobs*   A list of Office of Personnel Management offices nationwide, information about placement assistance and RIF (reduction in force) benefits for federal employees, information about the Department of Defense Outplacement Referral System, and programs to use with the federal jobs files (which you can access by typing j at the Main Menu).
- *Media*   Press releases from NTIS.
- *Misc*   Images from the Hubble Space Telescope in GIF format, a list of environmental BBSs, and information about governmentwide e-mail.
- *NPR*   The full text of the National Performance Review (a report about how to improve the federal government) and related documents.
- *NTIS*   Information about hundreds of NTIS products.
- *OTA-Pres*   Press releases about reports issued by the Office of Technology Assessment (OTA), along with the full text of the OTA report titled "Making Government Work: Electronic Delivery of Federal Services."
- *Sat-Imgs*   GIF images of North America and various hurricanes.
- *W-House*   Hundreds of documents issued by the White House, including press releases, transcripts of news conferences, speeches by the president and vice president, the president's schedule, and the full text of selected documents. These include the federal budget, the president's health care reform plan, the North American Free Trade Agreement (NAFTA), and the National Information Infrastructure report. Files are available dating back to January 1993.

O   Three sub-boards or databases:

   1. *Patent Licensing System*   This sub-board is designed to help companies learn about inventions developed in federal laboratories that are available for licensing. Journalists and interested citizens also can use the sub-board to help them monitor federal research activities. Inventions are available in ten subject areas: electrotechnology, biology and medicine, chemistry, food technology, instruments, mechanical devices and

equipment, metallurgy, optics and lasers, general, and nuclear technology. The sub-board has a summary of each invention, and full technical details can be ordered from NTIS. A favorite invention title: "Process for manufacture of nonbleeding maraschino cherries."

> 2. *Computer-aided Acquisitions and Logistic Support (CALS)*  This sub-board has bulletins, files, conferences, news, and an e-mail system about CALS and related subjects.

> 3. *National Health Security Act*  This database contains a searchable copy of the president's proposed health care reform bill and related documents.

E  More than a dozen forums for public messages on specific topics. The board has forums on CALS, government conferences, silly government regulations, government studies and reports, government e-mail and directory services, and government newsletters, among other subjects. There also are two forums for questions and comments about FedWorld and its gateways.

J  Lists of federal jobs available in the United States and overseas. The lists are provided by Office of Personnel Management offices nationwide.

P  An electronic mail system that allows users to send private messages to each other.

# GOVERNMENT PUBLICATIONS

## Consular Affairs Bulletin Board (CABB)

Overseas Citizens Services
U.S. Department of State
Room 4800
Washington, DC 20520

If you are planning a trip overseas, the Consular Affairs Bulletin Board (CABB) is the place to check first. It has everything from details about how to get a passport to extensive information about every country in the world. It also has information about adopting foreign-born children. All the files are updated daily.

Much of the material on the BBS also can be found on commercial services such as CompuServe. The advantage of this BBS is that it is free, whereas the commercial services charge a fee.

Information on the BBS is arranged in hundreds of files and searchable databases. Although the board contains lots of information, it is all easy to find because the BBS is well designed and menu driven.

To stop information that's scrolling on your screen, type s. If you get lost in the menu hierarchy and want to return to the Main Menu, type o. And if you want to back up one level to the previous menu, press the Escape key.

The Main Menu presents seven sub-menus, which you can select by typing the appropriate number:

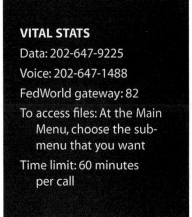

**VITAL STATS**
Data: 202-647-9225
Voice: 202-647-1488
FedWorld gateway: 82
To access files: At the Main Menu, choose the sub-menu that you want
Time limit: 60 minutes per call

1. **Passport information for U.S. citizens**   Files about passport eligibility, how to obtain a passport, passport fees, what to do about lost and stolen passports, and how to obtain a passport quickly.

2. **Emergency services available to U.S. citizens abroad**
   Files provide contact information and explain various emergency services provided by the Citizens Emergency Center. The center helps Americans abroad who die, become destitute, get sick, disappear, have accidents, or get arrested. The center is also the State Department's focal point for major disasters involving Americans abroad, such as plane crashes, hijackings, and natural disasters.

3. **Nonemergency information for U.S. citizens**   Information about acquiring U.S. citizenship, dual nationality, loss of U.S. citizenship, marriages abroad, marriages to foreigners, receipt of federal benefits abroad, Romanian adop-

tions, international adoptions, and international parental child abduction. The sub-menu also contains the text of The Hague Convention on the Civil Aspects of International Child Abduction.

4. **Consular information sheets and public announcements**  Consular information sheets replace the former travel advisories. They are available for every country in the world and list the location of U.S. embassies or consulates in the country, immigration practices, health conditions, minor political disturbances, currency and entry regulations, crime and security information, and drug penalties. Any areas of instability in the country are also listed. Separate travel warnings are posted for countries the State Department recommends American travelers should avoid. You can search the database by any term, but it is usually searched by country name. When you get a hit, enter the article's number to view the full text.

5. **Travel information on specific subjects or regions**  The subject files provide information on travel abroad in general, suggestions about how to have a safe trip, tips for Americans residing abroad, travel tips for older Americans, foreign entry requirements, HIV testing requirements for entry into foreign countries, and medical information for Americans abroad. The region files provide information on traveling to the Caribbean, Central and South America, China, Eastern Europe, Mexico, the Middle East and North Africa, South Asia, Subsaharan Africa, and Russia.

6. **Visa information**  Information for U.S. citizens who wish to travel abroad and for foreigners who wish to visit the United States. You can search the database of foreign entry requirements by country name.

7. **OSAC bulletin board**  A gateway to the Overseas Security Advisory Council Electronic Bulletin Board, which provides information about incidents in foreign countries that could affect travelers. The information is arranged in nine more sub-menus:

   - *Alert messages*  A database of travel alert messages that can be searched by country.

   - *Daily highlights*  A database of news briefs about events that may affect travel safety. The database can be searched by country.

   - *Current security/incident reports*  A database with information about security incidents that may affect travel. It can be searched by country.

   - *Consular information phone numbers*  A database, searchable by country, that lists telephone numbers for U.S. embassies and consulates and local police.

- *Special topics*   Lists of State Department publications and travel information telephone numbers.

- *Group profiles*   A database containing profiles of terrorist groups operating around the world. The database can be searched by the group's name or by region.

- *Anniversary dates*   A database, searchable by country, of anniversaries that may affect the safety of travel. For example, the database lists the anniversary of the Tiananmen Square massacre, which took place in China in 1989.

- *Consular information sheets and public announcements*   The same consular information sheets and travel warnings available through the main CABB BBS.

- *General crime information*   A database of reports about crime in foreign countries. The database is searchable by country.

## Consumer Information Center (CIC) BBS

U.S. General Services Administration
18th and F Sts., N.W.
Room G142
Washington, DC 20405

The Consumer Information Center (CIC) board offers a wealth of consumer information, including electronic copies of dozens of publications prepared by federal agencies and departments. The publications discuss such topics as understanding food additives, buying a house, choosing a nursing home, and using the Freedom of Information Act.

Here are some highlights of what's available:

- Electronic versions of publications available from the Consumer Information Center in Pueblo, Colorado. The Consumer Information Center is making more and more publications available in electronic form. All of the publications are available in both compressed and uncompressed versions. To access them, type **f** at the Main Menu. (The box lists some of the titles available.)

  One publication, the *Consumer's Resource Handbook*, is especially notable. This book describes how to get the most for your money, how to avoid consumer problems, and how to write complaint letters when problems arise. It also lists addresses for government and private agencies that can help you with problems and for consumer affairs representatives at hundreds of major companies. The book is split into two files on the BBS.

- Press releases geared toward newspaper reporters about Consumer Information Center publications.

- An electronic version of the Consumer Information Center's latest catalog.

- Scripts of public service announcements for radio and TV stations about publications listed in the Consumer Information Catalog.

- Various federal documents, including numerous documents related to health reform, the full text of the National Performance Review, a long list of

### VITAL STATS

Data: 202-208-7679
Voice: 202-501-1794
FedWorld gateway: 6
File list: ALLFILES.ZIP
To access files: At the Main Menu, type **f**
Time limit: 60 minutes per day
Note: If you get garbage characters, type **y** at the Main Menu. Then type **6** at the "Setting to change?" prompt and **n** for no color.

### Consumer Information Center Publications

AIDS and the Education of Our Children
The Americans with Disabilities Act: Q & A
Books for Children
Building Your Future with Annuities
Buying Medicine?
Choosing a Contraceptive
Choosing and Using Credit Cards
Chronic Fatigue Syndrome
Condoms and Sexually Transmitted Diseases
Consumer's Resource Handbook
Contact Lenses
Corporate Consumer Contacts
Depression
Diet, Nutrition, and Cancer Prevention
The Fair Credit Reporting Act
The Federal Information Center
Food Additives
Funerals: A Consumer Guide
Gas Mileage Guide
Guide to Choosing a Nursing Home
Guide to Federal Government Sales
Helping Your Child Do Better in School
A Home of Your Own
Homebuyer's Guide to Environmental Hazards
Lesser Known Areas of the National Park System
Lista de Publicaciones Federales en Espanol
Mortgage Money Guide
National Park System Map and Guide
Plain Talk About Wife Abuse
Protect Yourself From Telemarketing Fraud
Q & A about Breast Lumps
The Savings Bonds Q and A Book
Second Hand Smoke
Small Business Handbook
Staying Healthy & Whole: A Consumer Guide
Stress
Stripping Paint From Wood
Thrifty Meals for Two
Tips on Preventing AIDS
Your Right to Federal Records
Your Rights When Purchasing Products by Mail or Phone

pointers from the U.S. Postal Service, and a list of members of Congress with their addresses, telephone numbers, and fax numbers.

- A small collection of utility programs for DOS computers, including the latest version of PKUNZIP, a program for decompressing files, and Mailinfo, a program developed by the U.S. Postal Service.

- More than three dozen games for DOS computers.

- All Consumer Information Center BBS bulletins in one file, two lists of federal government BBSs, and a list of BBSs in the Washington, D.C., area.

The BBS also has a Bulletin Menu. It offers background about the Consumer Information Center and services available to the news media. Bulletins also are available that arrange the Consumer Information Catalog by subject.

The Doors Area, which can be reached by typing **d** at the Main Menu, has a database that allows users to "bank" time. This option helps users get around the time limit of sixty minutes per day. For example, if you want to download a huge file that will take seventy minutes, you can "deposit" ten minutes one day and then "withdraw" the time the day you download the file. The maximum bank "balance" allowed is thirty minutes. The Doors Area also leads to three online games: The Links, Hang Man, and Trivia Master.

## Federal Bulletin Board

Office of Electronic Information Dissemination Services
U.S. Government Printing Office
Washington, DC 20401

The Federal Bulletin Board is a perfect example of how not to set up a government information service. The board has two strikes against it: it is harder to use than most comparable systems, and almost everything on it costs money.

The board has two levels of access. Basic access is free, but you can't do much with it. You can download the few free files, browse in the file libraries, order publications from the Government Printing Office (GPO), and send and receive e-mail messages.

You can access the free files area by typing **a** at the Main Menu. Here are some examples of what's available:

- The text of a few White House documents, including the National Performance Review report, the National Export Strategy report, and the proposed Health Security Act. A much more extensive collection of White House documents can be found on FedWorld (see p. 20).
- A few hearing statements from the Subcommittee on Regulations and Government Information of the Senate Committee on Governmental Affairs.
- Lists of files available for sale.

If you want to purchase files, you must type **32** at the Main Menu and fill out a questionnaire that asks for the number on your credit card or GPO deposit account. The charge per file depends on its size, with the average file costing between $6 and $7. The minimum charge is $2 per file, which covers files of up to 50 kilobytes. Prices rise in dollar increments, with a file of 1 megabyte costing $21. For example, the first volume of the special prosecutor's Iran-contra report costs $30 to download.

Many users will object to paying steep fees for government information collected with their tax dollars, especially when they are printing the information themselves. However, some of the information that costs money here can be found elsewhere for free. For example, the board offers Supreme Court opinions for a fee, but the same opinions are available for free on SEARCH-BBS (p. 122) and on the Internet. An additional problem is that some files are compressed in a self-executing format that makes them unusable on Macintosh computers.

**VITAL STATS**
Data: 202-512-1387
Voice: 202-512-1530
FedWorld gateway: 22
Internet: telnet federal.bbs.gpo.gov 3001
Manual: USER.DOC
Available: 24 hours a day except from 3 a.m. to 5 a.m. EST

## Federal Register Electronic News Delivery (FREND)

Office of the Federal Register
National Archives and Records Administration
Washington, DC 20408

FREND provides limited information about federal laws and regulations. It has Public Law numbers for bills recently signed by the president, lists of documents that will appear in the next day's edition of the *Federal Register*, and tables of contents from recent editions of the *Federal Register*. The board does not provide the full text of federal laws and regulations or of the *Federal Register*. Nearly all information on the board can be read online or downloaded.

FREND's Top Menu has three major areas:

1. **News and announcements**  A schedule of public briefings about how to use the *Federal Register*, a list of senior Clinton administration officials who have been confirmed by Congress, and a list of all volumes of the Code of Federal Regulations available from the Government Printing Office.

2. **Public Law numbers**  Lists of bills passed by Congress and signed by the president that have been assigned Public Law numbers. The lists cover only those laws passed during the current session of Congress, and they do not provide the full text of the laws.

3. **Federal Register finding aids**  A list of documents that will appear in the next day's edition of the *Federal Register*. The lists normally are posted shortly after 8:45 a.m. each day that the *Federal Register* is published and are updated during the afternoon. This area also offers tables of contents from the *Federal Register*. Entries are alphabetized by the name of the agency and then are grouped as rules, proposed rules, and notice documents. The first posting, which occurs about midafternoon of the day before publication, does not include page numbers. A second posting after publication updates the file to include page numbers.

**VITAL STATS**

Data: 202-275-1538 or 202-275-0920

Voice: 202-523-3447

FedWorld gateways: 87 and 88 (they are identical)

Time limit: 60 minutes per call

# INFORMATION POLICY

## Information Infrastructure Task Force Bulletin Board

National Telecommunications and Information Administration
U.S. Department of Commerce
14th and Constitution Ave., N.W.
Room 4092
Washington, D.C. 20230

The Information Infrastructure Task Force Bulletin Board contains information about efforts to develop the National Information Infrastructure (NII). The NII is supposed to become a system of thousands of interconnected computer networks, televisions, fax machines, and telephones that will provide information cheaply and easily.

Several kinds of information are available on the BBS:

- News about upcoming meetings of various groups working on the NII.
- Answers to frequently asked questions about the NII.
- Names and telephone numbers of contacts.
- A fact sheet about the Information Infrastructure Task Force.
- Press releases.
- Minutes and reports from various committees.
- Numerous documents about the NII, including congressional testimony, speeches, and White House papers.
- Selected legislation.
- Information about the U.S. Advisory Council on the NII, including a list of members, press releases, and meeting notices.

**VITAL STATS**
Data: 202-501-1920
Voice: 202-482-1835
FedWorld gateway: 119
Internet: gopher iitf.doc.gov
  *or* telnet iitf.doc.gov
Note: You may need to experiment with the terminal setting in your communications software. A setting of VT100 works well. The login for either a dial-in or telnet connection is **gopher**.

## NTIA Bulletin Board

National Telecommunications and Information Administration
U.S. Department of Commerce
Herbert C. Hoover Building
Room 4090
Washington, DC 20230

**VITAL STATS**
Data: 202-482-1199
Voice: 202-482-6207
FedWorld gateway: 109
Internet: gopher
gopher.ntia.doc.gov *or*
ftp ftp.ntia.doc.gov *or*
telnet ntiabbs.ntia.doc.gov

Two kinds of files can be found on the NTIA Bulletin Board: highly technical documents about telecommunications standards and more general documents on telecommunications policy issues such as development of the National Information Infrastructure (NII). The National Telecommunications and Information Administration (NTIA), which serves as the president's chief adviser on telecommunications policies, is the lead agency in developing the NII.

Callers also can use the board to upload formal comments and testimony in NTIA proceedings.

Here are some highlights from the files:

- The National Information Infrastructure: Agenda for Action, a report about the NII.

- Information about where to send Freedom of Information Act requests pertaining to the NTIA or the Department of Commerce.

- An NTIA telephone directory.

- A list of documents published by the NTIA, along with ordering information.

- Transcripts of hearings, speeches, testimony, and committee meetings about the NII.

- A calendar of upcoming public events involving the NII.

- Press releases.

- An administration white paper on reform of the Communications Act.

- Notices about the availability of grants for NII projects.

# LIBRARIES

## Automated Library Information Exchange (ALIX)

FEDLINK
Library of Congress
Washington, DC 20540-5110

Although the Automated Library Information Exchange (ALIX) is aimed at librarians in federal government agencies, it offers information of interest to other librarians and the public as well. It has an especially strong collection of information about the Internet. The information is arranged into four areas: bulletins, files, conferences, and databases.

You can access the bulletins by typing **b** at the Main Menu. They are divided into two areas: general bulletins and online newsletters. The general bulletins provide a calendar of training classes, list job openings in federal and nonfederal libraries, and list telephone numbers for library and federal job hotlines. The online newsletters include copies of *FEDLINK TechNotes* and *Cataloging Newsline*.

Downloading files from ALIX is a nuisance. To download a file, you must be in the area where the file is located. If you want to download files from different areas, you have to move to each area. The ten file areas contain various types of files:

1. Utility programs for DOS computers to decompress files.

2. Lists of federal government BBSs, law-oriented BBSs, and BBSs in the Washington, D.C., area. This area also has numerous documents about the Internet, including a list of agriculture-related sites on the Internet, a list of Internet gophers, a bibliography of Internet books, and texts of *Special Internet Connections* by Scott Yanoff, the *SURANet Guide to Selected Internet Resources*, *Internet-Accessible Library Catalogs and Databases* by Art St. George, *Surfing the Internet* by Jean Armour Polly, and *Zen and the Art of the Internet*, a classic guide to the network.

3. Shareware and public domain programs to help librarians automate their work.

4. Library-oriented applications of hypertext and hypermedia software, expert systems, and other systems that use artificial intelligence.

5. Library-oriented templates in Lotus 1-2-3 and SuperCalc formats.

**VITAL STATS**

Data: 202-707-4888

Voice: 202-707-4800

FedWorld gateway: 3

Manual: For information about basic commands, type **?** at the Main Menu

To access files: At the Main Menu, type **f**

Time limit: 40 minutes per call

6. Bibliographies on library computer technology and software, directories of library associations, and lists of federal job openings from the U.S. Office of Personnel Management (updated biweekly).

7. Several newsletters including *FEDLINK TechNotes,* the *Library of Congress Cataloging Newsletter, OCLC Bits and Pieces,* and *OCLC Reference News.* The file area also has copies of the Americans with Disabilities Act, the National Performance Review report, and the Office of Management and Budget Circular A-130 on dissemination of government information. It also has information about telecommuting for federal employees and files about preserving photographs and other materials.

8. A limited number of utility programs for DOS computers.

9. Information about library applications of programming, expert systems, and artificial intelligence.

10. Copies of *ALCTS Network News,* a newsletter published by the Association for Library Collections and Technical Services.

ALIX has fourteen conferences where users can exchange messages. Many of the conferences also have useful bulletins. For example, the government information conference has abstracts of recent reports issued by the General Accounting Office. You can access the following conferences by typing c at the Main Menu:

- Archives and records management

- CD-ROM products

- Services to the disabled: access and computer accommodation

- FEDLINK member forum

- Government information

- Help on ALIX

- Libraries and technology

- Managing the library

- Networking and telecommunications

- OCLC news

- Preservation

- Reference desk

- Shareware on ALIX
- Tech services

ALIX also has four databases that can be searched online. To access them, type **u** at the Main Menu:

1. **Calendar database**   A text database that contains information on FLICC/FEDLINK events and training classes.

2. **Directory of federal libraries**   A database that includes the addresses of FEDLINK member libraries.

3. **Electronic mail address registry**   A database where ALIX users can list their electronic mail addresses on other computer systems such as CompuServe and the Internet. The database can be searched by a person's name or the name of an e-mail system.

4. **Internet glossary**   Definitions of terms and abbreviations used on the Internet.

## IMA BBS

Attn: ODISC4—IIAC (Major Fichten)
107 Army
The Pentagon
Washington, DC 20310-0107

The IMA (Information Mission Area) BBS is aimed at people in the U.S. Army and the private sector who work on information management issues. These issues include automation, telecommunications, records management, visual information, publications and printing, and libraries.

The board has electronic copies of numerous Army pamphlets and regulations. Some sample titles are "The Department of the Army Freedom of Information Act Program," "The Army Privacy Program," "The Army Information Resources Management Program," "Military Affiliate Radio System," "Record Communications and the Privacy Communications System," and "Preparing and Managing Correspondence."

**VITAL STATS**
Data: 703-275-6400
Voice: 703-275-6105
FedWorld gateway: 106
Internet: ftp 147.103.26.11
File list: BULLETIN 6
To access files: At the Main Menu, type **f**
Time limit: 90 minutes per call

## Library of Congress News Service

Public Affairs Office
Library of Congress
Room LM105
Washington, DC 20540-8610

The Library of Congress News Service offers information about Library of Congress (LC) programs, publications, hours of operation, and job opportunities. The BBS does not provide access to the library's computerized card catalogs.

On this board the files are called bulletins. To access them, type **b** at the Main Menu. This takes you to the Bulletin Menu, where the bulletins are divided into two dozen categories. You can read the bulletins online, but if you want to download them you have to return to the Main Menu. Before doing so, note the file names of any bulletins you want to download.

To download a bulletin, type **f** at the Main Menu and then type **d** for download. At the prompt, type **B** and the name of the bulletin you want. For example, to download Bulletin A152, you would type **BA152**.

You can also access many of the bulletins from the File Menu. The newer bulletins, however, are available only through the Bulletin Menu.

Here are some highlights of what's available:

- Guides to information about science fair projects, unidentified flying objects (UFOs), weather and climate data, career opportunities in science and technology, medical waste, women in the sciences, breast cancer, and other subjects.

- Press releases.

- Information about how to access Library of Congress resources through the Internet.

- Information of particular interest to librarians, such as news about new cataloging products, changes in LC cataloging procedures, major personnel appointments, and professional meetings.

- News about exhibit openings.

- A calendar of events such as lectures, readings, films, and concerts.

> **VITAL STATS**
> Data: 202-707-3854
> Voice: 202-707-9217
> Time limit: 45 minutes per call

- Lists of job openings at the Library of Congress.
- Lists of LC publications and other products.
- A list of hours of operation of the various reading rooms, telephone numbers, and addresses.
- Information about services to people with disabilities.
- Basic information about copyright.

# AGRICULTURE

## Agricultural Library Forum (ALF)

National Agricultural Library
U.S. Department of Agriculture
10301 Baltimore Blvd.
Beltsville, MD 20705-2351

Although the primary focus of the Agricultural Library Forum (ALF) is agriculture, this BBS contains information on a wide range of other subjects as well. It has information about the Internet, lists of reports published by the General Accounting Office, and bibliographies on nutrition.

ALF's greatest strength is its bibliographies on subjects as diverse as alternative agriculture, catfish farming, diet and cancer, food irradiation, and crime in rural America. The bibliographies are compiled from AGRICOLA, a fee-based database. Many can be downloaded from ALF, while others can be ordered for free from the National Agricultural Library (NAL).

The time limit on ALF is seventy-five minutes per day per password. If you need more time, go to the Main Menu and type **u** before your seventy-five minutes are up. This takes you to the Utilities Menu, where you should type **p**. Change your password, and ALF will give you another seventy-five minutes. You can change your password a maximum of three times each day, meaning the effective time limit on ALF is five hours per day.

ALF has three major areas:

**Bulletins**   ALF's bulletins describe the NAL, explain how to download files from ALF, list agriculture-related BBSs around the country, list upcoming agricultural events, and describe how to use compressed files. They also list telephone numbers for NAL contacts, state colleges of agriculture, U.S. Department of Agriculture (USDA) field libraries, and contacts at land grant colleges. In addition, they describe and list contacts for NAL's Information Centers on agricultural trade and marketing, alternative farming, animal welfare, aquaculture, biotechnology, food and nutrition, global change, plant genome data, rural information, technology transfer, water quality, and youth development. The bulletins cannot be downloaded, but you can capture them by using your communications software's capture feature.

---

**VITAL STATS**

Data: 301-504-6510
Voice: 301-504-5113
FedWorld gateway: 2
Manual: ALFGUIDE.TXT
To access files: At the Main Menu, type **f**
Time limit: 75 minutes daily per password, up to 5 hours daily with 4 passwords

**Conferences**   ALF has fourteen public conferences on various subjects, including the AGRICOLA database, animal welfare, biotechnology, rural development and health, and water quality. Each conference has bulletins that you can capture to disk by using the capture feature in your communications software.

**Files**   ALF has hundreds of files, including newsletters, other publications, software, and the full text of bibliographies prepared by the NAL.

Two documents are particularly valuable for new users:

- ALFGUIDE.TXT   This user's guide is extremely helpful, especially for people who expect to spend lots of time on ALF.
- NALQBLST.TXT   This file lists all the bibliographies produced by the NAL. Many can be downloaded from ALF, and others can be ordered for free from the NAL.

ALF has more than a dozen file areas. To get a list of files in an area, type the letters that appear in caps:

**AFS (Alternative Farming Systems)**   A list of publications produced by the Alternative Farming Systems Information Center, a list of periodicals about alternative farming, a calendar of upcoming events related to sustainable agriculture, and a list of educational and training opportunities in sustainable agriculture. The file area also contains numerous issues of a newsletter called *Small-Scale Ag Today.*

**AGRICOLA database**   Documents about the fee-based AGRICOLA database. The file area, however, does not provide access to the database itself. It has a keyword index to NAL publications, information about searching AGRICOLA, a list of all journals indexed in AGRICOLA, AGRICOLA training schedules, and utilities for using CD-ROM versions of AGRICOLA.

**AGRITOPics**   Background information, extensive bibliographies, and contact lists on a wide range of subjects, including the North American Free Trade Agreement (NAFTA), production and marketing of cut flowers, greenhouses, business overseas, organic farming, gardening books, and cheese and yogurt making at home.

**Information ALERTS**   Information about activities and publications of the NAL.

**ANIMAL welfare**   A list of publications available from the Animal Welfare Information Center, newsletters from the center, bibliographies on animal welfare issues, descriptions of animal welfare legislation before Congress, contacts for information on animal welfare, and a list of databases that contain biomedical, veterinary, and animal science information.

**Bulletin BOARDS**  Lists of environmental and technology BBSs, BBSs with Internet access, and BBSs in the Washington, D.C., area.

**COMPUTER stuff**  Communications and decompression software. This shareware works only with IBM and compatible computers.

**DCRC Reference Center files**  Keyword indexes to USDA Agriculture Handbooks and Agricultural Information Bulletins, along with user's guides to various CD-ROM versions of the AGRICOLA fee-based database.

**FAS**  Extensive information on foreign markets, trade policy, and outlooks. The file area includes newsletters from the Agricultural Trade and Marketing Information Center and food market reports for fifty-five countries. The reports discuss the market overview, U.S. position in the market, competition, trends, opportunities, distribution systems, and domestic food processing. They are written by U.S. agricultural attachés posted in the countries. The file area also provides dozens of files on agricultural markets and prices in Mexico.

**GENERAL Reference**  A little bit of everything, including lists of hundreds of NAL bibliographies and other publications, many of which can be downloaded from ALF or obtained free from NAL. There are also keyword indexes to NAL publications, USDA Agricultural Handbooks, and Agriculture Information Bulletins; descriptions of the NAL's Information Centers; lists of publications available from the Agricultural Trade and Marketing Information Center, the Aquaculture Information Center, and the Alternative Farming Systems Information Center; newsletters of the Agricultural Trade and Marketing Information Center and the Plant Genome Research Program; a guide to NAL services; a calendar of events related to aquaculture; a calendar of agriculture-related meetings and events; a list of agriculture-related resources on the Internet and BITNET; issues of the *Agricultural History Newsletter;* a list of General Accounting Office (GAO) reports and testimony on all topics; and a list of GAO reports and testimony on agriculture-related topics.

**NETWORKs**  Information on networks such as the Internet and BITNET. This area includes a list of agriculture resources on the Internet, a list of other resources available on the Internet, an index to Internet Requests for Comments, and a list of library-oriented computer conferences and electronic serials on BITNET and the Internet.

**FNICPUBS** Bibliographies of books and articles about diet and cancer, diet and dental health, nutrition and people with disabilities, nutrition and the elderly, nutrition and cardiovascular disease, nutrition and diabetes, nutrition and behavior, nutrition and adolescent pregnancy, sports nutrition, vegetarian nutrition, anorexia nervosa and bulimia, food allergies, and weight control. It also includes a bibliography of children's books on food and nutrition and a calendar of food and nutrition meetings.

**OLE** Lists of network resources for education and colleges that offer fully accredited degrees through correspondence study.

**QBSERIES** Extensive bibliographies on more than fifty topics, including economic aspects of alternative farming, public perceptions of biotechnology, biological control of weeds, medicinal plants, catfish farming, biofuels, breeding for cold tolerance in plants, crime in rural America, ethical and moral issues relating to animals, biotechnology legislation and regulation, transport and handling of livestock, women in agriculture, instructional materials on agricultural education, wildflowers, air pollution effects on crops and forests, agricultural and farmer cooperatives, and rural entrepreneurship and small business development. The bibliographies list books, reports, audiovisual materials, and articles from journals, newspapers, and newsletters. The listings are derived from online searches of the fee-based AGRICOLA database.

**RURAL** Information about the Rural Information Center, a list of rural development contacts by state, calendars of rural events, a list of Rural Health Research Center activities, rural health news and announcements, a list of rural development resources in the NAL, and a newsletter for rural and small libraries.

**SEEDS** A list of protected plants, information about seed import laws, and lists of noxious weed seeds by state.

**SPECIAL reference briefs** Annotated bibliographies on a wide range of subjects, including growing and using herbs, sustainable agriculture, exercise for dogs, animal euthanasia, aging, the meat industry, substance abuse, and food irradiation.

**WATER** Bibliographies from AGRICOLA about drinking water standards for various contaminants, wetland construction to treat livestock wastes, water quality and forestry, and streambank protection.

## Call-ERS / NASS

Economic Research Service
U.S. Department of Agriculture
1301 New York Ave., N.W.
Washington, DC 20005-4788

Call-ERS/NASS, which is operated by the Economic Research Service (ERS) and the National Agricultural Statistics Service (NASS), offers a wealth of statistics and other information about agricultural economics and rural America. Here are some highlights of what's available:

- Descriptions and ordering information for new paper reports from ERS on such topics as U.S. agricultural exports and economic indicators of the farm sector.

- Summaries of the most recent ERS Situation and Outlook reports about farm credit, U.S. agriculture in general, agriculture in the former Soviet Union, exports, vegetables, livestock and poultry, tobacco, feeds, and other subjects. Most files contain text and charts. Many also list contact names and telephone numbers to call for further information.

- Samples of data files available from ERS. Each sample is a compressed file that includes the complete README file from the original data product and one or more Lotus 1-2-3.WK1 files. The README contains a list of files distributed with the complete data product and the name, address, and telephone number of a contact person with detailed knowledge of the data. Sample files are "East European Agriculture," "Vegetable Outlook," "Food Consumption," and "Rural Public Water Systems."

- Catalogs of ERS data products, monographs, magazines and periodicals, and video tapes.

- Outdated reports from the National Agricultural Statistics Service on crop prices, agricultural production, and related topics. Current reports can be accessed for a fee.

### VITAL STATS

Data: 800-821-6229 or 202-219-0377 or 202-219-0378 (toll-free number available only Monday through Friday from 7:30 a.m. to 4:30 p.m. EST)

Voice: 202-219-0304

FedWorld gateway: 113 and 114 (they are the same)

Manual: At the Main Menu, type **u**

To access files: At the Main Menu, type the letter for the file area you want

Time limit: 30 minutes

## Hay Locator Service

Department of Agronomy
Purdue University
LILY
West Lafayette, IN 47907-1150

Farmers can use the Hay Locator Service to learn about hay and straw for sale or to advertise their own hay and straw crops. Most of the listings are for hay and straw in Indiana, but there also are listings for crops nationwide. You can search the listings, enter a new listing, or delete old listings.

When you start a search, the board takes you through a series of questions to narrow your request. It asks whether you want:

- Buyers, sellers, or both.

- Hay, straw, or both.

- Listings nationwide, in Indiana, in a specific Indiana county, or in a state other than Indiana

And, finally, it asks what type of bale or package type is desired.

The listings of crops available for sale generally include the type of crop, when it was cut, where it is located, how it is baled, the quantity available, the chemical analysis, whether it is stored inside, whether it suffered any rain damage, and the name, address, and telephone number of the seller.

**VITAL STATS**
Data: 317-494-6643
Voice: 317-494-8233

## NBCI BBS

National Biological Control Institute
U.S. Department of Agriculture, APHIS, OA
Federal Building, Room 350
6506 Belcrest Rd.
Hyattsville, MD 20782

You will find information about sustainable agriculture, biological control of pests and weeds, and integrated pest management on the National Biological Control Institute (NBCI) BBS. The board is intended primarily for researchers.

Most of the information on the board is duplicated. You can read a file online by choosing a particular category from the Main Menu, or you can download the file by typing **d** at the Main Menu and then choosing a category from the Library System Menu.

Here are examples of what's available:

**VITAL STATS**

Data: 800-344-6224 or 301-436-7487
Voice: 301-436-4329
FedWorld gateway: 129
Time limit: 30 minutes per call

- A calendar of events relating to biological control, entomology, integrated pest management, sustainable and organic agriculture, plant pathology, weed science, nematology, and invertebrate pathology.

- Lists of jobs in biology, primarily at universities.

- Newsletters about biological control. Titles available include *Alternative Agriculture News, Association of Applied Insect Ecologists News, ExSel Newsletter, Natural Enemy News, The Ladybeetle Flyer, Southeastern Biological Control Working Group, Tachinid Times, Association of Natural Bio-control Producers Newsletter, Biocontrol Flash, International Bioherbicide Group News, Plant Protection News, STING: Newsletter on Biological Control in Greenhouses, The Entomophagus* (Mexico), and *Pesticides Coordinator Report*.

- Minutes from professional meetings of the Coordinating Committee for Russian Wheat Aphid Biology and other groups.

- Summaries of newspaper articles about biological control.

- Detailed information about training and grant opportunities.

- Information about databases, hotlines, and other BBSs about sustainable agriculture.
- Results of surveys by various organizations.
- Forums on the sweet potato whitefly, Russian wheat aphid, and Aphis BC operations.

## National Biological Impact Assessment Program (NBIAP)

Virginia Polytechnic Institute and State University
120 Engel Hall
Blacksburg, VA 24061

The National Biological Impact Assessment Program (NBIAP) BBS, which is operated by Virginia Tech under a grant from the U.S. Department of Agriculture, offers news, files, searchable databases, and messages about agricultural and environmental biotechnology.

To access the files, type **f** at the Main Menu. This area offers the biotechnology policy of the federal Office of Science and Technology Policy, the Environmental Protection Agency's policy on microbial products, and the Food and Drug Administration's policy on foods derived from new plant varieties.

In addition, files list free publications on biotechnology, articles from industry publications, reports from the U.S. Department of Agriculture, databases and BBSs about biotechnology, biotechnology directories, newsletters about agricultural biotechnology, videocassettes and slide sets on biotechnology, and meetings, symposia, and workshops.

To access the databases, type **open** at the Main Menu. The databases contain listings of biotechnology companies, state biotechnology centers, state regulators and state laws, international biotechnology researchers, current literature titles, and institutional biosafety committees. You can search each database by a range of variables. For example, you can search the database of biotechnology companies by state, company name, or industry code.

Macintosh users may have trouble accessing the databases, which are designed for access by DOS computers. Mac users will need to experiment with their telecommunications programs to see what works. A terminal setting of VT100 is one option that should be tried.

The BBS has a monthly news report that you can read online or download. To download the report, type **d** at the Main Menu, and then type **news.rpt** as the file name.

Although users can access the BBS with the toll-free number for only thirty minutes per day, more time can be arranged on the toll line. Users who want more time should call the sysop.

**VITAL STATS**

Data: 703-231-3858 (toll-free number available upon registering)

Voice: 703-231-3747

Internet: gopher ftp.nbiap.vt.edu *or* telnet nbiap.biochem.vt.edu *or* ftp ftp.nbiap.vt.edu

Time limit: 30 minutes per day

# TEKTRAN (Technology Transfer Automated Retrieval System)

Agricultural Research Service
Office of Technology Transfer
U.S. Department of Agriculture
Building 005, BARC-West, Room 415
Beltsville, MD 20705

The TEKTRAN database contains more than 12,000 summaries of research results obtained by scientists at the Agricultural Research Service (ARS). The research covers such topics as genetic engineering, safeguarding crops and animals from disease, biological control of pests, and human nutrition. The database also contains information about more than 1,000 ARS inventions that are available for licensing.

Entries typically include a brief summary of the research, a technical abstract, and the name, address, and telephone number of the ARS scientist who conducted the research. You can search the database by a number of variables, including keyword, multiple keywords, scientist's name, commodity, and date.

To access TEKTRAN, you must call the TEKTRAN office. The staff will send you an ID, password, modem number, and user's manual.

TEKTRAN is designed to be accessible with VSterm and Crosstalk, two communications programs for IBM and compatible computers. It may not be accessible with some other programs, especially those designed for Macintosh computers. If you cannot access the database, call the TEKTRAN office and ask the staff to run a search. They will send you a printout with the results.

**VITAL STATS**

Data: Number must be obtained from TEKTRAN office

Voice: 301-504-5345

Manual: Call TEKTRAN office to obtain.

# BUSINESS, TRADE, AND ECONOMICS

# BUSINESS

## Office of Economic Conversion Information

Economic Development Administration
U.S. Department of Commerce
Room 7231
Washington, DC 20230

The Office of Economic Conversion Information BBS has tons of information for people, businesses, and communities affected by the closing of military bases and defense conversion. The BBS is a joint project of the U.S. Department of Commerce and the U.S. Department of Defense.

Here are some examples of the information that's available:

- A list of the most recent military base closures.

- Extensive bibliographies of government reports, books, and newspaper and magazine articles about base closings and defense conversion.

- An annotated list of private voluntary organizations that are active on defense conversion issues.

- Press releases about federal defense conversion initiatives.

- Speeches by President Clinton on defense conversion.

- Employment statistics by major industry for each state.

- Information about federal conversion assistance programs for military and civilian employees, businesses, and communities.

- The text of the Defense Base Closure and Realignment Act of 1990.

- The text of the National Historic Preservation Act, the Resource Conservation and Recovery Act, the Clean Air Act, Superfund legislation, the McKinney Act, the Clean Water Act, the National Environmental Policy Act, and the Endangered Species Act.

- Guidelines for the disposal of surplus government property.

- Policies for fast-track cleanup of closed and realigned bases.

- A list of contacts for each of the closed or realigned bases.

- Lists of contacts in various federal offices.

**VITAL STATS**

Data: 800-352-2949 or
202-377-2848
Voice: 800-345-1222
FedWorld gateway: 130
Internet: gopher
cher.eda.doc.gov

- Case studies of defense conversion in selected cities.
- The text of the "Governor's Guide to Economic Conversion."
- Information about technology centers in various states.

## PTO Bulletin Board System

Patent and Trademark Office
U.S. Department of Commerce
OEIPS CP2, Room 9D30
Washington, DC 20231

The PTO Bulletin Board System contains extensive information about patents and trademarks, though it does not include registration documents for patents and trademarks. You can reach the board's areas from the Main Menu by typing the letters that appear in bold type:

N  News releases, bulletins about how to use the BBS, and reports about patent trends, patent counts by state and country, and the ten companies that received the most patents in various years. All of the files can be read online or downloaded.

S  Information about how to use the Patent and Trademark Office's public search room as well as booklets about patent information on CD-ROM, other electronic products produced by the PTO, and publications about patents.

D  A list of Patent and Trademark Depository Libraries around the country.

P  A list of expired patents (the list is almost 2 megabytes).

F  Electronic copies of the *Official Gazette of the United States Patent and Trademark Office*; a list of all patents issued during the week, which includes the names of inventors and abstracts describing the inventions; hearing transcripts; and three manuals. The manuals are the *Manual of Patent Examining Procedure*, the *Trademark Manual of Examining Procedure*, and the *Goods and Services Manual*.

### VITAL STATS

Data: 703-305-9157

Voice: 703-305-9000

FedWorld gateway: 116

Manual: USER.ASC (ASCII text) or USER.WP5 (WordPerfect)

Time limit: 1 hour per call, 4 hours per day

Note: If you get garbage characters when you log in, type **a** at the first available prompt to bring up the Change User Profile Menu. Select **a** to turn off the ANSI codes and **g** to turn off the IBM graphics.

## SBA Online

Small Business Administration
409 Third St., S.W.
Washington, DC 20416

The primary focus of SBA Online is helping people to start and run small businesses. It has lots of business-related information and computer programs for small businesses.

The Small Business Administration has made things a little complicated by granting different levels of access depending on what number you use to call the board. The box lists the three options.

> ### SBA Telephone Options
>
> **202-401-9600**  Provides full access to the board. You can download any files, use the gateway to about three dozen other federal government BBSs, send e-mail to other users, and send and receive e-mail through the board's Internet gateway.
>
> **900-463-4636**  Also provides full access; however, the first minute costs thirty cents and each additional minute is ten cents. For example, a thirty-minute call costs $3.20.
>
> **800-697-4636**  Toll-free but provides somewhat limited access. You can download all SBA files and send e-mail to the sysop. You cannot exchange e-mail with other users, access the gateway to other federal BBSs, download software, or use the Internet e-mail gateway.

**VITAL STATS**

Data: 800-697-4636 (limited access), 202-401-9600 (full access), 900-463-4636 (full access for a fee)

Voice: 202-205-6400

FedWorld gateway: 40 (full access)

Internet: telnet sbaonline.sba.gov *or* gopher www.sbaonline.sba.gov

File list: SBAFILES.TXT

To access files: At the Main Menu, type **f**

Time limit: 90 minutes per call

Available: 24 hours a day except from 6:30 a.m. to 8:30 a.m. EST

The Main Menu presents nine numbered choices, most of which lead to sub-menus. Here are highlights for each choice:

1. **General information**  Information about the SBA, employment opportunities at the SBA, employment opportunities at other federal agencies, and federal job programs.

2. **Services available**  Information about services available from the SBA and articles from the *Small Business Advocate* newsletter.

3. **Local information**  Lists of local SBA offices, SBA Disaster Area Offices, Small Business Development Centers, and offices of the Service Corps of Retired Executives (SCORE). In addition, this area includes extensive overviews of the small business situation in individual states, including economic projections.

4. **Outside resources**  Numerous resources including the following:

    - A gateway to about three dozen other BBSs operated by federal agencies and departments.

    - A gateway that allows you to send and receive messages through the Internet.

    - Information from the Census Bureau, including business statistics, telephone numbers for key contacts at the Census Bureau, and articles from the *Census and You* newsletter.

    - A list of members of Congress by state with their addresses, telephone numbers, and fax numbers.

    - Limited information about Internal Revenue Service programs that help small businesses.

    - A list of state chambers of commerce with contact names, addresses, telephone numbers, and fax numbers.

    - Information about patents from the U.S. Patent and Trademark Office.

5. **Quick search menu**  Allows searching of information in the other Main Menu areas by dozens of keywords.

6. **White House information**  Various documents from the White House, including the National Information Infrastructure report and the National Performance Review report.

7. **Talk to your government**  A list of more than 150 federal government BBSs and an area where users can offer suggestions about how the federal government can improve services to citizens.

8. **SBA Online access changes**  Information about the various ways to access SBA Online.

9. **New items**  Duplicates of items found in the other areas.

SBA Online also has a Files Area that can be reached by typing f at the Main Menu. The files, which offer everything from White House documents to business-related shareware programs for DOS and Windows computers, are separated into more than two dozen directories. All callers can access the first eighteen directories, but those using the toll-free number cannot access directories 19–29, which contain the shareware (see box).

> **File Categories in SBA Online**
> 1. Women
> 2. International trade
> 3. Veterans
> 4. General business development files
> 5. Business initiatives, education, and training
> 6. Service Corps of Retired Executives (SCORE)
> 7. Government contracting
> 8. Minority small business
> 9. Small business innovation research
> 10. Surety guarantee
> 11. Small business investment
> 12. Financial assistance
> 13. Disaster assistance
> 14. Legislation and regulations
> 15. Small Business Development Center files
> 16. Miscellaneous files
> 17. White House files
> 18. Health Security Act files
> 19. Off-line mail readers and help
> 20. Files for starting up a business
> 21. Files for managing a business
> 22. Files for financing a business
> 23. Files for marketing your business
> 24. Files that help run your business
> 25. Miscellaneous file uploads
> 26. New files
> 27. List of all SBA Online files
> 28. Access to SBA Online information
> 29. Internet information files

# ECONOMIC DATA

## Census-BEA Electronic Forum

Bureau of the Census
Data Users Services Division
State and Regional Program Staff
U.S. Department of Commerce
Washington, DC 20233

The Census-BEA Electronic Forum is one of the best federal government BBSs. It contains a wealth of statistical information on the nation's people and economy. The BBS has information on income, poverty rates, population growth, the impact of AIDS on population loss, marriage and divorce rates, state-to-state migration, immigration, tax rates, living conditions, occupational shifts, commuting times, business trends, government revenue, and school financing, among other data.

The board's name is somewhat misleading, since the Bureau of Economic Analysis (BEA) files are not available to the public. The files can be accessed only by members of the BEA users group, which includes people at state universities, state government agencies, and similar institutions. The BEA files, which provide regional economic statistics, are available to the public on the fee-based Economic Bulletin Board (see p. 61).

Nonetheless, the Census files are extremely valuable. After logging on, you will be asked to join a special interest group (SIG). You have to join a SIG before you can access the files. SIG titles are Open Forum, 1990 Census, TIGER (Topologically Integrated Geographic Encoding Reference), Census Economic, CD-ROM, Agriculture Census, Population Estimates and Projections, Industry, Survey of Income and Program Participation, and 1992 Economic Census. At some point, the board plans to add a SIG on the 2000 census. If you just want to download files, it does not matter which SIG you join because they all access the same files. But if you want to exchange messages with other users or ask questions of Census Bureau employees, make sure you join the relevant SIG.

Once you are in the SIG, select option f to go to the Files Transfer Menu. Here are highlights of what's available:

**VITAL STATS**

Data: 301-763-7554

Voice: 301-763-1384 (Census)

Voice: 202-606-5360 (BEA)

FedWorld gateway: 64

Internet: telnet cenbbs.census.gov *or* ftp ftp.census.gov

Manual: Several files available on the Tutorial Menu

To access files: Join any special interest group (SIG), then type **f**

Time limit: 60 minutes per call

- Press releases about recent Census Bureau reports. These press releases are invaluable in learning about paper reports that may be of interest.
- Files for each state that list the urban and rural population, school enrollment, educational attainment, disabled population, use of English in the home, and ancestry for the state, its five largest cities, and its five largest counties.
- Information about machine-readable data.
- Help in using CD-ROMs produced by the Census Bureau.
- Shareware programs for communicating with the BBS and decompressing files. The programs are for DOS computers only.
- An exchange rate table comparing rates since 1980, a monthly analysis of U.S. foreign trade, and reports on imports and exports.
- Descriptions of electronic products available from the Census Bureau.
- Summaries of county business pattern reports for all fifty states, along with information on ordering paper copies of the full reports.
- Extensive information from the 1987 Census of Agriculture by state. County-level reports are available upon request.
- Miscellaneous information, including the text of President Bill Clinton's economic plan, tips about upcoming Census Bureau reports and activities, a list of government BBSs, and telephone contacts at the Census Bureau, the Bureau of Economic Analysis, the Bureau of Labor Statistics, the Office of Business Analysis, and the Office of the Under Secretary for Economic Affairs.
- State rankings in population, schools, educational attainment, civilian labor force, nonfarm employment, poverty status, farms, and other areas. The numbers are taken from the *Statistical Abstract of the United States*.
- State profiles taken from the *Statistical Abstract of the United States*. The files contain statistics on population, housing units, low-weight births, hospital beds and physicians per 100,000 population, average teacher salaries, educational attainment, federal defense spending, Social Security recipients, civilian labor force, disposable income, number of persons below the poverty level, average value of farmland, number of hazardous waste sites, and motor vehicle deaths, among other subjects.
- Reports on a wide range of industries, including aerospace, aluminum ingot and mill products, apparel, civil aircraft and aircraft engines, carpets and

rugs, computers and office and accounting machines, fabrics, fats and oils, fertilizer, flour milling, footwear, glass, industrial air pollution control equipment, inorganic chemicals, major household appliances, steel mills, titanium dioxide, and truck trailers. The reports typically include detailed data on inventories, unfilled orders, quantity and value of shipments, production, exports, imports, and consumption.

- National population projections for 2001, 2011, 2021, 2031, and 2041; state age, sex, and race data for 1980 and 1990; county population data for 1980 and 1990; and estimates of current state populations.

## Economic Bulletin Board (EBB)

Economics and Statistics Administration
Office of Business Analysis
U.S. Department of Commerce
Washington, DC 20230

The Economic Bulletin Board (EBB) is a one-stop source of current economic information. It contains statistical data, trade leads, and press releases from the Bureau of the Census, Bureau of Economic Analysis, Bureau of Labor Statistics, Bureau of Export Administration, Federal Reserve Board, Department of the Treasury, Office of the U.S. Trade Representative, Economics and Statistics Administration, International Trade Administration, Department of Energy, and the Foreign Agricultural Service, among others.

Technically speaking, the EBB is not a free BBS. Some parts of it can be accessed without charge, however, and the cost of using the rest is quite low. If you have an Internet account, you can access all the EBB's files for free on a gopher operated by the University of Michigan library. The address is gopher gopher.lib.umich.edu and the path to the files is

> Social Sciences Resources/Economics/Economic Bulletin Board

To explore EBB before subscribing, type **guest** when the board asks for your user ID. Guests can download bulletins, send but not receive messages, examine sample files, and access some information for exporters. Guests cannot access the files area. Guests are limited to twenty minutes per call, but they can call back immediately once their time has expired.

Subscribers have full access to all files. Subscriptions cost $45 annually, but they come with $20 worth of connect time. At 300 to 2400 baud, connect time costs between $3 and $12 per hour, depending on what time of day you call. At 9600 baud or through the Internet, connect time costs between $6 and $24 per hour. Flat-rate annual subscriptions are also available. One hour of access daily costs $250 annually, and four hours of access daily costs $400 annually. You can subscribe by calling the voice number or by downloading and filling out a registration form.

The EBB is menu driven, a setup that makes it extremely

### VITAL STATS

Data: 202-482-3870 (300-2400 bps); 202-482-2584 (9600 bps)

Voice: 202-482-1986

FedWorld gateway: 13

Internet: telnet ebb.stat-usa.gov

Manual: EBB QUICKSTART MANUAL (in Bulletin area I)

File list: LIST OF ALL EBB FILES (in Bulletin area I)

To access files: Most files available only to subscribers

Time limit: 60 minutes per call (subscriber); 20 minutes per call (guest)

easy to use. For example, to enter one of the areas, you just type the first letter of the area name at the prompt.

So what can you get for free as a guest? Here are some of the most valuable resources, by area:

## Bulletins

- A description of the EBB and information about how to subscribe.
- The Quickstart Manual, an excellent user's guide.
- A list of all files on the board and their location.
- A description of the types of files available by agency.
- A good list of federal government BBSs, though some of the telephone numbers are outdated.

## Files

After you reach the Files Menu, type **d** to see a list of files available to guests.

- Lists of telephone contacts at the Bureau of Economic Analysis, Bureau of Labor Statistics, Bureau of the Census, Office of the Under Secretary for Economic Affairs, and the Office of Business Analysis.
- Schedules of document release dates for the Bureau of Economic Analysis and the Office of Management and Budget.

## News

- A list of reports to be issued during the upcoming week by the Commerce Department.
- News items about the board's operation.

## Trade Promotion

- A list of resources for U.S. exporters.
- A calendar of upcoming trade promotion events.
- An explanation of where for go for export assistance.
- A list of U.S. and Foreign Commercial Service district offices.
- A list of key officers at U.S. embassies.
- A description of U.S. and Foreign Commercial Service export assistance programs.
- A state-by-state list of export resources.

Here are examples of files available to subscribers in the EBB's twenty file areas:

**Area 1, Statements by officials and summaries of current economic conditions**   The full text of President Clinton's economic plan, statements by the Federal Reserve Board chairman and the Bureau of Labor Statistics deputy commissioner, and numerous economic reports on gross national product, single-family home sales, durable goods orders, housing starts, and personal income.

**Area 2, National income and product account data from the Bureau of Economic Analysis**   Press releases with the latest gross domestic product data, the gross national product by industry, and data on national income.

**Area 3, Economic indicators**   Foreign direct investment data, weekly economic indicators, business conditions indicators, construction data, and current press releases from the Bureau of Economic Analysis, the Bureau of the Census, and the Bureau of Labor Statistics.

**Area 4, Employment statistics**   A wide range of employment and unemployment statistics.

**Area 5, Price and productivity statistics**   Consumer price index, producer price index, and the export-import price index.

**Area 6, Foreign trade data**   Exchange rates, U.S. foreign trade updates, merchandise trade data, data on U.S. direct investment abroad, data on foreign spending in the U.S. to acquire or establish businesses, and import and export trade data by product.

**Area 7, Industry statistics**   Highlights from the industrial outlook, industrial production and capacity utilization data from the Federal Reserve Board, and retail shipments data.

**Area 8, Fiscal and monetary policy data**   Daily Treasury statements, data on state and local government bond rates, and reports from the Federal Reserve Board on bank credit, consumer credit, foreign exchange rates, and selected interest rates.

**Area 9, Special studies and reports**   Reports on the business situation from the Bureau of Business Analysis, the economic and budget outlook from the Congressional Budget Office, and financial ratios for various industries from the Office of Business Analysis.

**Area 10, U.S. Department of Treasury auction results**   Results of Treasury bill, bond, and note auctions.

**Area 11, Regional economic statistics and press releases** Population projections for metropolitan areas and economic areas, state economic and population projections to 2000, gross state products, state per capita personal income, state personal income and earnings, state income and wages, state wages by industry, and personal income by county.

**Area 12, Energy statistics from the Energy Information Administration** Production, consumption, and net imports of energy by source, crude oil and petroleum products overview, natural gas supply and disposition, crude oil price summary, U.S. energy supply and demand summary, and international and U.S. petroleum supply and demand.

**Area 13, Daily trade opportunities from the U.S. and Foreign Commercial Service** Trade Opportunity Program (TOP) files are posted on the EBB every workday at 3 p.m. The files contain leads reported by overseas posts of the U.S. and Foreign Commercial Service.

**Area 14, Current business statistics** Data on general business indicators, commodity prices, construction and real estate, domestic trade, labor force and earnings, finance, and foreign trade of the U.S. This area also includes files on numerous specific industries, such as textile products and transportation equipment.

**Area 15, Press releases and reports from the Office of the U.S. Trade Representative** Press releases on trade negotiations and agreements, the North American Free Trade Agreement, nominations to trade posts, and foreign trade barriers.

**Area 16, International Marketing Insight (IMI) reports from the U.S. and Foreign Commercial Service** Discussions of important developments in particular countries that have implications for U.S. traders and investors. These reports, prepared by U.S. embassies and consulates abroad, cover a wide range of subjects, such as new laws, procedures, and trade regulations; changing marketplace dynamics; recent statements by influential people; and emerging trade opportunities. They also include travel profiles for many countries.

**Area 17, Miscellaneous files** Information from the Office of Foreign Assets Control of the U.S. Treasury Department about embargoes, economic sanctions, and executive orders affecting Cuba, Haiti, Iran, Iraq, Libya, North Korea, and Vietnam. The files also list telephone contacts at the Bureau of Economic Analysis, Bureau of Labor Statistics, Bureau of the Census, Office of the Under Secretary for Economic Affairs, and Office of Business Analysis (these telephone directories are also available in the File Area's free section).

**Area 18, Former Soviet Union and Eastern European trade leads** Information about trade opportunities provided by the U.S. Department of Commerce, Business Information Service for the Newly Independent States (BISNIS).

**Area 19, USDA agricultural leads** U.S. Department of Agriculture files, posted most days at 3 p.m. They list agricultural trade opportunities in foreign countries.

**Area 20, Defense Conversion Subcommittee information for Russia and the newly independent states** Information about defense conversion in Russia and the newly independent states.

## FED FLASH!

Federal Reserve Bank of Dallas
Research Department
2200 N. Pearl St.
Dallas, TX 75201

FED FLASH! makes available economic and banking data for the southwestern United States and the entire country. The BBS covers the Federal Reserve System's Eleventh District, which includes Texas and parts of Louisiana and New Mexico.

The files are separated into more than two dozen directories. Here are some of the most interesting:

**FEDPUB**   Electronic copies of publications produced by the Federal Reserve Bank of Dallas.

**AGSVY**   Results of the agricultural survey conducted by the Federal Reserve Bank of Dallas.

**REGION**   Regional economic indicators.

**SALES**   Retail sales figures for Dallas, Houston, Texas, Louisiana, and the United States.

**CONST**   Various kinds of construction data for Texas, Louisiana, and New Mexico.

**AGLAND**   Values of agricultural land in the Eleventh District.

**ENERGY**   Oil drilling statistics for Texas, Louisiana, and New Mexico.

**HHUNEMP**   Unemployment rates for Dallas, Fort Worth, the three states served by the Federal Reserve Bank of Dallas, and the United States.

**BANKFIN**   A wide range of financial data for Eleventh District banks, including assets, financial ratios, income and expenses, liabilities and capital, and nonperforming assets.

---

**VITAL STATS**
Data: 214-922-5199
Voice: 214-922-5178
File list: MASTER
To access files: At the Main Menu, type **f**

## Federal Reserve Economic Data (F.R.E.D.)

Research and Public Information Department
Federal Reserve Bank of St. Louis
P.O. Box 442
St. Louis, MO 63166

F.R.E.D., operated by the Federal Reserve Bank of St. Louis, has hundreds of files of economic and financial data. It specializes in regional economic data for Arkansas, Illinois, Indiana, Kentucky, Mississippi, Missouri, and Tennessee, although it also has current and historical national data as well.

The files are divided into more than two dozen directories. To get a directory list, type **f** at the Main Menu. To get a list of files in a directory, type the number of the directory at the prompt.

Much of the economic information on the board is historical. The first ten file directories offer only historical numbers, many dating from decades ago. For example, you can get figures for the consumer price index from 1913 to the present, savings deposits at commercial banks from 1959, prime rate changes from 1929, federal government debt from 1953, the gross national product from 1946, and civilian employment from 1948.

Here are some of the most interesting files in other directories:

12. **International data**   Historical numbers for foreign countries, such as the German consumer price index since 1957, the French gross domestic product from 1970, and the exchange rate of the dollar with numerous foreign currencies.

13. **Regional business indicators**   Historical employment and unemployment numbers for states served by the Federal Reserve Bank of St. Louis.

25. **Employment and population**   U.S. employment and population data for the most recent twelve months.

26. **International data**   International economic data for specific countries covering the past one or two years.

27. **Regional business indicators**   Monthly indicators for the states served by the Federal Reserve Bank of St. Louis.

> **VITAL STATS**
> Data: 314-621-1824
> Voice: 314-444-8562
> Manual: NEWUSER
> File list: FILESEXE.EXE (self-extracting) or FILESZIP.ZIP
> To access files: At the Main Menu, type **f**
> Time limit: 1 hour daily

# KIMBERELY

Public Affairs Department
Federal Reserve Bank of Minneapolis
250 Marquette Ave.
Minneapolis, MN 55401-2171

KIMBERELY offers tons of regional and national economic data in addition to information about the Federal Reserve System. The Federal Reserve Bank of Minneapolis, which operates KIMBERELY, serves the Ninth Federal Reserve District. The Ninth District includes Minnesota, Montana, North Dakota, South Dakota, the upper peninsula of Michigan, and twenty-six counties in northwestern Wisconsin.

Information on the board is presented in hundreds of files. To download a list of all the files, type f at the Main Menu, type k at the File Menu, and then select a transfer protocol from among those listed.

Here are some highlights of what's available:

> **VITAL STATS**
> Data: 612-340-2489
> Voice: 612-340-2443
> File list: KIM.TXT
> To access files: At the Main Menu, type **f**

- National economic data regarding the gross national product, unemployment, disposable personal income, retail sales, housing starts, inventories, consumer prices, producer prices, the money supply, and other economic factors. There is also a list of dates indicating when economic data will be released.

- District economic indicators such as money market rates, mortgage loan delinquency rates, home sales and prices, cash farm receipts, savings rates, crop prices, livestock prices, dairy and poultry prices, annual cash farm receipts, and other economic data for the Ninth District.

- Economic forecasts for the Ninth District and the United States, issued quarterly.

- Directories of district banks by state (in Lotus 1-2-3 format).

- Ninth District bank ratings under the Community Reinvestment Act.

- Press releases about the economy of the upper Midwest, bank performance, and other issues.

- Background information about the Federal Reserve Bank of Minneapolis, a list of directors and advisory council members, and information about touring the building.

- Background information about the Federal Reserve System, a guide to Federal Reserve regulations, addresses and phone numbers for the twelve Fed district banks, and a history of the Federal Reserve.

- Glossaries of terms related to financial regulators and institutions, monetary policy, foreign banking, consumer credit, and securities credit.

- Polls of business and community leaders published in the *FedGazette*, a quarterly regional business and economics newspaper. The polls report opinions on the regional economy, new banking regulations, the quality of schools, health care, and other issues.

- Articles from the *FedGazette*. Some sample titles are "When a 'Company Town' Loses Its Company, No Magic Formula for Recovery," "From the Ashes of Economic Crises, Jackson, MN, Builds Economic Diversity," "District States Struggle with Budgets," and "Banking 2000: More Technology and Fewer Banks."

- Information about agricultural credit conditions, reported quarterly. The file contains data going back four years.

- Abstracts of research reports prepared by Ninth District staff.

- Lists of various publications and audiovisual materials that can be ordered.

- The text of recent speeches by top Federal Reserve System officials.

- Biographies of governors of the Federal Reserve System, presidents of Federal Reserve banks, and senior officials at the Federal Reserve Bank of Minneapolis.

- Materials and programs for teachers of grades K-12.

- Facts about U.S. coins and paper money and detailed information about counterfeit detection.

- Information about consumer credit protection and publications from the Federal Reserve about consumer finance.

## New England Electronic Economic Data Center

Department of Economics
University of Maine
Orono, ME 04469

The New England Electronic Economic Data Center provides information about the New England economy. The BBS is sponsored by the University of Maine, the Federal Reserve Bank of Boston, the U.S. Bureau of Economic Analysis, and the National Trade Data Bank.

To save aggravation, access this resource with the BBS number rather than through the Internet. The FTP site has a nonstandard interface that is difficult to use.

The bulletins, which you can access by typing **b** at the Main Menu, provide general information about how to use the BBS and tips on using specific features.

The BBS also offers a door that leads to a CD-ROM containing economic data for states, counties, and metropolitan areas from the Bureau of Economic Analysis. To access the door, type **d** at the Main Menu.

The files offer a variety of economic information. All of the data files are compatible with Lotus 1-2-3 and Quattro. Here are some examples of what's available:

- Economic indicators from the Federal Reserve Bank of Boston.

- Gross state product data from the Bureau of Economic Analysis.

- Data on employment, retail sales, personal income, corporate income tax collections, construction, and housing.

- Aggregate financial statements for commercial banks and savings banks in Connecticut, Massachusetts, Maine, New Hampshire, Rhode Island, and Vermont.

- Gross state product data for regions nationwide from the Bureau of Economic Analysis.

- Shareware communications programs for DOS computers.

**VITAL STATS**

Data: 207-581-1867 (2400 baud) or 207-581-1860 (9600 baud)
Voice: 207-581-1863
Internet: ftp neeedc.umesbs.maine.edu
File list: ALL.LST
To access files: At the Main Menu, type **f**

# FOREIGN TRADE

## Customs Electronic Bulletin Board (CEBB)

U.S. Customs Service
Office of Information Management
1301 Constitution Ave., N.W.
Washington, DC 22209

The Customs Electronic Bulletin Board (CEBB) features vast amounts of information for importers and others interested in global trade issues. It also provides currency conversion rates for fifty countries. The conversion rates are updated daily. Here are examples of the information available:

- A glossary of abbreviations and acronyms used by the Customs Service.
- *Federal Register* notices.
- News about the North American Free Trade Agreement (NAFTA).
- A notice prohibiting the importation of specific merchandise from the People's Republic of China made by convict, forced, or indentured labor.
- Information about the availability of Customs rulings on computer disks.
- Notices about increased duties on a wide range of foreign goods, including beer from Ontario.
- A notice about counterfeit visas on textile shipments from China.
- News about the awarding or withdrawal of most-favored-nation trading status.
- A list of Customs Service representatives at American embassies around the world, with addresses, telephone numbers, and fax numbers.
- A list of Customs Service regional and district offices, with addresses and telephone numbers.
- A telephone list for headquarters and regional Customs Service staff.

The files are divided into twenty directories, which are listed below. To get a list of the files in a particular directory, type the directory's number at the Files

**VITAL STATS**
Data: 703-440-6155
Voice: 703-440-6236
FedWorld gateway: 47
File list: See discussion
To access files: At the Main Menu, type **f**
Time limit: 75 minutes per day
Available: 24 hours a day except Monday from 6 a.m. to 9 a.m. EST

Menu prompt. To get a list of all files in the first sixteen directories, download the file called FILEINFO.DAT. But be forewarned that it takes thirty-six minutes to download this file at 2400 baud. The file also does not list what is available in the last four directories.

1. Excerpts/Global Trade Talk
2. News releases
3. From the commissioner
4. Federal records and notices
5. Proposed or final rulings
6. Trade meeting schedules
7. Quota threshold status
8. Currency conversion rates
9. Customs directives
10. Trade operations instructions
11. ADD/CVD instructions
12. Customs extra
13. Customs valuation encyclopedia
14. ADD/CVD archive data
15. Currency archive data
16. Quota archive data
17. NAFTA information
18. Canadian customs information
19. Mexican customs information
20. Intellectual property rights

# Eximbank Bulletin Board

Marketing Division
Export-Import Bank of the United States
811 Vermont Ave., N.W.
Washington, DC 20571

The Export-Import Bank (Eximbank) is an independent federal agency that helps finance exports of U.S. goods and services. Its BBS is designed for exporters, bankers, government officials, and others involved in exporting. It has no files of interest to general users.

An opening message says the BBS is a subscription board. That message is incorrect. The BBS is public, and there are no fees for using it.

Information on the BBS is separated into bulletins and files. The board has more than three dozen bulletins. You can access them by typing **b** at the Main Menu. The bulletins describe the Eximbank and its services, list key telephone numbers and Eximbank seminars, and explain Eximbank programs.

The files are separated into more than a dozen directories:

1. Eximbank press releases
2. Bank referral list (available by state)
3. Country information guide
4. Business development group fact sheet
5. Selected program descriptions
6. Working capital guarantee program
7. Eximbank seminar schedule
8. Eximbank summary of board minutes
9. Master guarantee and funding agreement
10. Project financing
11. Credit guarantee facilities
12. Procedures for economic impact analysis
13. Russia
14. Reinventing Eximbank: The results

**VITAL STATS**

Data: 202-565-3835
Voice: 202-565-3906
FedWorld gateway: 24
To access files: At the Main Menu, type **f**
Time limit: 30 minutes per call

## Export License Information Status Advisor (ELISA)

Defense Technology Security Administration
U.S. Department of Defense
400 Army Navy Drive, Suite 300
Arlington, VA 22202

Exporters can use ELISA to check the status of their export license applications at the Department of Defense. General users cannot use the license system, since an export license application number is required.

The only information of use to general users is Bulletin 6, which describes export assistance available from the Department of Commerce's Trade Information Center.

**VITAL STATS**

Data: 703-604-5902

Voice: 703-604-5176

FedWorld gateway: 14

Available: 24 hours a day except weekdays from 7 a.m. to 8 a.m. EST

# GOVERNMENT CONTRACTS AND GRANTS

## Criteria Bulletin Board System (CBBS)

Sacramento District
U.S. Army Corps of Engineers
CESPK-EB-A
1325 J St.
Sacramento, CA 95814-2922

The Criteria Bulletin Board System (CBBS) contains design criteria and technical specifications used by the Sacramento District of the U.S. Army Corps of Engineers, which serves California, Nevada, Utah, and part of Colorado.

The files are primarily of interest to contractors. They explain the specifications required for constructing both military installations and civil works projects.

If you are interested in using the board, call the voice number to receive login instructions.

**VITAL STATS**

Data: 916-556-7997

Voice: 916-557-7670

Internet: telnet 130.165.2.1

Note: Call the voice number for login instructions.

## Defense Communications Agency Acquisition Bulletin Board System (DABBS)

Defense Commercial Communications Office Communications Center
2300 East Dr.
Scott AFB, IL 62225-5406

The purpose of the Defense Communications Agency Acquisition Bulletin Board System (DABBS) is to solicit bids from telecommunication companies for services to various Defense Department agencies. The board includes full requests for proposals (RFPs).
   There are no files of interest to general users.

### VITAL STATS
Data: 618-256-9200
Voice: 618-256-9380
Manual: BULL93.BBS
To access files: At the Main Menu, type **f**

# ED Board

U.S. Department of Education
400 Maryland Ave., S.W.
ROB Room 3616
Washington, DC 20202-4726

ED Board provides information about grants and contracts available from the Department of Education. The board also has a database of announced grant programs.

You can search the database for grant information by announcement date, current availability, or sponsoring program office. To access the database, type **g** at the Main Menu and **3** at the Grant Information sub-menu.

The following files are among the board's highlights:

**Guide to U.S. Department of Education Programs**
Information about the purpose and eligibility requirements of every grant program. The guide also lists the name and telephone number of the office responsible for each program.

**Combined Application Notice (CAN)**   Information about certain Department of Education grant programs, including the purpose of the program, eligibility requirements, applicable regulations, selection criteria, program priorities, projected number of awards, and program contact names and telephone numbers.

**Doing Business with the Department of Education**
General information about the contract process.

**ED's Bidder List**   Information about the contract bidders list and an application to sign up.

**RFP Information**   A list of current contracting opportunities at the Department of Education. Callers can ask for an RFP (request for proposal) package through the BBS.

---

**VITAL STATS**

Data: 202-260-9950

Voice: 202-708-6775

FedWorld gateway: 110

Manual: To read or download the manual, type **b** at the Main Menu

To access files: At the Main Menu, type **c** for contracts or **g** for grants

## NASA SBIR/STTR Bulletin Board

National Aeronautics and Space Administration
Mail Code CR
Washington, DC 20546

The SBIR/STTR Bulletin Board provides information for businesses that want to participate in NASA's Small Business Innovation Research or Small Business Technology Transfer programs. It contains annual solicitations, award lists, procurement information, contact information, and news about both programs. The board does not contain general information about NASA or space flights.

The BBS is divided into three sections: the Main Board, the Small Business Innovation Research Conference, and the Small Business Technology Transfer Conference. You can join a conference by typing j at the Main Menu. Each section has its own bulletins, files, and e-mail functions:

**Main Board**  This section contains information about how the BBS operates. The bulletins describe the board and provide help in using it. The files include two manuals and decompression programs for both DOS and Macintosh computers.

**Small Business Innovation Research Conference**  Under the SBIR program, NASA provides competitive research contracts to businesses with fewer than 500 employees. NASA's SBIR program is aimed at developing technologies in more than a dozen areas, including aeronautical propulsion and power, materials and structures, teleoperators and robotics, instrumentation and sensors, spacecraft systems and subsystems, and human habitability and biology in space. Bulletin 1 in the SBIR conference provides a short description of the program.

**Small Business Technology Transfer Conference**  The SBTT program encourages the transfer of technology to commercial markets by teaming small businesses and research institutions. Teams that develop research proposals can receive research contracts. Bulletin 1 in the SBTT conference provides a short description of the program.

### VITAL STATS

Data: 800-547-1811 or 202-488-2939

Voice: Telephone support is not provided; you may leave questions on the board.

FedWorld gateway: 36

Internet: ftp coney.gsfc.nasa.gov

Manuals: QUIKSTRT.TXT (short version) and MANUAL.TXT (long version)

# NIH Grant Line

John C. James, Moderator
National Institutes of Health
Westwood Building, Room 109
Bethesda, MD 20892

If you are looking for a grant to support biomedical research, NIH Grant Line from the National Institutes of Health is the place to check. Files on this BBS announce the availability of grants from various agencies of the Public Health Service. The BBS also has monthly listings of new grants awarded.

There are three ways to access this BBS:

1. **Through FedWorld**  You must switch to a half-duplex communications setting when you move from FedWorld. If your communications program does not have a half-duplex setting, turn on local echo instead. You will get a message telling you when to make the change. If you do not change the setting, what you type will be invisible on the screen.

2. **Through the dial-up connection**  This access requires special settings in your communications software of even parity, 7 data bits, 1 stop bit, and half duplex. If your communications program does not have a half-duplex setting, turn on local echo instead. In addition, you will need to experiment with your terminal setting to see what works. A VT100 setting seems to work well. After you connect, type **,gen1** (the comma is essential) and press the Enter key. You will not be prompted to do this. Next, you will get a prompt asking for initials. Type **bb5** and press Enter. Finally, a prompt will ask for your account. Type **ccs2** and press Enter.

3. **Through the Internet**  After you connect, type **,gen1** (the comma is essential). At the "Initials?" prompt, type **bb5** and then type **ccs2** at the "Account?" prompt.

Getting a file list requires a few steps. First, type **f** at the Main Menu. At the first prompt, type **d** to get a list of file directories. At the next prompt, type either the name of the directory you would like listed or **all** to get a list of all files on the board.

**VITAL STATS**

Data: 301-402-2221

Voice: 301-594-7270

FedWorld gateway: 70 (you must switch to a half-duplex communications setting when you move from FedWorld)

Internet: telnet wylbur.cu.nih.gov

To access files: At the Main Menu, type **f**

Note: Dial-in callers require special communications settings: even parity, 7 data bits, 1 stop bit, and half duplex (or local echo)

Most of the files contain information about research opportunities available through the Public Health Service. Much of this information is derived from the *NIH Guide for Grants and Contracts,* a weekly print publication. Monthly and quarterly indexes to the guide are available on the BBS. The files area also contains an edited version of the NIH telephone directory.

All users, including those who access the BBS through FedWorld or the dial-up connection, can download files to their NUnet, BITNET, or Internet e-mail addresses. The sysop reports that downloading to an e-mail address is faster than downloading through a modem. To download a file to an e-mail address, after selecting the file to be downloaded choose Option 2 ("Transmitted to a NUnet, BITNET, or Internet userid") and then type in your e-mail address.

## On-Line Schedules System (OSS)

Information Resources Management Services
U.S. General Services Administration
18th and F Sts., N.W.
Washington, DC 20405

The On-Line Schedules System is designed for federal government buyers and contract specialists who wish to purchase computers or telecommunications equipment. It has information from vendors who are authorized to participate in the General Services Administration (GSA) Multiple Award Schedule Program.

The BBS has information about 150,000 products, electronic copies of more than 400 contracts, and GSA price lists. You can search the product information by manufacturer's part number, contract number, product category, and other parameters.

The bulletins, which you can access by typing **b** at the Main Menu, describe new features of the BBS and provide brief news items about government procurement.

You can access the user's manual by typing **4** at the Main Menu. This takes you to another menu, where you have the choice of reading the manual online or downloading it to your computer. However, the version of the manual for downloading has been compressed in a self-executing format that is unusable by Macintosh computers. Mac users can read the manual online and save the session by using their communications software's capture feature.

The board also has the following:

**VITAL STATS**
Data: 202-501-7254
Voice: 202-501-0002
FedWorld gateway: 23
Internet: telnet oss.gsa.gov 2020
Manual: At the Main Menu, type **4**

- Information about changes in federal acquisitions regulations, as published in the *Federal Register*. To access these files, type **2** at the Main Menu.

- An extensive list of companies and people barred from selling goods to the federal government. The list includes the company name, its address, the names of the people involved, and a code about why the company is excluded from federal procurement programs. To access the list, type **3** at the Main Menu.

- Numerous files for vendors.

## Science and Technology Information System (STIS)

DAS/IRM
National Science Foundation
4201 Wilson Blvd.
Arlington, VA 22230

The Science and Technology Information System (STIS) offers access to more than 40,000 documents, including the *National Science Foundation Bulletin*, the *NSF Guide to Programs*, program announcements, press releases, statistical reports from the NSF's Division of Science Resources Studies, the NSF telephone book, reports of the National Science Board, NSF job vacancy announcements, and descriptions of research projects funded by the NSF.

The BBS does not provide general information about scientific topics. Instead, it focuses on how the NSF supports scientific research. You will find information about how to apply for grants and descriptions of research funded by NSF but no information about the results of the research. The box lists some sample document titles.

Finding documents is a bit cumbersome because this system is really designed for access through the Internet. If you have Internet access, use it instead of calling direct.

If you do call direct, once you reach the Main Menu you may want to start by choosing Option 4, "Download STIS Manual." The manual provides excellent help in using this complex board.

Next, you may want to choose Option 5, "Download Index to Files for FTP." The index is arranged by Internet FTP directory. Don't worry about that—just note the names of any documents that interest you.

After you have compiled a list of those names, at the Main Menu, select Option 1, "Search/Browse Documents (TOPIC)." This will take you into the board's full-text search and retrieval system. Choose to do a word search, and type in the name of the document you want. TOPIC will find the document and allow you to read it onscreen, download it, or send it to your e-mail address. With TOPIC, you also can ignore the index and simply search for documents by keywords.

If you expect to use this system much, you should download several documents:

### VITAL STATS

Data: 703-306-0212
Voice: 202-357-7555
FedWorld gateway: 61
Internet: telnet stis.nsf.gov
  or gopher stis.nsf.gov
  or ftp stis.nsf.gov
Manual: NSF9410 (or call the NSF Information Center at 703-306-1234 to request a printed copy of NSF 94-10)

Note: After connecting, you must press the Enter key. Type **public** at the login prompt. If you are accessing by direct dial, your communications software must be set to emulate a VT100 terminal.

> **Selected National Science Foundation Documents**
>
> America's Academic Future
> Antarctic Research Program Guide
> Arctic Science, Engineering, and Education
> Beyond National Standards and Goals: Excellence in Math and Science Education, K-16
> Career Opportunities in Science and Technology
> Federal Funds for Research and Development
> Funding Opportunities for Astronomers
> Human Resource Development for Minorities in Science and Engineering
> In the National Interest: The Federal Government and Research-Intensive Universities
> The National Science Foundation Global Change Research Program
> NSF Blue Ribbon Panel on High Performance Computing
> The NSF in the Decade of the Brain
> Research Experiences for Undergraduates
> Research on Digital Libraries
> Research Priorities in Networking and Communications
> Women Continue to Earn Increasing Percentage of Science and Engineering Baccalaureates

- NSF9410, the STIS User's Guide (if you have not already downloaded this as Option 4).

- ACCESFAQ, which provides answers to frequently asked questions about accessing STIS and its files.

- DWNLDFAQ, which offers lots of information about downloading files, especially through the Internet.

- STISDIRM, which explains how to get summaries of new documents, full documents, or press releases automatically delivered to you by e-mail.

## VA Vendor BBS

IRM Planning, Acquisitions, and Security Service (711)
U.S. Department of Veterans Affairs
810 Vermont Ave., N.W., Room 744
Washington, DC 20420

The VA Vendor BBS contains extensive information for firms that wish to sell goods or services—anything from pencils to X-ray machines—to the Department of Veterans Affairs (VA).

The board has the following information:

- Special announcements from the VA.

- VA telephone directories.

- Procurement regulations.

- VA advertisements from *Commerce Business Daily*.

- Requests for proposals, comments, and quotes.

- Various VA reference publications, including the Five-Year Information and Resources Management program plan and the Forecast of Nationwide Contracting Opportunities.

**VITAL STATS**

Data: 800-735-5282 or 202-233-6971

Voice: 202-633-7088

Fax: 202-233-4726

FedWorld gateway: 21

Time limit: 40 minutes per day

Available: 8 a.m. to 8 p.m. EST

# SPECIFIC BUSINESSES AND INDUSTRIES

## Bureau of Mines Bulletin Board Network (BOM-BBN)

Bureau of Mines
U.S. Department of the Interior
Mail Stop 9800
810 7th St., N.W.
Washington, DC 20241-0002

You can find detailed data about mineral availability, demand, and production on the Bureau of Mines bulletin board. After a series of opening messages, the BBS presents the Bulletin Menu. By typing the number of any bulletin, you can read it onscreen. You can also download bulletins from the File Management Menu.

Three bulletins are particularly useful:

6. A list of commodity specialists at the Bureau of Mines, listed by mineral; their telephone numbers are included.

7. A list of country specialists at the Bureau of Mines, listed by foreign country; their telephone numbers are included.

9. A description of a free service that you can call to get current information about minerals; information is delivered to your fax machine.

The file directories contain various kinds of information:

1. **Bulletins**   Copies of bulletins that can be downloaded.

2. **USBM tip sheets**   A list of mineral production totals by state and story tips for reporters.

3. **Bimonthly list of BOM publications**   A list of Bureau of Mines publications and articles written by Bureau of Mines personnel in nonbureau publications. Many of the publications are free. Some sample titles are "Effects of Horizontal Stress Related to Stream Valleys on the Stability of Coal Mine Openings," "Gallium and Germanium Recovery from Domestic Sources," and "Mine Fire Diagnostics Applied to the Carbondale, PA, Mine Fire Site."

4. **Mines data (mineral commodity data)**   Data on mineral production, availability, and demand, listed by commodity. Statistics are available for the following commodities: abrasives, aggregates, aluminum, antimony, arsenic, bauxite, bismuth, cadmium, cement, chromium, cobalt, copper, crushed

**VITAL STATS**
Data: 202-501-0373
Voice: 202-501-0406
FedWorld gateway: 4
To access files: At the Main Menu, type **f**
Time limit: 60 minutes per call

stone, feldspar, gallium, gold and silver, gypsum, indium, iron and steel, iron ore, lead, lime, magnesium, manganese, molybdenum, nickel, phosphate rock, platinum, sand and gravel, silicon, soda ash, sulfur, tin, titanium, thallium, tungsten, vanadium, and zinc.

5. **USBM tech transfer tech news**   Descriptions of technical research about mining, with contact information. Some sample titles are "Expert System for Determining the Spontaneous Combustion Potential of Coal" and "Abandoned Mine Lands Program: Subsidence Monitoring Using Seismic Activity."

6. **Software products listing**   A list of software programs and databases developed by the Bureau of Mines. Contact information is listed for each product.

7. **USBM abandoned mine lands research**   A list of publications about research on abandoned mine lands.

## FCC Public Access Link (PAL)

Authorization and Evaluation Division
Federal Communications Commission
7435 Oakland Mills Rd.
Columbia, MD 21046

The FCC Public Access Link (PAL) is aimed at people who are trying to obtain authorizations for electrical equipment from the Federal Communications Commission (FCC). These authorizations certify that the equipment's emissions do not interfere with radio frequency devices. The BBS also offers a small amount of general information about the FCC. Most of the information on the board is technical, and there is nothing of interest to general users.

Information on the board is separated into thirteen categories:

1. **Access equipment authorization database** Information about the status of pending and granted applications. This database can be accessed only by people with proposed or validated FCC identification numbers, however.

2. **Definitions** Definitions of the alphabetical and numeric codes used in the access equipment authorization database.

3. **Applying for an equipment authorization** Information on preparing applications, fees, rules, forms, bulletins, and measurement procedures. The area also includes a list of test firms approved by the FCC for performing compliance testing.

4. **Other Commission activities and procedures** Information about obtaining FCC documents, forms, and rules and regulations. There is also a list of FCC field offices.

5. **FCC Laboratory operational information** Directions to the laboratory, a list of its hours, and a contact list.

6. **Public notices** Technical notices, primarily about radio frequency devices.

7. **Bulletins/measurement procedures** Technical documents about FCC regulations and procedures.

8. **Rulemakings** Descriptions of current rulemaking proceedings concerning radio frequency devices.

> **VITAL STATS**
> Data: 301-725-1072
> Voice: 301-725-1585, ext. 216
> Time limit: 8 minutes per call (but you can call as many times as you like)
> Note: If you have a high-speed modem (9600 baud or above), you may have trouble establishing a connection.

9. **Help**   Assistance in using the BBS, including a list of information found in the various categories.

   a. **Information hotline**   News about new forms and bulletins, a fee guide, and new filing instructions.

   b. **Processing speed of service**   Information explaining how long it takes the FCC Laboratory to process equipment authorizations.

   c. **Test sites**   A list of foreign and domestic firms that are authorized to test devices regulated by the FCC.

   d. **Advanced television service schedule of meetings**   A schedule of meetings of the Advisory Committee on Advanced Television Service.

# FCC-State Link

Industry Analysis Division
Federal Communications Commission
Mail Stop 1600 F
1919 M St., N.W.
Washington, DC 20554

FCC-State Link provides reports that telephone companies are required to file with the Federal Communications Commission (FCC). The reports include data on finances, quality of service, and infrastructure. The board is designed for use primarily by state public utility commissions, which regulate telephone companies on the state level. Most of the information is technical.

The *FCC Daily Digest* also is posted to the board. This document contains speeches by FCC officials, news releases, the titles of public notices, and brief descriptions of FCC actions in various cases. Normally, the *FCC Daily Digest* is posted by 1:30 p.m., Monday through Friday.

**VITAL STATS**

Data: 202-418-0241

Voice: 202-418-0940

FedWorld gateway: 84

Manual: RBBS-QRF.ZIP (compressed) or RBBS-PC.REF (uncompressed). The manual is a generic document for the BBS software.

File list: ALLFILES.ZIP (compressed) or ALLFILES.TXT (uncompressed)

To access files: At the Main Menu, type **f**

Time limit: 30 minutes per day

Available: Not available to the public Monday through Friday from 8 a.m. to 1:30 p.m. EST

### ITC Chemicals BBS

U.S. International Trade Commission
500 E St., S.W.
Suite 513-I
Washington, DC 20436

The ITC Chemicals BBS provides quarterly reports on U.S. production of selected synthetic organic chemicals, such as benzene, polypropylene, and acetone. The reports, which are available in ASCII text or Lotus 1-2-3 formats, can be accessed by typing **s** at the Main Menu. The BBS also has a few utilities for DOS and Windows computers and a few games. Most of the utilities and games are a few years old.

The BBS also includes a chemicals dictionary database. You can access it by typing **d** at the Main Menu. It lists chemical names, Chemical Abstract Service (CAS) registry numbers, and related chemical synonyms. This feature probably will not work for Macintosh users.

**VITAL STATS**
Data: 202-205-1948
Voice: 202-205-3352
To access files: At the Main Menu, type **s**
Time limit: 60 minutes per call

## National Marine Fisheries Service—NW Region

National Oceanic and Atmospheric Administration
7600 Sand Point Way N.E.
Seattle, WA 98115

Commercial fishermen in the Northwest are the primary audience for the National Marine Fisheries Service board. It provides commercial fishing regulations affecting northwestern states, statistics on seafood exports to the member states of the European Union, information about how to order reports on the market for fish in foreign countries, and weekly statistics on the commercial fish catch in Oregon.

> **VITAL STATS**
> Data: 206-526-6405
> Voice: 206-526-6119
> Manual: BBSUSER.DOC (a generic manual for the BBS software)

## NCUA BBS

National Credit Union Administration
1775 Duke St.
Alexandria, VA 22314-3428

The NCUA BBS contains manuals, legal opinions, proposed regulations, and press releases from the National Credit Union Administration. The NCUA regulates and insures all federal credit unions and insures those state-chartered credit unions that apply and qualify for insurance.

You can access a newsletter by typing **n** at the Main Menu. It lists upcoming meetings of the NCUA board, tells about important new files added to the BBS, and provides news about revisions of several NCUA manuals.

The files are divided into more than a dozen file areas. Here are some of the most interesting files:

**VITAL STATS**
Data: 703-518-6480
Voice: 703-518-6335
FedWorld gateway: 128
Manual: NCUABBS.TXT (the manual is excellent)
To access files: At the Main Menu, type **f**
Time limit: 2 hours per day

- The full text of various rules and regulations. Sample titles are "Organizing a Federal Credit Union," "Mergers of Federally Insured CUs," and "Trustees and Custodians of Pension Plans."

- The full text of the Truth in Savings Act. Like many other files on this board, however, this one has been compressed in a self-executing format that makes it unusable on Macintosh computers.

- A bylaw document titled "Operations Following an Attack on the U.S."

- The full text of the *Supervisory Committee Manual.*

  Opinion letters from the NCUA legal department dating back to January 1989.

- News about proposed legislation that would affect credit unions.

- A list of phone numbers at NCUA headquarters.

## Surety BBS

Surety Bond Branch
Financial Management Service
U.S. Department of the Treasury
401 14th St., S.W., Room 262C
Washington, DC 20227

The Surety BBS has the full text of Treasury Department Circular 570, which lists insurance companies that can insure or reinsure federal bonds. You can read the list online or download it. For each company listed, the following information is provided: company name, business address, telephone number, the financial limit on how many bonds it can underwrite, the states in which it has surety licenses, and the state where it is incorporated.

**VITAL STATS**
Data: 202-874-7214
Voice: 202-874-6850
FedWorld gateway: 34
Time limit: 30 minutes per call

# TAXES AND SOCIAL SECURITY

## Electronic Filing System (EFS) Bulletin Board

Internal Revenue Service
EFS Bulletin Board, T:I:I
1111 Constitution Ave., N.W.
Washington, DC 20224

The Electronic Filing System (EFS) Bulletin Board is aimed at developers of tax preparation software and tax preparation firms that file electronically. It provides technical specifications and documents for these two audiences. The board contains no information for individuals who wish to file electronic tax returns.

**VITAL STATS**
Data: 202-799-0221
Voice: 202-283-0459
FedWorld gateway: 33
Time limit: 60 minutes per call

## Information Systems Support BBS

Internal Revenue Service
1111 Constitution Ave., N.W.
Washington, DC 20224

The Information Systems Support BBS has more than 700 Internal Revenue Service tax forms and instructions. The documents are in portable document format (PDF). They can be viewed and printed with software that supports PDF, such as Adobe Acrobat Reader. If you would like a list of all the tax forms available, download the file PDF.LST.

The board also offers hundreds of shareware and freeware software programs copied from CD-ROMs produced by various organizations. There are files related to OS/2, Windows, Unix, and databases. You can access the files by typing l at the Main Menu.

Finally, the board "echoes" conferences on computer-related subjects from FidoNet, a worldwide electronic mail system. You can join an echomail conference by typing f at the Main Menu. The board echoes conferences about Clipper programming, mainframe computers, graphics, high-speed modems, Lotus 1-2-3, OS/2, computer viruses, and Windows, among other subjects.

**VITAL STATS**

Data: 202-219-9977
Voice: 202-501-4700, ext. 5173
FedWorld gateway: 5
Manual: BBSGUIDE.DOC
To access files: At the Main Menu, type l

## IRP-BBS

Information Reporting Program (IRP)
Internal Revenue Service
Martinsburg Computing Center
P.O. Box 1359
Martinsburg, WV 25401

The Internal Revenue Service's IRP-BBS is useful for businesses that must file information returns with the IRS. For example, if a bank pays you more than a certain amount of interest on an account, it must file an information return telling the IRS about the payment.

The BBS includes publications about how to file forms 1098, 1099, 5498, and W-2G electronically or on magnetic tape and how to report IRA contributions and distributions. It lists vendors that provide products or services related to electronic filing of information returns. It also has some publications from the Social Security Administration about how to file forms electronically and provides electronic copies of the *SSA/IRS Reporter*, a newsletter for employers. Businesses also can file IRS information returns through the BBS.

**VITAL STATS**

Data: 304-263-2749

Voice: 304-263-8700

Manual: 1527-92.ASC

Time limit: 60 minutes per call

Note: You may need to experiment with the terminal setting in your communication software. A setting of TTY works well.

# IRS Statistics of Income Division Bulletin Board

IRS—SOI Division
Jim Willis or Kristine Zahm R:S:F
Foreign Operations Section
Internal Revenue Service
P.O. Box 2608
Washington, DC 20013-2608

The IRS Statistics of Income Division Bulletin Board provides aggregate statistics from individual, corporate, and foundation tax returns. The board contains no tax information for individual persons or corporations. Instead, it provides summary statistics for different types of taxpayers.

Here are some examples of the information you will find:

- Individual income and tax data by state.
- Individual income returns by adjusted gross income.
- Highlights of corporate income tax returns by year.
- Highlights of tax returns for U.S. corporations controlled by foreign owners.
- Selected income and balance sheet items for tax-exempt organizations.
- Balance sheets and income statements for private foundations.
- A list of publications and data tapes produced by the IRS Statistics of Income division.

**VITAL STATS**

Data: 202-874-9574
Voice: 202-874-0277 or 202-874-0273
FedWorld gateway: 104
Manual: BLT6.ZIP (but not worth downloading)
File list: FILELST.TXT
To access files: At the Main Menu, type **f**

## Magnetic Media Bulletin Board System

Philadelphia Service Center
Internal Revenue Service
11601 Roosevelt Blvd.
Philadelphia, PA 19255

Businesses can use the Magnetic Media Bulletin Board System to upload electronic copies of IRS forms 940, 941, 941E, 1040NR, and 1041 to the Philadelphia Service Center. These forms include, among others, the Employer's Annual Federal Unemployment Tax Return, the Employer's Quarterly Federal Tax Return, and the Quarterly Return of Withheld Federal Income Tax and Medicare Tax. Individuals cannot use the board to upload tax returns.

The board also contains information about how to file the forms electronically. To access this information, type i at the Main Menu.

**VITAL STATS**
Data: 215-516-7625
Voice: 800-829-6945

# COMPUTERS

# COMPUTER LANGUAGES, STANDARDS, AND SECURITY

## Ada Information Clearinghouse Bulletin Board

c/o IIT Research Institute
P.O. Box 46593
Washington, DC 20050-6593

The Ada Information Clearinghouse Bulletin Board is operated by a private company under a Defense Department contract. It has anything and everything you ever wanted to know about Ada, a high-level programming language developed by the Defense Department that is used in military programming applications.

The BBS has more than 1,000 files, including the text of the Defense Department's policy on computer programming languages; a list of upcoming conferences, symposia, and programs on Ada; information on how to obtain various documents about Ada; a bibliography of books and articles about Ada; a newsletter of current events relating to Ada; information about how to access Ada information on the Internet; a list of classes and seminars about Ada; a list of sources for Ada source code; the *ADA Language Reference Manual*, the *Catalog of Resources for Education in Ada and Software Engineering*, and copies of the *Ada Information Clearinghouse Newsletter*.

All files on the board are compressed with PKZIP, a DOS program for compressing files. Decompression utilities for both DOS and Macintosh systems are available on the BBS.

The BBS also has six databases that you can search online. To reach them, type **d** at the Main Menu. The databases provide the following information:

1. The Validated Compilers (VCL) door enables users to determine what validated Ada compilers are available for various types of hardware.

2. The Ada Programming Tools (TOOLS) door contains information about more than 200 Ada vendors, more than 300 products they produce, and the hardware needed to run the products.

3. The Current Ada Articles (NEWS) door allows users to search abstracts of Ada-related articles published in trade and technical journals.

4. The Ada Bibliography (BIBS) door provides users with a comprehensive bibliography of Ada-related publications.

**VITAL STATS**

Data: 703-604-4624

Voice: 703-685-1477 or 800-232-4211

To access files: At the Main Menu, type **f**

Time limit: 3 hours per call

5. The Bibliography/Abstracts (ABS-BIB) door provides users with a bibliography of Ada-related documents as well as an abstract for each bibliographic citation.
6. The Ada Education (CREASE) door provides access to the *Catalog of Resources for Education in Ada and Software Engineering.*

## Ada Technical Support Bulletin Board System

Code N912.4
NCTANSLANT
9456 Fourth Ave., Suite 200
Norfolk, VA 23511-2199

Ada programmers and software engineers are the target audience for the Ada Technical Support Bulletin Board System. The board has the following major features:

- A files area that contains software for Ada programmers.
- An area where programmers can leave questions about the Ada language and get answers from the BBS staff.
- News items about Ada.
- A lengthy list of books about Ada.
- Ada product descriptions supplied by vendors.

**VITAL STATS**

Data: 804-444-7841

Voice: 804-444-4680

Manual: BBSGUIDE.TXT

To access files: At the Main Menu, type **f**

Time limit: 90 minutes per day

## Air Force CALS Test Bed BBS

DET2HQ ESC/ENC
Suite 300
4027 Col. Glenn Highway
Dayton, OH 45431-1601

The Air Force CALS Test Bed BBS has information about CALS (Continuous Acquisition and Lifecycle Support), which is a government initiative to standardize digital text and graphics information. The files area contains all of the CALS standards, files about the text and graphics standards, and test reports.

**VITAL STATS**

Data: 513-476-1273

Voice: 513-427-5869, ext. 351

Manual: BBSUSER.DOC (a generic manual for the BBS software)

To access files: At the Main Menu, type **f**

## Data Distribution System

Attn: CECPW-FM
Room 2B10
Kingman Building
Fort Belvoir, VA 22060-5516

The Data Distribution System supports users of two U.S. Army computer systems: the Housing Office Management System (HOMES) and the Integrated Facilities System Mini-micro (IFS-M). The board contains files and messages relating to these two systems. It also has a very small collection of DOS and Windows utilities.

**VITAL STATS**
Data: 703-355-3471
Voice: 703-355-0073
FedWorld gateway: 30
Internet: telnet
　160.147.90.240
Manual: BBSUSER.TXT

## NGCR BBS

SPAWAR 331
2451 Crystal Dr.
Arlington, VA 22245-5200

The NGCR BBS, which is operated by a contractor for the U.S. Navy, is aimed at government agencies and contractors involved in developing Next Generation Computer Resources (NGCR) standards. These are open system hardware and software standards that are designed to standardize interfaces, protocols, and services. The board includes bulletins from working groups, minutes of working group meetings, and a few utilities.

**VITAL STATS**

Data: 800-682-6809 or 703-902-3169

Voice: 703-902-5317

FedWorld gateway: 55

Internet: gopher ngcrbbs.jmb.bah.com 7070 *or* http://ngcrbbs.jmb.bah.com

To access files: At the Main Menu, type **f**

Time limit: 60 minutes per call

## NIST Computer Security BBS

National Institute of Standards and Technology
U.S. Department of Commerce
Building 225
Gaithersburg, MD 20899

Virtually anyone who uses a computer will find interesting and valuable information on the NIST Computer Security BBS from the National Institute of Standards and Technology. It contains hundreds of files about computer security—everything from detailed reviews of all the major anti-virus products for DOS and Macintosh computers to highly technical reports on encryption.

After a brief roundup of news about the board, users are presented with the Bulletin Topics Menu. Bulletins are available on eight topics, including use of the BBS, computer security alerts, upcoming events and activities, and computer security organizations. Instead of running up your phone bill by reading the bulletins online, you can download any that interest you and read them later.

To download bulletins, note the numbers of the bulletins you want. When you see the prompt "Read what bulletin(s)?" press the Enter key. This takes you to the Main Menu, where you should type **f** to get to the Files Menu. Then type **d**. When asked what file you want to download, type **bullet** and the bulletin's number. For example, if you want Bulletin 26, type **bullet26** without any spaces between the letters and numbers.

For anyone interested in learning how to fight computer viruses, this board provides a wealth of information. The computer security alert bulletins describe new viruses. The bulletins typically are posted far before the information shows up in major computer magazines. Besides describing how the virus operates, the bulletins explain efforts to upgrade all the major commercial and shareware anti-virus programs to fight the new virus and tell how to get the upgrades.

In addition, the board has extensive reviews of every major anti-virus product on the market for DOS and Macintosh computers. The reviews also reference reviews on the BBS of competing products and list reviews that appear in computer magazines.

### VITAL STATS

Data: 301-948-5717 (2400 baud) or 301-948-5140 (9600 baud)

Voice: 301-975-3359

FedWorld gateway: 10

Internet: telnet cs-bbs.ncsl.nist.gov *or* gopher csrc.ncsl.nist.gov *or* http://csrc.ncsl.nist.gov *or* ftp csrc.ncsl.nist.gov

Manual: BBSGUIDE.TXT

To access files: At the Main Menu, type **f**

Time limit: 60 minutes per call, 70 minutes per day

Some of the most useful files on the board are the following:

**INTERNET.TXT**   A detailed list of companies and organizations that provide public access to the Internet.

**800-LABS.ZIP**   The first of fifteen files providing an extensive bibliography of computer security publications.

**ANN_CONF.TXT**   A list of annual computer security conferences.

**ORGS.TXT**   A list of computer security organizations.

**HGI.ZIP**   *The Hitchhiker's Guide to the Internet*, a classic publication on the subject.

**CSA_87.TXT**   The text of the Computer Security Act of 1987.

**GUIDANCE.SLA**   A discussion of how to select anti-virus programs.

**FEDELI.TXT**   Information about how to organize a corporate anti-virus program.

**HACKER.ZIP**   A thesis about the social organization of the computer underground.

Some of the information on the BBS has been downloaded from the Internet. The BBS has copies of three electronic publications from the Internet that are moderated digests on computer issues. These publications are usually distributed several times each week:

1. The PRIVACY Forum Digest examines issues relating to both personal and collective privacy in the information age.

2. The RISKS-FORUM Digest examines risks to the public from computers and related systems.

3. The VIRUS-L Digest discusses computer viruses.

## NIST/NCSL Data Management Information Exchange (DMIE)

National Institute of Standards and Technology
National Computer Systems Laboratory
U.S. Department of Commerce
Building 225, Room A266
Gaithersburg, MD 20899

The NIST/NCSL Data Management Information Exchange (DMIE) is operated by the National Computer Systems Laboratory, which develops standards and conducts research about computers and related telecommunications systems. The board has only a handful of files, some of which are seriously outdated. The files describe the NCSL and its standards activities, list NIST and NCSL reports, and provide information about the SQL validation test service.

**VITAL STATS**

Data: 301-948-2059

Voice: 301-975-3272

FedWorld gateway: 12

To access files: At the Main Menu, type **f**

## NIU-Forum Bulletin Board

National Institute of Standards and Technology
National Computer Systems Laboratory
Advanced Systems Division (ISDN)
Gaithersburg, MD 20899

The NIU-Forum Bulletin Board provides information about research on the Integrated Services Digital Network (ISDN). This network, which is in the developmental stage, allows the simultaneous transmission of voice and data on the same line. The BBS is primarily of interest to ISDN researchers, since its information is extremely technical.

    The BBS is harder to use than many other boards and is not intuitive. For example, to download a file you must choose the Print command.

**VITAL STATS**

Data: 301-869-7281

Voice: 301-975-5685

Internet: telnet 129.6.53.11

Manual: USER'S GUIDE

Note: Your communications software must be set to emulate a VT100 terminal. The login is **dialin.**

## SHAREWARE

### CNSP/CNAP Bulletin Board

PRC Inc.
Suite 200
4065 Hancock
San Diego, CA 92110

The CNSP/CNAP Bulletin Board, which is operated for the U.S. Navy by a contractor, has thousands of shareware and freeware programs for DOS and Windows computers. There are no programs for Macintosh computers, and there are only a handful of files about Navy issues.

The board has one big flaw: its telephone lines are defective. This problem can cause lots of difficulties in connecting. If your first attempt at connecting fails, try again on a different day.

**VITAL STATS**
Data: 619-556-0135 or
619-556-0136
Voice: 619-236-9083

There are two major file areas on this board. The first, which you can access by typing f at the Main Menu, contains hundreds of DOS and Windows programs separated into more than three dozen directories. A few of the directories contain a handful of Navy documents, though there is nothing very exciting.

The second file area is the PC-SIG CD-ROM, 12th edition, which is published by a private California company and contains more than 5,000 freeware and shareware programs for DOS and Windows computers. To reach it, type j at the Main Menu, **10** at the "Conference # to join?" prompt, and finally f.

The board also has conferences on Windows, operating systems, hardware, software, Navy issues, virus information, contracts, and a few other topics. These conferences serve as collection areas for messages on the topic. You can access them by typing j at the Main Menu.

## HSETC BBS

Naval Health Science Education and Training Command
Building 1, Room 1710, Code 33
8901 Wisconsin Ave.
Bethesda, MD 20889-5612

The HSETC BBS, from the Naval Health Science Education and Training Command, provides a collection of utility programs for DOS computers, although many of the programs are at least several years old. There are no programs for Macintosh computers, and there are no files about Navy health science programs.

**VITAL STATS**
Data: 301-295-3917
Voice: 301-295-2373
FedWorld gateway: 92

## Judge Advocate General's Information Network (JAGNET)

JAGNET Information Center
U.S. Department of the Navy
200 Stovall St.
Alexandria, VA 22332-2400

Although JAGNET is aimed primarily at the U.S. Navy legal community, most of it is also open to the public. The board contains no files about activities of the Navy Judge Advocate General.

For the general user, the board's greatest strength is its collection of more than 700 shareware utilities and programs. These include a wide range of programs for word processing, communications, graphics, and Windows. There are even a few games. The board has programs only for DOS and Windows computers, and all the files have been compressed in the ZIP format.

File Directory 9 contains several files of general interest:

**FED-EVID.ZIP**   The Federal Rules of Evidence in ASCII text.

**FEDRCIVP.ZIP**   The Federal Rules of Civil Procedure.

**NAVAPP.ZIP**   A huge list of Navy acronyms and abbreviations.

**NWP9A001.ZIP**   The first of three files providing the Annotated Supplement to the Law of Naval Operations.

**USBBS106.ZIP**   A list of IBM-based BBSs around the country. The list is updated monthly.

**USCONST.ZIP**   The U.S. Constitution in ASCII text.

**USN0293A.ZIP**   A list of Navy BBSs and other BBSs of military interest worldwide. The list is updated regularly.

**VITAL STATS**
Data: 703-325-0748
Voice: 703-325-2924
FedWorld gateway: 25
File list: JAGNET.ZIP
To access files: At the Main Menu, type **f**

## MASC Library RBBS-PC

MASC Library, MCS
U.S. Department of Commerce
325 Broadway
Boulder, CO 80303

More than 25,000 freeware and shareware programs for IBM and compatible computers are available on the two MASC BBSs. The programs include utilities, spreadsheets, word processing packages, financial and scientific applications, home applications, and games. Users download the programs from the PC-SIG CD-ROM, which is published by a private California company. There are no programs available for Macintosh computers.

Examples of the programs available are a vacation planner with route information, a payroll system, federal tax return help, an online Bible, a program that helps automate rate calculations for packages sent by the U.S. Postal Service and United Parcel Service, an algebraic calculator, an electronic coloring book for kids, a form generator, a fractal drawing program, a picture database of dinosaurs, a personal information manager, a backup program, a weight-loss program, a program to help plan retirement, a client tracking system, a drawing and painting program, a project management program, an environmental database on global warming and ozone depletion, an anti-virus program, and an interactive typing tutor.

New users should read the bulletins that appear after the opening screen. The bulletins provide general information about using the board and detailed downloading instructions, list noteworthy programs available on the BBS, and explain how to call online library catalogs offered by the Colorado Alliance of Research Libraries and the Boulder Public Library.

Finding out what files are available is a bit tricky. There are three options:

- Read Bulletin 5, which lists some of the most popular files on the BBS.

- Order a book called *The PC-SIG Encyclopedia of Shareware: A Comprehensive Guide to Low-Cost Software for IBM and Compatibles*. The book, which describes all the files on the board, is available for $19.95 plus shipping

**VITAL STATS**

Data: 303-497-5848 (MASC I, with disks 1-2485) or 303-497-5567 (MASC II, with disks 1-2804)

Voice: 303-497-3271

Manual: BULLETIN 2

Time limit: 60 minutes per day

Available: Weekdays from 4:30 p.m. to 8 a.m. MST; weekends, 24 hours a day; other times by appointment and handling from PC-SIG Inc., 1030D East Duane Ave., Sunnyvale, CA 94086.

- Perform a system search. To do this, at the Main Menu choose the Library Menu. Then type **s**. The system will prompt you to type in a keyword or string of keywords from a program's name or description. Type in the keyword(s), but don't enter an extension. For example, type **procomm** instead of **procomm.exe**. The system will then ask you to choose a directory for searching. You can search the Master Directory, but this can take up to ten minutes. Alternatively, you can search a Range Directory if you have an idea of the disk number. When the system finds the keyword(s) you entered, it will display the disk number, file name, and description on your screen. Note the disk number.

To download the disk, type **c** and select the number of the disk you wish to download. Then type **d**. At the prompt, enter the disk's number and the ZIP file extension (for example, DISK2350.ZIP). The system will then ask you to choose from a list of communications protocols for downloading. Choose the one that works best with your software, and get your communications software ready to receive the file.

All files are archived in ZIP format. The program PKUNZIP, which decompresses files, is available on Disk 2486.

# PPCUG-RDAMIS

Pentagon PC User Group—Research, Development, and Acquisition Management Information System
c/o John Forbes
ASN (RD&A) R&E
The Pentagon, Room 5C730
Washington, DC 20350-1000

The PPCUG-RDAMIS BBS has hundreds of work-related shareware programs for IBM and compatible computers. There are no programs for Macintosh computers.

After logging on, you are greeted by a pair of intimidating messages warning against unauthorized use of the system. The BBS is open to the public, so don't worry about the messages.

The board has hundreds of programs, including system utilities, project management programs, math and science programs, database managers, communications programs, printer utilities, anti-virus programs, compression and extraction programs, word processing utilities, spreadsheet utilities, and graphics tools, among others.

The board also has more than 100 conferences on topics ranging from abortion to Zenith. Although some of the conferences originate locally, many are echoes of conferences from other BBSs.

In addition, you can find some interesting data files in three file areas:

**VITAL STATS**
Data: 703-614-4114
Voice: 703-614-0349
FedWorld gateway: 93
File list: ALL.LST
To access files: At the Main Menu, type **f**

- **Federal employment**   Lists of federal job openings around the country.

- **Government interest**   A list of country codes used on diplomatic license plates.

- **Bulletin board listings**   Lists of government and nongovernment BBSs around the country.

## Small Computer Support Center

Malmstrom Air Force Base
10 77th St. N.
Great Falls, MT 59405

The Small Computer Support Center offers hundreds of shareware and freeware programs for DOS and Windows computers. You can reach the board's major areas from the Main Menu by typing the letters shown in bold type:

**L** Hundreds of freeware and shareware programs for DOS and Windows computers, including decompression utilities, computer-aided design (CAD) programs, communications programs, and virus utilities.

**C** Access to a CD-ROM packed with shareware and freeware programs for Windows computers.

**O** Copies of the Malmstrom Base Bulletin and a list of technical support lines at computer companies.

**VITAL STATS**

Data: 406-731-2503 or 406-731-3910

Voice: 406-731-4612

Manual: BBSUSER.DOC (a generic manual for the BBS software)

# CRIMINAL JUSTICE

# National Criminal Justice Reference Service (NCJRS)

Office of Justice Programs
U.S. Department of Justice
Box 6000
Rockville, MD 20850

Although the National Criminal Justice Reference Service (NCJRS) uses archaic software that is extremely cumbersome, it contains a vast amount of information about criminal justice. The information is generated by several Justice Department agencies: the National Institute of Justice, the Office of Juvenile Justice and Delinquency Prevention, the Bureau of Justice Statistics, and the Bureau of Justice Assistance.

If you are using a DOS computer, the NCJRS offers a free communications program that makes the board easier to use. To get a copy, call the voice number. The special software is not available for Macintoshes or other types of computers. All other types of communications software work with the board, but only if you have patience.

When you connect to the board, at the prompt type **ncjrs** (be sure it's in lower case) and press the Enter key. Then follow the prompts to register.

The file areas are called topics. They frequently have a series of sub-topics, which in turn often have their own sub-topics. Each of these topics or sub-topics may have numerous files or databases. Navigating through all these layers is one of the board's greatest challenges.

To access any topic or file, use the up- and down-arrow keys until you highlight the topic or file you want. Then hit the Enter key. To go back one level, type **g**. To return to the main screen, type **h**.

Following are some of the major commands. In each case, you must hold down the Control key (Ctrl) at the same time you press the letter key:

**Ctrl-b**   Jump to the bottom of the current screen.

**Ctrl-n**   Display next page.

**Ctrl-p**   Display previous page.

**Ctrl-x**   Cancel command or operation.

## VITAL STATS

Data: 301-738-8895

Voice: 800-851-3420 or 301-251-5500

FedWorld gateway: 75

Manual: Choose the topic called Bulletin Board Assistance, which provides an online user's guide.

Note: Your communications software must be set to emulate a VT100 terminal. A delay of many seconds may occur between the time when the BBS answers and when it establishes a connection.

The file areas contain far more information than can be described in this book. Following are brief summaries of what each one offers:

**Current news, announcements and NIJ publications online**   A calendar of upcoming conferences, a list of criminal justice BBSs, information about new criminal justice publications, information about the Department of Labor's Substance Abuse Information Database for employers, files on various criminal justice issues, and a conferencing area called the User Information Exchange.

**National Institute of Justice topics (NIJ*NET)**   An NIJ staff directory, extensive files about police equipment such as armor and body-worn transmitters, Autobid software for choosing police patrol cars, the NIJ's program plan, and information about grant availability.

**Office of Juvenile Justice and Delinquency Prevention**   A list of publications available from the Juvenile Justice Clearinghouse, a list of upcoming conferences, a list of state juvenile justice advisory group chairs, and contact information for state criminal justice councils.

**Bureau of Justice Statistics topics**   Press releases with statistics on a wide range of justice topics, bulletins with statistics about various justice issues, information about criminal history records, a publications list for the Bureau of Justice Statistics (BJS), information about the BJS Clearinghouse, and a list of specialists at the BJS.

**Bureau of Justice Assistance topics**   Files on various criminal justice issues, information about the availability of topical searches and bibliographies, a staff directory of the Bureau of Justice Assistance (BJA), a list of nationwide criminal justice contacts, a national directory of Treatment Alternative to Street Crime (TASC) programs, information about upcoming conferences and seminars, and information about BJA publications.

**World Criminal Justice Library Network, U.S. Information Center**   International criminal justice news, a schedule of international conferences, a list of new publications about criminal justice, reviews of books about law and politics, country-by-country descriptions of criminal justice systems of Central America in English and Spanish, and articles from the *NIJ Journal* in Spanish.

**Order free documents from NCJRS**   An online system for ordering free publications from the National Institute of Justice.

**Bulletin board assistance**   Lists of key commands, menu commands and functions, and NCJRS BBS staff. In addition, there is information about downloading files, uploading files, and sending messages.

Downloading files is an adventure. You must follow this procedure:

1. Use your up- and down-arrow keys until you highlight the file you want.
2. Hit the Enter key.
3. Type o to activate the Output command.
4. When the output screen appears, press the space bar until "Xmodem" appears after the "to" prompt.
5. Hit the Enter key after Xmodem appears.
6. Activate your communications software to receive the file when you are prompted.
7. Enter the name of the file to download.
8. Hit the Enter key when the file transmission is completed.

With some communications programs, the NCJRS BBS does not allow Xmodem downloading. When you try to use Xmodem, you will get a message saying it is not available (even if your software supports Xmodem). In this case, you must go back to the output screen and choose "screen" after the "to" prompt. The file then will download to your screen, and you can capture it by using your communications software's capture feature.

# NJS BBS

Naval Justice School
360 Elliot St.
Newport, RI 02841-1523

The Naval Justice School's board, NJS BBS, offers the full text of numerous books about military justice. It also has hundreds of utility programs for DOS and Windows computers and seventy-six conferences.

The BBS has more than 1,000 files, which are divided into twenty-nine directories. The files are primarily of two types:

- The full text of textbooks and other books about military justice. Titles available include *Environmental Law Deskbook*, *NJS Military Justice Study Guide*, *NJS Civil Law Study Guide*, *NJS Evidence Study Guide*, *NJS Procedure Study Guide*, *NJS Criminal Law Study Guide*, *Staff Judge Advocate's Handbook*, *Evidentiary Foundations*, *Commander's Handbook for Military/Civil Law*, and *Staff Judge Advocate's Deskbook*.

- Hundreds of freeware and shareware utility programs for DOS and Windows computers. Among them are archiving utilities, menu and editor programs, communications programs, and WordPerfect utilities.

**VITAL STATS**
Data: 401-841-3990
Voice: 401-841-3800
File list: NJSFILES.ZIP

Nearly all of the conferences are echoes from MetroLink and the Military Echo Conference Network (MILECHO). Conferences echoed from MetroLink cover communications, hard disks, laser printers, Pascal programming, Star Trek, aviation, shareware, Windows, WordPerfect, veterans issues, student issues, and photography, among other topics. Conferences from MILECHO discuss government software, Macintoshes in the military, security issues, personnel issues, and the Ada programming language, among other topics.

## SEARCH-BBS

National Consortium for Justice Information and Statistics
7311 Greenhaven Dr.
Sacramento, CA 95831

The SEARCH-BBS provides the full text of Supreme Court opinions, dozens of software programs for criminal justice agencies, lists of job openings in criminal justice, and free e-mail access to the Internet. The board is sponsored by the U.S. Department of Justice and the National Consortium for Justice Information and Statistics.

Information on the board is divided into bulletins, files, publications, databases, and messages:

**Bulletins** The bulletins explain some of the board's functions, describe other criminal justice BBSs, and describe some criminal justice organizations.

**Files** The board's files on both criminal justice and general computer topics are divided into more than twenty file areas. To download a master file list, type 3 at the Files Menu. The file has been compressed in a format that makes it unusable on Macintosh computers.

The files area offers software programs for courts, software programs related to hazardous materials, dozens of programs for police departments, a legal spelling dictionary, several communications programs, database programs, a handwriting analysis program, and dozens of utility programs. Nearly all the files are for DOS computers.

**Publications** Here are some highlights of what's available:

- Supreme Court opinions, which are posted on the board the same day they are released by the Court. The board contains Supreme Court opinions dating back to the beginning of the 1992 term. You can download entire opinions or search opinions by keywords.

- The *FBI Law Enforcement Bulletin*.

- A publications catalog from the National Institute of Justice.

**VITAL STATS**
Data: 916-392-4640
Voice: 916-392-2550
Internet: See box, p. 124
File list: ALLFILES.EXE
 (not usable by Macintosh computers)
Time limit: 60 minutes per call

- Several dozen publications from the U.S. Bureau of Justice Statistics on such topics as pretrial release, drugs, state and local police departments, recidivism, and drunk driving.

**Databases**   The board has six searchable databases:

- *Automated Index*   The Automated Index of Criminal Justice Information Systems contains information about computer systems used by various agencies. You can search the database to identify systems that meet specific needs or to find out what systems other agencies are using.

- *Calendar of Events*   This database lists conferences, seminars, and training opportunities in criminal justice. It can be searched by date, title, location, and sponsoring organization.

- *CJBBS List*   This database lists other criminal justice BBSs nationwide. It can be searched by area code, name fragment, city, or state.

- *NELS Employment Service*   This database contains national listings of job openings in criminal justice. It includes jobs in academia and research, community services and corrections, institutional corrections, and law enforcement and security. Each listing includes the type of position, job description, salary, qualifications, agency name, location, and closing date for applications. Jobs are arranged by category, and each category can be searched by job title, state, salary, agency, and closing date.

- *PALS*   The Planning Abstract Listing Service database provides information about innovative programs, policies, and procedures developed by law enforcement agencies nationwide. Each listing includes the project title, sponsoring organization, a brief project summary, and contact information.

- *Training Facilities*   This database contains descriptions of criminal justice training facilities. Each listing includes availability, contact information, computer systems available, instructional aids, type of organization, fees, and accommodations. The database can be searched by location, agency name, contact name, and computer equipment.

**Messages**   The messages area performs several functions. It offers:

- Conferences for messages on law and policy, research and statistics, technology, training, vendors, and general topics.

- Free e-mail access to the Internet.

- Access to some Internet mailing lists and Usenet Newsgroups on information technology and criminal justice issues.
- Access to the FidoNet e-mail network.
- The ability to send messages to other SEARCH-BBS users.

> ### Internet E-Mail Access to SEARCH-BBS
>
> Much of the information on the board is available through Internet e-mail. Files available through the Internet include all of the shareware, the Supreme Court opinions, and many of the publications.
>
> To request a file, send an e-mail message to ftpmail@search.org. In the body of the message, type **get filename.ext**, where *filename* is the name of the file and *ext* is the extension. To get a list of the available shareware files, send the message **get allfiles.txt**. To get a list of the Supreme Court files, send the message **get hermes**.

## FEDIX and MOLIS

Federal Information Exchange
Suite 200
555 Quince Orchard Rd.
Gaithersburg, MD 20878

FEDIX and MOLIS is designed to be an information link between the federal government and colleges and universities. The BBS, which is operated by a private firm under contract to several government agencies, is actually two boards in one. FEDIX provides information about agency research opportunities, program contacts, scholarships, equipment available for sale, procurement notices, and minority opportunities. MOLIS provides information about colleges and universities that have historically served African Americans or Hispanics.

Unfortunately, the system is so poorly designed that it's far harder to use than comparable systems. There is a lot of useful information here, but finding what you want can be a challenge.

From the Main Menu you can access four major areas on the BBS, each of which has its own sub-menu:

**Federal Opportunities (FEDIX)**   This area provides information from six federal agencies: the Department of Energy, the Office of Naval Research, the National Aeronautics and Space Administration, the Federal Aviation Administration, the Air Force Office of Scientific Research, and the Department of Agriculture. For most of the agencies, information is provided about

- education and research programs (including eligibility requirements, funding, and deadlines);
- scholarships, fellowships, and grants;
- used government research equipment available for sale;
- the availability of funding for specific research and education activities;
- minority research and education programs;

**VITAL STATS**

Data: 800-783-3349 or 301-258-0953 (toll-free number available only Monday through Friday from 7 a.m. to 9 p.m. EST)

Voice: 301-975-0103

FedWorld file: 52

Internet: telnet fedix.fie.com *or* gopher fedix.fie.com *or* http://web.fie.com *or* ftp fedix.fie.com

Manual for FEDIX: UGUIDE.EXE (self-executing compressed format) or UGUIDE.TXT (ASCII text)

Manual for MOLIS: MOLGUIDE.EXE (self-executing compressed file) or MOLGUIDE.TXT (ASCII text)

- the agency's history, budget, and organizational structure;
- current events within the agency; and
- procurement notices.

In addition, this area has minority program information for the National Science Foundation, the Department of Housing and Urban Development, the Department of Commerce, and the Agency for International Development.

**Minority College and University Capability Information (MOLIS)** This area provides information about 107 historically black colleges and universities and 32 colleges and universities that primarily serve Hispanics. Information is available about

- research centers, facilities, and equipment;
- precollege and education programs;
- scholarships and fellowships (including application procedures and the names of contacts);
- degrees and enrollment;
- revenues and expenditures;
- faculty members and administrators;
- tuition, fees, and room and board;
- students;
- federal plans for support of these institutions;
- campus conferences, seminars, and meetings; and
- recent campus appointments.

This area also contains information about the Quality Education for Minorities Network and the Science and Engineering Alliance Inc.

**Higher Education Opportunities for Minorities and Women (HERO)** This area provides information about college and university programs, special services, and financial assistance for minorities and women. All colleges and universities have been invited to participate in HERO, but few have done so.

**Download FEDIX/MOLIS Files** This area has files that can be downloaded from five agencies: the Air Force Office of Research, the Department of Energy, the Federal Aviation Administration, NASA, and the Office of Naval Research.

Primarily, these files contain procurement notices, contact lists, information about education programs, program descriptions, information about the availability of lab equipment, research program descriptions, and lists of publications.

Sub-area 7 contains files of information from MOLIS, including general institution information, institution majors, a list of institution addresses and leaders, institutional expenditures, general financial information, and institutional revenues. It also contains the MOLIS User's Guide. Sub-area 8 has information about FEDIX and the FEDIX User's Guide.

# NIH EDNET

Office of Education
National Institutes of Health
Building 10, Room 1C129
Bethesda, MD 20892

NIH EDNET is designed primarily to allow students and teachers to communicate with scientists at the National Institutes of Health (NIH). The board also has a single file. It lists health-related topics and corresponding telephone numbers at the NIH.

Accessing the board requires a few steps, which vary depending on the access method you use:

1. **Dial-in** After you connect, type **,vt100** (the comma is essential) and press the Enter key. You will not be prompted to do this. Next, you will get a prompt asking for initials. Type **nak** and press Enter. You will get a prompt asking for your account. Type **zzyz** and press Enter twice.

2. **Internet** Telnet tn3270.cu.nih.gov. At the "Enter Command" prompt, type **logon 3270**. At the "Initials?" prompt, type **nak**. At the "Account?" prompt, type **zzyz**.

The board offers eight conferences that contain messages on specific topics:

**Speakers** A list of topics that NIH employees can speak about at high schools. Teachers can use the conference to request speakers for their classrooms.

**Resource** Messages describing educational materials and resources available to teachers and students.

**OE-News** Messages describing new educational and recruitment programs of interest to NIH employees.

**Postdoc** Messages listing available positions for postdoctoral training.

**Teachers** Messages describing educational opportunities for high school and middle school science teachers at the National Institutes of Health.

---

**VITAL STATS**

Data: 800-358-2221 or 301-402-2221 (see login instructions in the description)

Voice: 301-402-1708

Internet: telnet tn3270.cu.nih.gov (see login instructions in the description)

Note: Dial-in users will have to experiment with the terminal setting in the communications software. A setting of VT100 works well. Your software must be set to even parity, 7 data bits, 1 stop bit, and half duplex (or local echo).

**Forum**  A conference for students, teachers, scientists, educators, and others interested in topics in the biomedical sciences. Students and teachers can leave questions for NIH scientists.

**Students**  Messages listing internship and employment opportunities for high school, college, medical, and graduate students at the National Institutes of Health.

**Middle**  A conference for students in junior high and middle schools. Students can use this conference to seek assistance in their biomedical research projects from students in the Montgomery Blair High School Magnet Junior/Senior Science Project in Silver Spring, Maryland. Teachers and NIH scientists provide oversight and scientific support.

## OERI Bulletin Board System

Office of Educational Research Improvement
U.S. Department of Education
555 New Jersey Ave., N.W.
Washington, DC 20208-5725

Anything and everything you ever wanted to know about education is located somewhere on the OERI Bulletin Board System. It has two strengths: (1) hundreds of files of statistics about education; and (2) hundreds of shareware and public domain education programs that teachers or parents can use with children. The board is operated by the Office of Educational Research Improvement, the primary research agency at the Department of Education.

The board has nearly 3,000 files, which are divided into more than twenty directories. You can access the files by typing 1 at the Main Menu. Here are some highlights of what's available:

- A guide to Department of Education programs that describes funding available from federal education programs.

- ERIC Digests, which are brief reports on a variety of topics from the ERIC Clearinghouse on Reading and Communication Skills. Some titles are "Educating the Consumer about Advertising," "Computer Uses in Secondary Science Education," "School Role in Sexual Abuse Prevention," and "Teaching Students to View TV Critically." Each report includes a bibliography.

- A huge collection of statistics about public libraries nationwide.

- Electronic copies of brochures called "Help Your Child Learn to Write Well," "Helping Your Child Improve in Test-Taking," and "Helping Your Child Learn Science."

- An electronic copy of *Educational Programs That Work,* which describes successful education programs around the country. A print version of the report costs $14.95, but you can download the electronic version for free.

- The State Education Performance Chart, which lists twenty-two statistics on educational attainment and reforms.

- The *Digest of Education Statistics,* which has nearly 400 tables of education statistics. It provides data on school enrollment, dropouts, spending on

**VITAL STATS**
Data: 800-222-4922 or 202-219-1511
Voice: 202-219-1526
Internet: gopher gopher.ed.gov *or* http://www.ed.gov *or* ftp ftp.ed.gov
To access files: At the Main Menu, type **1**

schools, items most frequently cited by the public as major problems facing local public schools, pupil-teacher ratios and expenditures in public schools from 1960–1961 to 1990–1991, average teacher salaries for 1969–1970 to 1990–1991, administrative roadblocks reported by secondary school principals from 1965 to 1987, participation by high school seniors in extracurricular activities, trends in drug use by high school seniors from 1975 to 1989, revenues for public schools from 1919–1920 to 1988–1989, state spending on education from 1959–1960 to 1990–1991, selected statistics for historically black colleges and universities, trends in faculty salaries at colleges and universities, changes in scores on the Graduate Record Examination from 1964 to 1988, average undergraduate tuition and fees from 1964–1965 to 1989–1990, and international comparisons of education, among other subjects.

- The *OERI Bulletin,* which discusses information, publications, and data sets generated by the Office of Educational Research Improvement as well as events sponsored by OERI.

- Projected education statistics on the national and state levels to the year 2002.

- Hundreds of shareware and public domain education programs for computers. Although the largest number of programs work with IBM and compatible computers, the board also has smaller numbers of programs for Commodore, Atari, Tandy, and Apple computers. You'll find math and vocabulary games, programs that use PC speakers to teach children to count, a talking program that teaches children their ABCs, a geography test, a program that teaches anatomy, astronomy-related programs, library card catalog programs, a vocational program for culinary arts, chemistry drills, gradebook and attendance programs, a planetarium simulator, the periodic chart of the elements, American history quizzes, typing practice programs, an SAT verbal prep program, virus checkers, spelling programs, test writing programs, a Civil War timeline, the U.S. Constitution with amendments, and word processors for children.

# EMERGENCY RESPONSE AND FIRE SAFETY

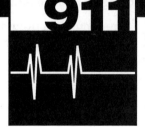

## Building and Fire Research Bulletin Board System (BFRBBS)

Building and Fire Research Laboratory
National Institute of Standards and Technology
U.S. Department of Commerce
Gaithersburg, MD 20899

The Building and Fire Research BBS specializes in technical information about fire research. Several types of information are available:

**Bulletins** Lists of upcoming fire research conferences and meetings, news about fire-related research, lists of other fire-related bulletin boards and fire safety computer programs, and information about how to download files.

**Fire simulation programs** Copies of numerous fire simulation programs for computers.

**Publications** Bibliographic information for publications produced by the Building and Fire Research Laboratory. There is also a manual for FIREDOC, an online bibliographic database of reports, articles, books, and audiovisual materials in the collection of the Fire Research Information Service. The database is designed to be accessed with either ProComm, a DOS communications program, or DynaComm, a Macintosh program. ProComm is shareware that costs about $35, while DynaComm costs about $300.

**Utility programs** Copies of PKUNZIP, which can be used to decompress files, and the ProComm communications program. Both are DOS programs.

**Forums** Areas where users can discuss fire-related issues.

---

**VITAL STATS**
Data: 301-990-2272
Voice: 301-975-6862
Manual: BULLET08
To access files: At the Main Menu, type **f**
Time limit: 45 minutes per call, 120 minutes per day

## CAMEONet

Environmental Health Center
National Safety Council
Suite 401
1019 19th St., N.W.
Washington, DC 20036

CAMEONet supports users of Computer-Aided Management of Emergency Operations (CAMEO), a software program developed by two federal agencies. The board is operated by the National Safety Council, which is not a federal agency.

CAMEO is designed to help government and industry officials who use hazardous chemicals or respond to chemical emergencies. The board provides files that can be used with CAMEO. These include data from the Toxic Release Inventory, historical weather data, and data from the 1990 census. The files are formatted for use with CAMEO, but some other software programs may be able to read them as well.

**VITAL STATS**

Data: 703-560-1650

Voice: 800-992-2636 or 202-293-2270

To access files: At the Main Menu, type **j**

## Hazardous Materials Information Exchange (HMIX)

Federal Emergency
 Management Agency
Preparedness, Training, and
 Exercises Directorate
Preparedness Division
500 C St., S.W.
Washington, DC 20472

Department of Transportation
Research and Special Programs
 Administration
Office of Hazardous Materials
 Initiatives and Training
400 7th St., S.W.
Washington, DC 20590

**VITAL STATS**

Data: 708-972-3275

Voice: 800-752-6367 (in Illinois, 800-367-9592)

Manual: GUIDE.TXT (ASCII text) or GUIDE.WP (WordPerfect) (the manual is excellent)

File list: PCBFILES.LST

Time limit: 30 minutes per call

The Hazardous Materials Information Exchange (HMIX) provides information about numerous topics regarding hazardous materials, including emergency management, training, resources, technical assistance, and regulations. Much of the material on the board is quite technical.

Information is presented in bulletins and files. There are more than forty bulletins, which you can access by typing **b** at the Main Menu. The bulletins describe various regulations, discuss communications software programs, and provide tips on using the board. Here are a few examples:

- Bulletin 10 describes Mexico's regulations for transporting hazardous materials and wastes, rules of increasing importance with the passage of the North American Free Trade Agreement (NAFTA).

- Bulletins 34–38 provide information about such popular communications programs as ProComm and SmartCom.

- Bulletin 43 answers common questions about the board.

You can read bulletins onscreen or download them. To download a bulletin, type **d** at the Main Menu, and at the next prompt type **blt** and the bulletin's number. For example, to download Bulletin 2 you would type **blt2** (with no space between blt and the number).

You can access a few files by typing **f** at the Main Menu. The available files include the user's manual and the master file list. To access most of the files, however, you must type **j** at the Main Menu to "join a topic." Each of the more than two dozen topics has its own menu and its own file directory. Here are some highlights of what's available:

- Information about training in incident response, emergency preparedness, enforcement, and motor carrier safety offered by the Federal Emergency Management Agency, the Department of Transportation, the Department of Energy, the Occupational Safety and Health Administration, and the Environmental Protection Agency.
- A calendar of conferences.
- Lists of instructional literature, videos, software, and newsletters about fire protection and prevention, training, transportation, laws and regulations, emergency management and response, emergency medicine and decontamination, industrial hygiene and worker safety, and waste management.
- Information about toll-free technical assistance available from the federal and state governments, in addition to lists of federal, state, commercial, and private online databases and hazardous materials bulletin boards.
- Various laws and regulations from the Department of Transportation, the Environmental Protection Agency, the Occupational Safety and Health Administration, and other agencies.
- Lists of contacts at federal agencies, professional associations, trade associations, research centers, and environmental groups.
- A variety of materials about Department of Transportation programs, including the Motor Carrier Safety Program and the hazardous materials program.
- Files for each Environmental Protection Agency region. These include a regional calendar, news items, transportation and emergency response contacts, a list of Local Emergency Planning Committee contacts, and lists of training courses offered by private groups, state training offices, colleges and universities, and local agencies.
- Information about upcoming international meetings relating to transportation of dangerous goods.
- Information about the National Task Force on Hazardous Materials Emergency Preparedness.
- A list of resources on firefighting and emergency medical services (EMS), federal rules and regulations affecting firefighting and EMS, and related information.

## OEPC BBS

Office of Environmental Policy and Compliance
U.S. Department of the Interior
Mail Stop 2340
1849 C St., N.W.
Washington, DC 20240

The OEPC BBS is operated by the Interior Department's Office of Environmental Policy and Compliance, which is involved in hazardous waste cleanup, natural resources damage assessments, and emergency responses to incidents such as oil spills. The sysop reports that the board's primary purpose is to present drafts of regulations and other documents to the public. The board contains few such documents, however.

**VITAL STATS**

Data: 202-208-7119
Voice: 202-208-3811
FedWorld gateway: 80
Manual: OEABBS.HLP
File list: ALLFILES.TXT (uncompressed) or ALLFILES.ZIP (compressed)
To access files: At the Main Menu, type **f**
Time limit: 1 hour per day

The board provides a dozen public conferences on such topics as water resources, hazardous materials management, mineral resources, and urban transportation. It also offers a hodgepodge of files, including information about national parks in the Washington, D.C., area, a list of BBSs nationwide, and a small number of graphics images.

Here are a few of the files that are available:

- An update on new memorials in Washington, D.C., and background information about cherry blossoms and national parks in the Washington area.

- Lists of military BBSs and BBSs in Washington, D.C.

- Lists of OEPC headquarters staff and regional environmental officers.

- Graphics images, all in GIF format. Images are available of an astronaut in space; a butterfly; Washington, D.C., as seen from Landsat; Earth from space; an Earthrise as seen from the moon; and a U.S. map with state boundaries.

- A few documents about transportation, including the section of the U.S. Code pertaining to highways and the text of the Intermodal Surface Transportation Efficiency Act.

# State and Local Emergency Management Data Users Group (SALEMDUG) BBS

Federal Emergency Management Agency Headquarters
500 C. St., S.W.
Washington, DC 20472

The SALEMDUG BBS has hundreds of files about emergency management issues. During natural disasters, it offers daily situation reports from the Federal Emergency Management Agency (FEMA). The BBS is aimed at emergency management personnel at the national, state, and local levels.

The board presents information in bulletins, conferences, and files. Most users can skip the bulletins, which offer little of interest.

The board has dozens of conferences, which you can access by typing j at the Main Menu. There are conferences on fire and emergency medical services, hazardous materials response, fire prevention and safety, search and rescue, earthquakes, severe weather, the Civil Air Patrol, occupational safety and health, CD-ROM, Windows, database development, phones, and communication, among other topics. Many of the conferences are "echoes" from other systems, such as the RelayNet International Message Exchange.

The files are separated into six directories:

1. **Emergency management**    Information about radio and TV stations, civil preparedness agencies, hospitals, medical personnel, shelters, nuclear reactors, airports, dam safety, highway structures, wholesale businesses, and crisis relocation in south Florida; a series of reports about Hurricane Andrew; copies of *Disaster Research News;* an emergency management plan for Texas; copies of *EmergencyNet NEWS;* a shareware personnel, training, and equipment database organizer for fire departments; a special report about flooding in the Midwest; a list of major high-rise fires in the twentieth century; two DOS programs for tracking hurricanes; a list of earthquakes in Oklahoma from 1897 through 1993; a list of state police frequencies around the country; a list of federal government frequencies; and FEMA situation reports on Hurricane Emily and Midwest flooding.

2. **Communications**    A list of citizens band frequencies, communications programs for DOS and Windows, and a utility program for checking modems.

**VITAL STATS**
Data: 202-646-2887
Voice: 202-646-3110
FedWorld gateway: 39
Manual: SALEMBK.ZIP (the manual is excellent)
To access files: At the Main Menu, type **f**
Time limit: 60 minutes per day

3. **Utilities**   Dozens of utility programs, primarily for DOS computers; however, a few Windows and Macintosh utilities are included.

4. **Leisure**   Games and utilities for DOS and Windows.

5. **General**   A wide range of programs, primarily for DOS and Windows. These range from a meal planning and grocery shopping program to a personal information manager.

6. **Recent uploads**   An automated telephone directory for the Federal Emergency Management Agency and various utility programs and games for DOS and Windows.

# ENERGY

## Bibliographic Retrieval System (BRS)

Public Document Room
U.S. Nuclear Regulatory Commission
Washington, DC 20555

**VITAL STATS**
Data: Number provided after registration
Voice: 202-634-3273
Fax: 202-634-3343
Note: You must register before using this database.

If you want to track what's happening at your local nuclear power plant, the Bibliographic Retrieval System (BRS) is the place to do it. Technically speaking, the BRS is not a BBS. Instead, it is a huge database that you can access with your computer and modem. For many years the BRS was just a bibliographic system; however, as this book was being written, thousands of full-text documents were being added. These documents are being transferred from the NRC's NUDOCS records system, which used to be accessible by the public but now is available only to NRC employees. Once the transfer is completed, the BRS will offer thousands of full-text documents.

Most of the documents cover the licensing, regulation, and inspection of nuclear power plants. Here are some examples of what's available:

**Licensee Event Reports**   Reports that nuclear power plant operators must file with the NRC when something goes wrong.

**Notice of Violation**   An NRC notice to a licensee that it has violated a rule and must correct the problem.

**IE Information Notice**   A letter from the NRC to licensees alerting them to some problem relating to health and safety, safeguards, or protection of the environment that has developed at other nuclear plants.

**Inspection Reports**   Reports arising from regular inspections of nuclear power plants that identify any problems found.

The NRC is also responsible for regulating companies that process, transport, or handle nuclear materials and nuclear waste. For example, it regulates hospitals' use of nuclear materials in radiation treatments. Documents about licensing of these firms and institutions are also included in the database.

Because the BRS is a huge database, it is much harder to use than the typical BBS. However, if you have any interest in the regulation of nuclear power plants and other facilities that use nuclear materials, it is well worth learning how to use the database.

To gain access to the BRS, you must call, fax, or send a letter to the NRC's Public Document Room. You will be sent a form to fill out. After you return it, you will receive a password, an extensive manual, and other materials.

The NRC offers free BRS training in Washington, D.C., which it strongly encourages users to attend. The database provides an online tutorial for those who cannot travel to Washington.

## Commission Issuance Posting System (CIPS)

Federal Energy Regulatory Commission
ED-23.2
Room 3026
941 N. Capitol St., N.E.
Washington, DC 20426

The Commission Issuance Posting System (CIPS) BBS provides information about federal regulation of public utilities. It has documents issued by the Federal Energy Regulatory Commission (FERC), press releases, a daily listing of all documents filed by utilities, and a list of upcoming FERC meetings. The BBS contains only documents filed during the previous thirty days. You can obtain a useful brochure about using CIPS by calling the BBS's voice number.

FERC has broad powers. It regulates mergers and purchases of electric utilities, rates charged by interstate oil and gas pipelines, operation of oil and natural gas pipelines, and rates for interstate sales of wholesale electricity, among other areas. It also issues licenses for construction of hydroelectric dams and is responsible for ensuring dam safety.

In most instances, the BBS contains only documents issued by FERC. Thus you can see how FERC rules in a case, but you usually cannot see the original documents filed by the utility.

The Bulletin Menu, which appears after the opening message, contains several useful documents that you can read online and save with your communications program's capture feature. Three bulletins are particularly useful:

**Bulletin 2—Commission Meeting Schedule**  A schedule of FERC meetings for the coming year.

**Bulletin 7—CIPS Instructions**  An excellent user's guide.

**Bulletin 10—Topic Words**  A list of one- or two-word terms used to help identify the type of document. Topic words can be used in searching for documents. The list also briefly describes each topic word.

The board's files are separated into dozens of categories, all identified by a one- or two-letter prefix. To search the files, type s at the Commands Menu. At the prompt, enter the search string. This

### VITAL STATS

Data: 202-208-1397 (2400 baud) or 202-208-1781 (9600 baud)

Voice: 202-208-2474

FedWorld gateway: 19

Manual: BULLETIN 7

To access files: At the Commands Menu, type I for a list of the directory categories

Time limit: 60 minutes per call

Available: 24 hours per day except Monday through Friday from 8 a.m. to 9 a.m. EST

can be a utility name, a keyword, or a topic word. After typing the search string, leave a space and type the prefix of the directory you want searched. If you want to search all directories at once, type a instead of a directory prefix. For example, you would type **Detroit Edison a** if you wanted to search all directories for documents about Detroit Edison. Then, when you hit the Enter key, the system would produce a list of documents.

Alternatively, you can get a list of all files added since a given date or since the last time you logged on. To do this, type **n** at the Commands Menu. Then at the prompt, type the desired date and the name of a directory. For example, you would type **050894 cp** to create a list of all the files added to the CP category since May 8, 1994.

Technically, the documents on CIPS are not the official versions. The official paper documents are available in the Public Reference Room in Washington, D.C. For all practical purposes, though, the electronic versions are the same as the paper versions.

Here are some of the most interesting directories to search:

**EC**  Applications by public utilities to sell themselves, purchase other utilities, or merge with other utilities.

**ID**  Documents identifying interlocking directorships between utilities or between utilities and nonutility firms.

**DF**  The daily list of all filings made at the FERC. Each entry includes the date of the filing, the applicant name, the type of filing, the filer or originator, and the docket number; it also notes whether the filing is an intervention. This list covers documents filed the previous day.

**FD**  A list of all documents issued on a particular day. Each entry includes the document number, the applicant name, the date issued, and the document's title.

**NR**  FERC news releases.

**DC**  The daily calendar of FERC events.

## Energy Information Administration Electronic Publishing System (EPUB)

U.S. Department of Energy
1000 Independence Ave., S.W.
Washington, DC 20585

Virtually anything you want to know about energy supply, demand, and prices can be found on EPUB. This board includes everything from trend data on the number of offshore oil and gas wells to statistics on the cost of electricity nationwide.

EPUB is one of the easiest boards to use. The files are separated into more than a dozen file areas by type of report. They can be read online or downloaded.

The reports contain statistics on subjects such as coal production and consumption, use of electric power, prices of winter fuels, natural gas production and consumption, petroleum production, the short-term energy outlook, energy consumption by source, energy imports by source, crude oil supply, drilling activity, electricity generation by utilities, the cost of imported crude oil, retail gasoline prices, world crude oil production, natural gas prices, the amount of electricity generated by nuclear power plants, and U.S. energy supply and demand.

Three files in File Area 8 provide useful lists of contacts:

• ME-FIRST lists contacts at the National Energy Information Center who can refer callers to experts or provide Energy Information Administration (EIA) publications, tapes, and computer disks.

• DATA lists dozens of contacts at the EIA by topic. The contacts are experts on coal, electric power, electric utilities, nuclear power, uranium, renewable energy, natural gas, petroleum, energy consumption, energy economics, and international energy issues such as foreign investment and greenhouse gases.

• FORECASTS lists contacts who can provide information about forecasts of energy production and use.

**VITAL STATS**
Data: 202-586-2557
Voice: 202-586-8959
FedWorld gateway: 16
Time limit: 60 minutes per call

# Fossil Energy Telenews

Office of Fossil Energy Communications
U.S. Department of Energy
Mail Stop FE-5
1000 Independence Ave., S.W.
Washington, DC 20585

Press releases, speeches, congressional testimony, and federal budget documents about fossil energy can be accessed through Fossil Energy Telenews. The Office of Fossil Energy in the Department of Energy (DOE) is responsible for research and development programs involving coal, petroleum, and natural gas. It also oversees the Clean Coal Technology program, which seeks to design and build clean coal-burning facilities; the Strategic Petroleum Reserve; the Naval Petroleum and Oil Shale Reserves; and the Liquefied Gaseous Fuels Spill Test Facility.

The BBS supports three basic functions:

1. **Bulletins** Provide the most recent press releases about fossil energy, lists of key Fossil Energy staff, the status of the Fossil Energy budget, and schedules for upcoming speeches, congressional testimony, and special events. Sample news release headlines are "Energy Department Names 26 Winners in Annual University Coal Research Competition," "DOE Selects Five Projects in Fifth Round of Clean Coal Technology Program," and "DOE Concludes Negotiations for Three More Oil Recovery Projects in Program to Slow Abandonment of Oil Fields." Bulletins also list Fossil Energy procurement notices published in *Commerce Business Daily*. These notices have titles like "Paving and Road Surfacing at the Weeks Island and West Hackberry SPR," "Clean, Inspect, Repair and Epoxy Line Crude Oil Tank Number 2," and "Replace Brine Disposal Pipeline at One DOE Facility."

2. **Files** The files, which are arranged by subject, contain Fossil Energy press releases dating back to 1985, copies of speeches, copies of congressional testimony, and detailed Fossil Energy budget documents. No recent testimony or speeches are included because Fossil Energy officials have

> **VITAL STATS**
>
> Data: 202-586-6496
> Voice: 202-586-6503
> FedWorld gateway: 45
> Manual: A printed user's guide is available upon request. Type **c** at the Main Menu, and leave a message requesting the guide and listing your name and address.
> To access files: At the Main Menu, type **f**.

been speaking without prepared texts. The files section also contains a couple of utilities for IBM and compatible computers to help callers use the files.

3. **Communications**  Allows users to leave messages for Fossil Energy public information officers and for other BBS users.

## Office of Statistics and Information (OSI) BBS

Minerals Management Service
Operations and Safety Management
U.S. Department of the Interior
Mail Stop 4610
381 Elden St.
Herndon, VA 22070-4817

Statistics about offshore oil and gas exploration and development are available through the Office of Statistics and Information (OSI) BBS. The statistics are compiled by the Minerals Management Service, which leases oil and gas rights on the Outer Continental Shelf.

Typing **f** at the Main Menu gets you a list of the thirty-six file areas on the board, but only some of them actually have files. You can get a list of files in an area by typing its number.

Some of the most interesting files provide the following information:

- Details about oil and gas leasing in each of the four Outer Continental Shelf regions.

- Estimates of undiscovered oil and gas reserves in the four OCS regions.

- Details about exploratory wells drilled in each region.

- Data about the number of permits approved in federal and state waters from 1960 to 1989.

- Lists of the top twenty-five companies holding interests in leases, ranked by total acreage held.

- An electronic version of *Federal Offshore Statistics,* a publication that lists a variety of statistics about offshore oil and gas leasing.

- An electronic version of the *Annual Report to Congress* prepared by the Office of Statistics and Information in the Minerals Management Service.

- An electronic version of the Federal Oil and Gas Royalty Management Act.

- An electronic version of the Outer Continental Shelf Lands Act.

**VITAL STATS**
Data: 703-787-1181
Voice: 703-787-1043
FedWorld gateway: 67
File list: ALLFILES.ZIP
To access files: At the Main Menu, type **f**

- An electronic version of the Submerged Lands Act.
- A nationwide list of all Minerals Management Service employees that includes their telephone numbers and mail stop numbers.

## Tech Specs Plus BBS

Technical Specifications Branch
Division of Operating Reactor Support
Office of Nuclear Reactor Regulation
U.S. Nuclear Regulatory Commission
Washington, DC 20555

The Tech Specs Plus BBS contains documents about the operation of nuclear power plants. Some of them can be very helpful in identifying generic problems affecting various types of nuclear plants. However, the board does not contain documents about individual plants. You can find them on the Bibliographic Retrieval System (BRS), another computer system operated by the Nuclear Regulatory Commission (see p. 142).

The bulletins, which you can access by typing **b** at the Main Menu, provide an introduction to the board, explain how files are named, and list brief news items.

The files are basically of two types:

- Documents sent by the NRC to operators of nuclear power plants lumped under the broad title "Generic Communications." Most of these documents alert operators to new NRC policies or to problems at other nuclear plants that the NRC believes could be widespread. The BBS has files of these documents dating back many years. Five specific titles are available:

    1. Bulletins—1971 to the present.
    2. Circulars—1976 to 1981 (this document has been discontinued).
    3. Generic Letters—1977 to the present.
    4. Information Notices—1979 to the present.
    5. Administrative Letters—1993 to the present.

- Technical specifications for operating nuclear power plants. The specifications detail which systems have to be operable, what tests must be performed, what administrative procedures must be followed, and what other requirements must be met. There are separate specifications available for nuclear plants produced by different manufacturers. The sysop reports that members of the public who have a rudimentary knowledge of nuclear power should be able to understand the specifications.

**VITAL STATS**

Data: 800-679-5784 or 301-504-1778

Voice: 301-504-3138 or 301-504-1189

FedWorld gateway: 63

To access files: At the Main Menu, type **f**

# ENVIRONMENT

## GENERAL

### Gulfline BBS

Gulf of Mexico Program Office
Building 1103
Room 202
Stennis Space Center, MS 39529

The Gulfline BBS is a joint project of the Environmental Protection Agency and the National Oceanic and Atmospheric Administration. The board primarily covers environmental issues affecting the Gulf of Mexico and the five states that border it: Alabama, Florida, Louisiana, Mississippi, and Texas. But it also has a wide range of other environmental information and hundreds of shareware and freeware programs for DOS computers. The board presents information in bulletins, files, conferences, and databases.

The bulletins, which you can access by typing **b** at the Main Menu, describe the Gulf of Mexico Program, provide limited information about the BBS, and list environmental BBSs around the country.

The files, which you can access by typing **f** at the Main Menu, are divided into three dozen directories. There are publications from the Gulf of Mexico Program, a few files about regulatory and legislative issues, files from each of the states served by the Gulf of Mexico Program, and hundreds of freeware and shareware programs for DOS computers.

The BBS has more than two dozen conferences, most of which are public. They provide users with the opportunity to exchange messages on specific issues, but they contain no files or bulletins. There are public conferences on coastal and shoreline erosion, habitat degradation, living aquatic resources, marine debris, nutrient enrichment, public health, and other issues.

The BBS also has four databases, or doors, that are available to the public. You can access them by typing **d** at the Main Menu:

**SEARCH** A database of environmental specialists, primarily in the five Gulf states. It also contains listings for members of Congress from the Gulf states and references to other environmental databases.

**TIRES** Hundreds of files that include copies of the Gulf of Mexico Program Office's newsletter, press releases and public events calendars, the text of en-

**VITAL STATS**

Data: 800-235-4662 or 601-688-2677

Voice: 601-688-7671

FedWorld file: 57

Manual: SRCHMAN.TXT (ASCII) or SRCHMAN.WP5 (WordPerfect 5.1)

To access files: At the Main Menu, type **f**

Available: 24 hours a day except from 3 a.m. to 4 a.m. CST

vironmental bills introduced in Congress and information about their progress, news articles about Gulf of Mexico environmental issues, and information about conferences and symposia about the Gulf of Mexico. You must choose a database within TIRES, and then you can either get a list of all files in the database or search it by keywords.

**EPAPHONE**   Telephone numbers and addresses of Environmental Protection Agency employees nationwide. The database can be searched by first and last name.

**NOAPHONE**   Telephone numbers and addresses of National Oceanic and Atmospheric Administration employees nationwide. It can be searched by first and last name.

## OAQPS Technology Transfer Network

Office of Air Quality Planning and Standards
Technical Support Division
U.S. Environmental Protection Agency
Mail Stop 14
Research Triangle Park, NC 27711

The OAQPS Technology Transfer Network is a group of fourteen Environmental Protection Agency BBSs that provide information about air pollution. Boards on the network contain the text of the Clean Air Act amendments of 1990, numerous summary files from the Toxic Release Inventory, the EPA Fuel Economy Guide for automobiles, and information about accessing EPA libraries and documents.

After connecting, new users are presented with the Unregistered Users Main Menu. It provides descriptions of the fourteen boards and a registration option. You must register to have full access to the network.

After registering, you will see the Technology Transfer Network Top Menu. Type **t** to access the BBSs.

Here are descriptions of the fourteen boards available through the network:

1. **Aerometric Information Retrieval System (AIRS)** The focus of this BBS is encouraging the exchange of information among state and local agencies that use AIRS, the national database for ambient air quality, emissions, and compliance data. The BBS has newsletters; brochures and pamphlets about AIRS; information about upcoming meetings, conferences, and training sessions; AIRS contacts and telephone numbers; and AIRS-related software programs.

2. **Ambient Monitoring Technology Information Center (AMTIC)** This BBS specializes in information about ambient monitoring technology. It has copies of the *AMTIC News* and *IMPROVE* newsletters; sections of the Code of Federal Regulations about ambient monitoring; files about the effects of acidic pollution on auto finishes, recent observations in the Great Lakes Basin, the effect of acid rain on wood coatings, and the effect of benzene exposure; extensive information about how

**VITAL STATS**

Data: 919-541-5742

Voice: 919-541-5384

Internet: telnet ttnbbs.rtpnc.epa.gov

Available: 24 hours a day except Monday from 8 a.m. to noon EST

Note: Your communications software must be set to emulate a VT100, VT102, or ANSI terminal.

to access EPA documents and libraries, including a list of all EPA libraries; and information about air pollution publications.

3. **Air Pollution Training Institute (APTI)**   Funded by the EPA, the institute develops instructional materials relating to air pollution abatement. The board has information about courses offered by APTI.

4. **Best Available Control Technology/Lowest Achievable Emissions Rates Information System (BLIS)**   The BLIS BBS contains information from the Reasonably Achievable Control Technology (RACT)/Best Available Control Technology (BACT)/Lowest Achievable Emission Rate (LAER) Clearinghouse. The heart of the BBS is the BLIS database. It contains information about pollution limits and process modifications required under air pollution permits issued by state and local air pollution control programs around the country. You can search the database by state, region, pollutant, process, or a combination of options. The database is designed to help state and local officials determine what types of controls other air pollution agencies have applied to various sources. A database of federal, state, and local air pollution regulations is also available.

5. **Clean Air Act Amendments (CAAA)**   This BBS contains extensive information about the Clean Air Act amendments of 1990. It has the text of the amendments; policy and guidance documents; an index to the BBS that you can search by topic; a text search feature that allows you to search the Clean Air Act by topic; files that define terms, explain acronyms, and provide summaries about topics such as dispersion modeling and ambient monitoring; congressional testimony about the Clean Air Act amendments; recently signed rules that have not yet been published in the *Federal Register;* and monthly updates of EPA's activities under the Clean Air Act amendments.

6. **Clearinghouse for Inventories and Emission Factors (CHIEF)**   CHIEF is designed to provide access to tools for estimating emissions of air pollutants and performing air emission inventories. It is operated by the EPA's Emission Inventory Branch. The board has contact lists, electronic copies of important memos and letters, EPA emission inventory guidance reports, emission estimation software, information on EMA emission factors for air pollutants, and a newsletter about emission factors.

7. **Control Technology Center (CTC)**   The CTC provides state and local agencies and EPA regional offices with technical support in implementing air pollution control programs. The BBS has a computer modeling system for surface impoundments, a computer model for estimating landfill air

emissions, electronic copies of the CTC newsletter, a list of ongoing CTC projects, and summaries of all documents available from the CTC.

8. **Emission Measurement Technical Information Center (EMTIC)**   Aimed at people who conduct or oversee emissions tests, this BBS provides technical guidance on stationary source emission testing issues. It contains highly technical files and bulletins on emission testing, information about acid rain, and contact lists.

9. **New Source Review (NSR)**   This BBS provides information about New Source Review permitting. The board has the abstracted index of the *New Source Review Prevention of Deterioration and Nonattainment Area Guidance Notebook,* which you can search by keywords; numerous EPA documents about NSR rulemaking and implementation; and news about upcoming meetings on NSR issues.

10. **Support Center for Regulatory Air Models (SCRAM)**   Computer codes for regulatory air models can be obtained from this BBS. The board also has bulletins and news about model modifications.

11. **National Air Toxics Information Clearinghouse (NATICH)**   This BBS is aimed at helping federal, state, and local agencies control toxic air pollutants. It offers numerous summary files from the Toxic Release Inventory, in spreadsheet format; electronic copies of the NATICH newsletter; lists of local, state, and EPA regional contacts; state and local regulatory program descriptions and contact lists; acceptable ambient guidelines; emissions inventory data; a NATICH publications list; and a list of publications from the Health Effects Research Laboratory.

12. **COMPLIance Information (COMPLI)**   The COMPLI BBS has three databases: the National Asbestos Registry System (NARS), which lists all asbestos contractors, inspections of the firms, and the inspection results; the Determinations Index, which is a compilation of clarifications and determinations issued by the EPA concerning selected subparts of the *Federal Register;* and Woodstoves, which lists EPA-certified woodstoves and woodstove manufacturers.

13. **Office of Mobile Sources (OMS)**   This BBS is operated by the EPA's Office of Mobile Sources and its National Vehicle and Fuels Emissions Laboratory. It includes the EPA Fuel Economy Guide for automobiles, emissions rules for various types of vehicles, and tips for better gas mileage. It also provides files about ozone pollution from automobiles,

clean fuels, methanol as a fuel, electric vehicles, nonattainment cities, and milestones in automotive pollution control.

14. **Office of Radiation and Indoor Air (ORIA)**   This BBS provides information about controlling exposure to radiation and indoor air pollution.

## Online Library System (OLS)

National Library Network Program
U.S. Environmental Protection Agency
Mail Stop 291
26 W. Martin Luther King Dr.
Cincinnati, OH 45268

The Environmental Protection Agency's Online Library System (OLS) provides nine databases that offer bibliographic citations for books, reports, and journals held by EPA libraries nationwide. The publications cover such topics as air quality, hazardous waste, laboratory methods, pollution prevention, toxic substances, water pollution, and health effects caused by pollution.

The databases can be searched by title, author, corporate source, keywords, call number, year of publication, and report number. Three of the databases contain citations for holdings in EPA regional libraries in Boston, Chicago, and San Francisco. Here are descriptions of the other six databases:

**National catalog** Citations and summaries of documents on topics related to biology, chemistry, ecology, and other basic sciences. This database also contains citations for EPA reports distributed through the National Technical Information Service. Contains about 150,000 entries.

**Hazardous waste** Bibliographic information and abstracts for publications and databases about hazardous waste. Materials covered include books, EPA reports, policy and guidance directives from the Office of Solid Waste and Emergency Response (OSWER), periodicals, and commercial databases containing information about hazardous waste. Contains about 5,000 entries.

**Environmental financing information network** Information about financing alternatives for state and local environmental programs and projects. The database contains abstracts and case studies that describe successful financing alternatives, in addition to information about contacts in government and nonprofit organizations who are familiar with public financing and environmental programs.

### VITAL STATS

Data: 919-549-0720

Voice: 202-260-2080 (to request free manual) or 513-569-7183 (for technical questions)

Internet: telnet epaibm.rtpnc.epa.gov (at the first menu, select Public Access; at the second menu, select OLS)

Manual: Available by calling the voice number

Note: Your communications software must be set to 7 data bits, 1 stop bit, even parity, and half duplex (or local echo). After connecting, type **d** at the "Selection?" prompt.

**Chemical collection system**  Bibliographic information for items relating to chemicals. Contains about 140,000 entries.

**Access EPA**  Listings from *Access EPA,* a publication that provides contact information for about 300 sources of environmental information.

**National Center for Environmental Publications and Information (NCEPI)**  A list of EPA publications that is updated biweekly.

## Pesticide Information Network (PIN)

Leslie Davies-Hilliard
U.S. Environmental Protection Agency
Mail Stop H7507C
401 M St., S.W.
Washington, DC 20460

The Pesticide Information Network (PIN) provides information about pesticides that have restricted uses and pesticide monitoring projects around the country. Its databases allow detailed searches by numerous variables.

When you first connect, you may think you have entered in the middle of a session. That's because the board offers lots of information before formally greeting you and asking you to log in. Just follow the prompts.

The Main Menu has six directories:

A. Instruction manuals

B. Search the Chemical Index/view the chemical classes

C. Search the PMI File

D. Search the RUP File

E. Use the mailroom

F. Send the system operator a message

New users should begin in the instruction manuals directory. It contains manuals for all three databases that can be read online or captured to your computer by using your communications software's capture feature. The manuals are extremely useful, especially for users who lack extensive knowledge about chemicals.

The three databases contain the following information:

1. **Chemical Index**   A cross-referenced list of the names, synonyms, and CAS (Chemical Abstract Service) numbers for all chemicals contained in the other two databases. The index also identifies the database(s) in which the chemical can be found. The Chemical Index is helpful when you are unsure about the correct chemical name to use or when you want to do a quick search to see whether the databases have information about a specific chemical. The index is completely menu

**VITAL STATS**
Data: 703-305-5919
Voice: 703-305-7499
FedWorld gateway: 77
Manual: Three manuals can be found in the instruction manuals directory.
Note: You must enter all commands in capital letters. The BBS does not recognize lower-case letters.

driven. It allows you to search by chemical name or CAS number and also has a list of chemical classes.

2. **PMI File**   A compilation of pesticide monitoring projects being performed by federal, state, and local governments and private institutions. For each project, the database lists the chemicals, substrates, and location, in addition to the name, address, and telephone number of a person to contact for more information. You can search the database by chemical, CAS number, chemical class, chemical category, substrate, substrate breakdown, state, EPA region, country, sponsoring agency, revision date, body of water, or combinations of these categories. Searching this database is a complex process, so it's a good idea to read the manual before attempting a search.

3. **RUP File**   A listing of all pesticide products that have been classified as restricted use pesticides (RUPs) under 40 CFR Part 152, Subpart I. For each pesticide, the file contains the EPA chemical code number, active ingredient name, EPA registration number and product name, product manager number, criteria for classification, formulations and uses restricted, and the EPA actions that led to the classification. The file is updated monthly. You can access the file in three ways:

   - Download the entire file, a process that takes about forty minutes. To do this, turn on your communications software's capture feature and choose option B.

   - Download the list of Product Managers. This list contains the name, address, and telephone number of the manager who is assigned to each product. To do this, turn on your communications software's capture feature and choose option C.

   - Search the file to develop a unique list. Doing a search is complicated, so it's a good idea to read the manual first.

## Remote Access Chemical Hazards Electronic Library (RACHEL)

Environmental Research Foundation
P.O. Box 5036
Annapolis, MD 21403

Among other features, RACHEL offers documents from the U.S. Coast Guard and the U.S. Environmental Protection Agency about toxic chemicals. The BBS is operated by the Environmental Research Foundation, a private organization.

The federal government documents are located in the RACHEL database, which you can access by typing **r** at the Main Menu. You can search the database by document number, keywords, publication date, and other variables.

Two types of federal government documents are available:

**VITAL STATS**
Data: 410-263-8903
Voice: 410-263-1584
(answered only from 3 p.m. to 6 p.m. EST)
Manual: RACHEL.DOC

- U.S. Coast Guard fact sheets on chemicals. There are more than 1,000 documents from the Coast Guard's Chemical Hazard Response Information System (CHRIS). Each document has extensive information about a toxic chemical.

- Information about polluters sued by the U.S. Environmental Protection Agency from 1972 to 1990. These documents are from EPA's Civil Enforcement Docket. Each document lists the name and address of the company that was sued, the outcome of the case, any penalties assessed, the law involved, the violation charged, the date filed and concluded in federal court, the judicial district, and the court docket number, among other information.

The BBS also has extensive nonfederal information about toxic chemicals, including abstracts from newspapers and magazines, New Jersey Department of Health fact sheets on chemicals, reference information about the environment, copies of *Rachel's Hazardous Waste News,* and information about landfills, incinerators, and waste-handling companies.

# Research and Development Electronic Bulletin Board

U.S. Environmental Protection Agency
Office of Research and Development
Mail Stop G75
26 W. Martin Luther King Dr.
Cincinnati, OH 45268

The Research and Development Electronic Bulletin Board provides a bibliographic database of more than 18,000 publications prepared by the Environmental Protection Agency's Office of Research and Development (ORD) and its contractors. The database has abstracts of all ORD publications from 1976 to the present. They cover a wide range of environmental issues. For example, a search of the topic word *PCB* turned up 137 hits.

To access the database, type **open 1** at the Main Menu. You can search the database by title and abstract words, authors, laboratories, sponsoring agencies, performing organizations, EPA report number, National Technical Information Service (NTIS) order number, contract or grant number, and report year. Documents identified through the database can be ordered online.

More than a dozen bulletins are available on the Bulletin Menu, which you can reach by typing **b** at the Main Menu. Bulletins provide information about using the BBS, note upcoming Office of Research and Development meetings, list contacts who can provide technical assistance about groundwater, and explain how to access EPA's Online Library System.

The board also has more than 100 files, divided into file directories. Here are highlights of what you'll find:

- SWAMI 2.0, a software program that uses process analysis for identifying waste minimization opportunities for industries.

- The Surface Water Treatment Rule from the Code of Federal Regulations.

- The Total Coliform Rule from the Code of Federal Regulations.

- A database containing the coordinated list of chemicals.

- A list of engineering BBSs.

- A hydrogeologic unit conversion program.

**VITAL STATS**
Data: 513-569-7610
Voice: 513-569-7272
Manual: HELPFILE.TXT (uncompressed) or HELP.ZIP (compressed)
To access files: At the Main Menu, type **f**

- Periodic Table of the Elements for Windows.
- The EPA-ERT Air Methods Database.
- The RREL Treatability Database.
- Municipal solid waste options software.
- Numerous freeware and shareware utility programs for DOS computers.

There also are nine conferences, five of which are public. Three of the public conferences are automatically open to everyone, and the other two (denoted by an asterisk in the following list) require you to register with the sysop to gain access. To register, type **c** (for "Comment to Sysop") at the Main Menu, and leave a brief message requesting access. Here are brief descriptions of the public conferences:

1. **Expert systems**   Support, distribution, updates, and discussion on ORD's expert systems.

2. **Biotechnology**   A forum for discussing biotechnology engineering and technology, including the use of genetically and nongenetically engineered microbes.

3. ***Regional operations**   A conference aimed primarily at regional scientists but open to others in EPA to further the exchange of technical support.

4. ***Water regulations**   A forum to exchange information about the Office of Water's regulatory agenda and ORD's research activities to support it.

5. **Environmental Monitoring and Assessment Program (EMAP)**   A forum for exchanging information about EPA's EMAP program.

## U.S. EPA Region 10 BBS

U.S Environmental Protection Agency
Region 10
1200 Sixth Ave.
Seattle, WA

The U.S. EPA Region 10 BBS includes a wide range of environmental information for Alaska, Idaho, Oregon, and Washington. It also offers nearly two dozen conferences on everything from environmental education to pesticides to Alaska rural sanitation.

You can join the conferences by typing **j** at the Main Menu. The conferences serve as collection areas for messages on specific topics. Some of the topics covered are toxics, indoor air quality, wetlands, sustainable development, air toxics, chemical emergency planning, and Alaskan seafood processors.

Here are examples of some of the information available in the files:

- Information about sites contaminated with hazardous chemicals, including Superfund sites, in Alaska, Idaho, Oregon, and Washington. The file A_SFFACT.TXT explains how to use this information.

- A list of threatened and endangered species in EPA Region 10.

- Information about nonpoint source control practices for forestry in each Region 10 state.

- Drinking water regulations.

- Water quality standards for Alaska.

- Copies of a newsletter called *WaterTalk*.

- An electronic copy of the National Performance Review, a report about how to improve the federal government.

- Information about community-based electronic networks.

- Copies of a newsletter called *Networks and Community* that discusses resources on the Internet.

- Utility programs for DOS computers.

**VITAL STATS**

Data: 206-553-2241

Voice: 206-553-1026

Manual: HELP.TXT (uncompressed) or HELP.ZIP (compressed). This is a generic manual for the BBS software.

To access files: At the Main Menu, type **f**

# HAZARDOUS WASTE

## Alternative Treatment Technology Information Center (ATTIC)

SDC
Suite 300
200 N. Glebe Rd.
Arlington, VA 22203

The Alternative Treatment Technology Information Center (ATTIC) offers extensive information about technologies available for treating hazardous waste. Its core consists of two searchable databases. To reach a database, type its number at the Main Menu:

**1. Treatment Technology Database** Contains about 2,000 abstracts and citations of articles and technical reports on biological, chemical, physical, solidification/stabilization, and thermal treatment technologies. The database can be searched by keywords, free text, ATTIC control number, region or state, title, site name, and site history. Entries provide information on the treatment process, contaminants, cost, and performance.

**2. Risk Reduction Engineering Laboratory Treatability database** Contains information about the removal and destruction of chemicals in water, soil, debris, sludge, and sediment. It includes data on thirty-three alternative technologies.

The board also has more than 100 technical bulletins, which are divided into nine directories. You can access the bulletins by typing **6** at the Main Menu. Here are some highlights from selected directories:

**Environmental Information Resources Bulletins** Descriptions and contact information for databases, hotlines, and BBSs about environmental issues.

**EPA Superfund Innovative Technology Evaluation (SITE) Emerging Technology Bulletins** Descriptions of various projects around the country. Some sample titles are "Removal and Recovery of Metals from Groundwater" and "Alternating Current Electrocoagulation."

### VITAL STATS

Data: 703-908-2138
Voice: 703-908-2137
FedWorld gateway: 74
Manual: MANUALG.ZIP (the manual is excellent)
Note: If you prefer a paper copy of the manual, call the voice number or leave a message on the board for the sysop.

**Training Courses and Workshop Highlights**  Lists of upcoming seminars and conferences.

**Database Help Bulletins**  Explanations of how to use ATTIC.

The procedure for accessing files is a bit different from that used by most other BBSs. Type **b** at the Main Menu, and then type **5** at the ATTIC BBS Options Menu. Following are some of the more interesting files:

- The MSW Factbook, a huge electronic reference manual about municipal solid waste. But a warning: at 2400 baud, it can take more than an hour to download this enormous file.

- A list of agriculture-related BBSs.

- A list of environmental BBSs.

- A few utility programs for DOS and Macintosh computers.

Finally, the board has a calendar of events. To access it, type **8** at the Main Menu.

## Cleanup Information Bulletin Board (CLU-IN)

Office of Solid Waste and Emergency Response
Technology Innovation Office
U.S. Environmental Protection Agency
Mail Code 5102W
401 M St., S.W.
Washington, DC 20460

The Cleanup Information Bulletin Board (CLU-IN) specializes in information about hazardous waste. The most valuable file on the board, however, may be ECOLINK.ZIP, an annotated guide to using BBSs and online databases for finding environmental information.

The board has several interesting bulletins that you can access by typing **b** at the Main Menu. These include the following:

**VITAL STATS**
Data: 301-589-8366
Voice: 301-589-8368
FedWorld gateway: 7
To access files: At the Main Menu, type **f**

- Summaries of *Commerce Business Daily* procurement and contract award notices about hazardous waste, solid waste, underground storage tank remediation, and other environmental topics.

- A list of Superfund sites around the country, divided by state.

- Information about other Environmental Protection Agency (EPA) databases.

The board also has many useful files. To get a current list of all files on the board, begin by typing **f** at the Main Menu. Then type **1** at the next prompt. When that directory finishes scrolling, type **2** at the next prompt. Continue until all five file directories have scrolled on your screen.

Here are some highlights from the file directories:

### 1. Publications

- A bibliography about innovative treatment technology.

- A newsletter about bioremediation in the field.

- A list of products to use in containing oil spills.

- *Federal Register* bulletins and abstracts on hazardous waste.

- The EPA Library's *OERR Infoline Newsletter* about the hazardous waste Superfund collection.
- Some sections of the Code of Federal Regulations about hazardous waste.

## 2. Databases, Models, Expert Systems, and Other Programs

- The Hazardous Waste Collection database for DOS computers (requires twelve files).
- The EPA ERT's Air Methods database for DOS computers (requires four files).
- RREL Treatability Database for DOS computers (requires three files).
- Coordinated List of Chemicals database for DOS computers.
- Pesticide Treatability Database (requires six files).

## 3. CLU-IN BBS Files

- A list of environment-oriented BBSs.
- Information about the Audubon BBS.
- A BBS demonstration program for DOS computers.
- A glossary of computer terms.

## 4. Public Domain Utilities

- Anti-virus utilities.
- Utilities for both DOS and Macintosh computers for decompressing files.

## 5. User Uploads

- A program for DOS computers for converting hydrogeologic units.
- A text file that provides a tour of the Internet.
- An excellent, annotated list of environment-related BBSs.
- A file that describes how to find environmental information online using BBSs and databases.

## Cleanup Standards Outreach (CSO) BBS

Radiation Studies Division
U.S. Environmental Protection Agency
Mail Code 6603J
401 M St., S.W.
Washington, DC 20460

The Cleanup Standards Outreach (CSO) BBS seeks public comments on proposed rules for cleaning up sites that are contaminated with radioactivity. Previously, there were no specific cleanup standards for such sites. The new regulations will apply to Superfund sites, facilities operated by the departments of Energy and Defense, and sites operating under licenses issued by the Nuclear Regulatory Commission.

The board has only a few files. They explain the rulemaking, provide background information about radiation cleanup, and summarize meetings. All of the files are in a compressed, self-extracting format that makes them unusable on Macintosh computers.

Callers can use the board to submit comments about the rulemaking. However, those who want their comments included in the official regulatory docket must also mail paper copies to the Environmental Protection Agency.

**VITAL STATS**

Data: 800-700-7837 or 703-790-0825
Voice: 202-233-9340
FedWorld gateway: 134
To access files: At the Main Menu, type **f**
Time limit: 60 minutes per day

# INFOLINK

Civilian Radioactive Waste Management Information Center
U.S. Department of Energy
P.O. Box 44375
Washington, DC 20026

INFOLINK provides information about the Department of Energy's efforts to find a repository for the nation's high-level radioactive waste. The board is not for the weak of heart. The software is awkward, at least some of the phone lines are noisy, and the staff who run it for a Department of Energy contractor are not very reliable. It took several telephone calls to get the entire login procedure and several more calls to get the user's manual.

New users must first call the voice number to request an account. You will be asked for your name, address, and telephone number. Energy Department staff in Washington will pass along the information to the contractor in Oak Ridge, Tennessee. The contractor is supposed to call you back within a day with your password and login details. It is also supposed to ship a user's manual immediately. Good luck.

All but the most expert BBS users will need a copy of the user's manual to navigate the board. The manual is clearly written and contains lots of screen shots to help new users.

The BBS has five major areas that you can access from the Opening Menu:

1. **Current OCRWM program information**  This area has eleven sub-areas that are supposed to contain background information, Department of Energy (DOE) reports and studies, new publications, speeches and testimony, and other information. However, most of the sub-areas have no files. Only the newsflash, current bulletin, and press releases sub-areas currently contain significant numbers of files.

2. **Product record system**  This database contains descriptions and abstracts of more than 700 publications and audiovisual materials produced by the Office of Civilian Radioactive Waste Management. It can be searched by DOE/RW number, subject, publication date, or type of product. Sample document titles are "Reducing the Likeli-

---

**VITAL STATS**

Data: Number provided after registration

Voice: 800-225-6972 or 202-488-5513

Manual: A paper copy will be sent to you when you request an account.

Note: You must call to request an account before accessing this BBS. In addition, the board requires special terminal settings in your communications software. A setting of VT100 works well, and some others also should work.

hood of Future Human Activities that Could Affect Geologic High-level Waste Repositories" and "Area Recommendation Report for the Crystalline Repository Project." Available OCRWM products are free and can be ordered through the database.

3. **Publications catalog**   This database is an online version of the OCRWM publications catalog, which lists selected documents about high-level radioactive waste from OCRWM and other sources. Most of the documents are produced by federal agencies or their contractors. Citations were collected from online searches of DIALOG and databases maintained by the National Technical Information Service; the *Federal Register* and related publications; lists of OCRWM publications; and the documents themselves.

4. **OCRWM Bulletin index**   This section contains the complete text of the *OCRWM Bulletin* from January 1988 to the present. Articles are listed and indexed separately and can be retrieved by keywords. For example, users interested in a particular company can search the article database by the company's name. A listing of keywords can be accessed online.

5. **System services**   This section provides several services, including electronic mail for BBS users.

## Nuclear Regulatory Commission Decommissioning Rulemaking Bulletin Board

U.S. Nuclear Regulatory Commission
Washington, DC 20555

The purpose of the Nuclear Regulatory Commission Decommissioning Rulemaking Bulletin Board is to help the NRC develop rules for decontaminating nuclear facilities that are removed from service. Most of these facilities are nuclear power plants.

Previously, decisions about the extent to which radioactive contamination had to be cleaned up before a site could be closed were made on a case-by-case basis. The purpose of the rulemaking is to develop consistent rules about the required level of decontamination.

It is expected that this BBS will be discontinued when the decommissioning rulemaking is completed, which is scheduled for the middle of 1995. The NRC is considering replacing it with a BBS on rulemaking in general.

Files on the board provide the following information:

- Comments from various parties about the decommissioning rules.

- Background documents about the decommissioning rulemaking.

- Case studies about decommissioning reactors.

- A list of decommissioned and shutdown reactors.

- Notices from the *Federal Register* about NRC policy changes regarding radioactive waste.

- A list of hotline numbers for people who participated in radiation experiments in past decades.

- A list of telephone numbers for selected NRC offices.

**VITAL STATS**
Data: 800-880-6091
Voice: 301-492-3999
FedWorld gateway: 133
File list: ALLFILES.TXT
To access files: At the Main Menu, type **f**
Time limit: 2 hours per day

# MODELS

## Applied Modeling Research Branch (AMRB) BBS

Chief, Applied Modeling Research Branch (MD-80)
Atmospheric Characterization and Modeling Division
U.S. Environmental Protection Agency
Research Triangle Park, NC 27711

The Applied Modeling Research Branch BBS contains computer models of air dispersion. The models, which run on IBM and compatible computers, can be used in support of the Clean Air Act.

**VITAL STATS**
Data: 919-541-1325
Voice: 919-541-1376
Time limit: 3 hours per call

## CEAM BBS

Center for Exposure Assessment Modeling
U.S. Environmental Protection Agency
Office of Research and Development
Athens Environmental Research Laboratory
960 College Station Rd.
Athens, GA 30605-2720

About a dozen environmental models for DOS computers are available on the CEAM (Center for Exposure Assessment Modeling) BBS. In addition, the board includes files that support the software models. The models are designed to help federal, state, and local environmental officials make risk-based decisions concerning the protection of air, water, and soil.

The models simulate urban and rural nonpoint sources, tidal hydrodynamics, geochemical equilibrium, aquatic food chain bioaccumulation, and conventional and toxic pollution of streams, lakes and estuaries. All of the models are in the public domain, so they are free.

A file called INFOPACK.ZIP contains nine basic files for the board in a compressed package. They include a list of CEAM models and files, an overview of the BBS, and descriptions of CEAM models.

The board also has a number of useful bulletins. They provide information about accessing CEAM through the Internet, list CEAM-supported models, and list CEAM model documentation. Most of the bulletins also can be downloaded as files.

More than a dozen conferences serve as collection areas for messages on specific issues. Topics covered include ecological risk assessment, water quality modeling, and risk assessment, among others.

**VITAL STATS**

Data: 706-546-3402
Voice: 706-546-3549
Internet: ftp earth1.epa.gov
After you log in with your user name (anonymous) and Internet address, type **cd epa_ceam**. Only certain models are available through the Internet.
Manual: CEAMBBS.TXT
File list: CEAMFILE.LST
To access files: At the Main Menu, type **f**
Time limit: 5 hours per day

## National Ecology Research Center (NERC) Bulletin Board System

National Ecology Research Center, NBS
4512 McMurry Ave.
Fort Collins, CO 80525-3400

The National Ecology Research Center (NERC) Bulletin Board System contains software for modeling environmental habitats. The software, which is available only for IBM and compatible computers, is quite technical.

The software is designed for environmental officials in the federal and state governments. It allows them to determine the effects of various management practices on large projects, to establish in-stream flows for rivers, and to model other environmental conditions.

The board also has special interest groups about the software programs and a small collection of utility programs.

**VITAL STATS**
Data: 303-226-9365
Voice: 303-226-9335
Manual: NEWUSER.TXT
To access files: At the Main Menu, type **f**

# WATER

## Nonpoint Source Program Electronic Bulletin Board

U.S. Environmental Protection Agency
Mail Stop WH553
401 M St., S.W.
Washington, DC 20460

The primary focus of the Nonpoint Source Program Electronic Bulletin Board is water pollution, although it also includes lots of information about other environmental issues. Whether or not you're interested in water pollution, at least log on long enough to download the user's manual. Besides providing information specific to the Nonpoint BBS, it offers lots of details about navigating around BBSs in general. It includes an excellent online tour of the BBS that you can read and then perform online. If you are new to BBSs, this manual is indispensable.

The BBS has four major areas: bulletins, files, special interest groups, and doors to online databases.

The board has about 100 bulletins. To get a list of them, type **b** at the Main Menu. You can read the bulletins online or download them. Following are some highlights:

- A list of environment-related newsletters and publications.
- Information about EPA libraries and their water-related materials.
- Information about groundwater.
- Information about pollution prevention and environmental activities around the home.
- A list of contacts for federal job information.
- A description of sources for White House press releases.
- Press releases from the White House about environmental issues.

**VITAL STATS**
Data: 301-589-0205
Voice: 202-260-3665
FedWorld gateway: 79
Manual: MAN-ASCI.ZIP (ASCII text) or MAN-WP51.ZIP (WordPerfect 5.1)
To access files: At the Main Menu, type **f**

The files are separated into four directories. To get a list of the directories, type **f** at the Main Menu. At the next prompt, type the number of the directory you want to list. Here are some highlights:

## Directory 1

- A background report about wetlands.
- A large list of environment-related BBSs and hotlines.

- A list of national toll-free numbers for motor oil recycling.
- The Earth Charter from the environmental summit in Rio de Janeiro.
- A calendar of water-related events.
- A description of software and services available from EPA's Center for Exposure Assessment Modeling.
- A list of state Clean Lakes Program contacts and EPA Clean Lakes Program coordinators.
- Portions of an EPA report on pesticides in drinking water.
- A list of EPA contacts who can provide assistance on groundwater issues.
- A file about how to have a beautiful (and environmentally responsible) lawn.
- An extensive file for consumers about lead poisoning (available in English and Spanish versions).
- Electronic copies of the Nonpoint Source Program newsletter.
- A bibliography of NPS-related documents.
- Electronic copies of the EPA Headquarters library newsletter.
- Numerous files about wetlands.
- A partial list of database files available from the U.S. Geological Survey.

## Directory 2

- Anti-virus programs for DOS computers.
- A program for converting WordPerfect files.
- A list of engineering-related BBSs.
- A program that provides a "fog index" for text.
- All of the board's help files in one file.
- A file defining computer communications and BBS jargon.
- Utility programs for decompressing files on both DOS and Macintosh computers.

## Directory 3

- An article about a Senate bill to amend and reauthorize the Clean Water Act.
- Numerous files of congressional testimony about clean water issues.

## Directory 4

- A promotional flier about the BBS.
- A flier about the Watershed Restoration SIG (special interest group).
- Several files containing the text of bills introduced in Congress about clean water.
- Numerous files of congressional testimony about clean water issues.

The board also has special interest groups devoted to various issues. SIGs frequently have bulletins or files, and each one has its own e-mail system. To join a SIG, type j at the Main Menu, a space, and the SIG's number. There are eight SIGs:

1. **Agricultural issues**   This is a forum for discussing issues related to agricultural nonpoint source pollution. The SIG contains more than forty bulletins that list agriculture-related newsletters, key personnel at the National Agricultural Library, and recommended publications about agriculture and the environment. The bulletins also contain news items about pesticides. In addition, the forum has files that list periodicals about alternative farming, describe educational and training opportunities in sustainable agriculture, provide facts about Atrazine (a chemical used on farms), and offer numerous case studies about projects in agricultural conservation.

2. **Fish consumption**   This forum is concerned with the health risks of eating contaminated fish. Its bulletins list keywords used in the Fish Consumption Database (Door 1), discuss the potential effects of global warming on common freshwater fisheries, list new fish advisories, provide updated information about mercury contamination, and provide information about the Great Lakes Human Health Effects Research and Information Exchange Network. The files list state contact persons for fish advisories and describe the life history of the lake trout. The SIG also contains a door to the Fish Consumption Database. Users can search the database for fish bans and advisories, documents, and contacts. To get help with your search, see Appendices III and IV of the SIG's user's manual.

3. **Waterbody system**   This forum supports EPA's Waterbody system. Its files include a list of Waterbody system contacts at the EPA and states and a manual for the WBS computer program, which must be requested separately.

4. **Nonpoint source research**   This forum is about EPA activities and products that may be of interest to professionals in nonpoint source pollution prevention. The SIG's bulletins describe technical assistance available from EPA's Office of Research and Development (ORD), list recent ORD publications, describe agricultural research, and describe global climate research.

5. **Watershed restoration network**   This forum for exchanging information about watershed restoration has more than two dozen bulletins. Some sample titles are "A Watershed Approach to Fisheries Restoration on the Klamath River," "Guidelines for Collection of Cuttings to Maintain Genetic Diversity," and "California Native Grass Association Founded." The SIG also has doors to EPA's Watershed Registry, where users can provide or read information about specific watershed projects.

6. **Total Maximum Daily Load** (TMDL)   This forum is intended for people engaged in water resources management on a watershed/basin scale. Its files provide numerous case studies of Total Maximum Daily Load projects.

7. **Volunteer monitoring**   This forum covers monitoring of waterways by volunteers. Its bulletins provide information about state volunteer monitoring programs, including program names, addresses, and coordinators; list keywords to use in the SIG's doors; note upcoming conferences and meetings about volunteer monitoring; and provide news about volunteer monitoring. The files include documents about citizen action, a fact sheet about getting started in volunteer monitoring, documents that describe volunteer monitoring programs nationwide, and copies of newsletters about volunteer monitoring.

   The SIG also has two doors to online databases. The first contains information about volunteer monitoring programs sponsored by state agencies. Each record discusses a specific program and provides the program name, a contact person, the type of monitoring performed, the type and number of water bodies monitored, and the number of program participants. The second door provides references to documents that can help volunteer monitors. Subjects include citizen action programs, environmental education, monitoring methods, and pollution control approaches. Each record provides a citation and abstract and, where available, a contact and cost information.

8. **Coastal nonpoint pollution**   This SIG covers issues related to Section 6217 of the Coastal Zone Act Reauthorization Amendments of 1990. It is intended to help states develop and implement their Coastal Nonpoint Pollution Control Programs. The SIG's files include chapters from EPA's Management Measures Guidance, a directory of agricultural extension program leaders, a list of EPA nonpoint source coordinators, and a list of state extension water quality coordinators.

The BBS also has three doors to databases. To access them, type **open** at the Main Menu and then choose the database you want:

**Clean Lakes Database**   Abstracts and citations of technical material and information from journal articles, Clean Lakes Program reports, conference proceedings, and government documents. Subjects covered include lake ecology, lake management and protection, in-lake restoration techniques, watershed management, point and nonpoint sources of pollution, water quality assessment, modeling, and lake problems such as nutrients, acidification, and toxic substances. The database can be searched by title, subject, author, and region or state.

**NPS News-Notes Database**   The full text of articles from the *NPS News-Notes Newsletter,* produced by EPA's Office of Wetlands, Oceans, and Watersheds. The database can be searched by article number, title, and keywords.

**Educational Materials Database**   Lists of projects, videos, pamphlets, posters, and other items produced by states and local governments as outreach materials for their nonpoint source programs. The database contains information about outreach activities, public education programs, educational materials, communication techniques, and public involvement projects. It can be searched by title and description.

## Technology Transfer BBS

U.S. Environmental Protection Agency
Region IV
4WM-MF
345 Courtland St., N.E.
Atlanta, GA 30365

Files and conferences on the Technology Transfer BBS focus on the design, operation, maintenance, and regulation of wastewater treatment plants, although information is also available about drinking water, storm water, and water quality.

The bulletins, which you can access by typing **b** at the Main Menu, explain how to use the board, provide details about the conferences, explain how to decompress files and display graphics files available on the BBS, list new technology transfer publications, and provide news about rules and regulations.

The ten conferences are available only to users who request access from the sysop. To do so, type **c** at the Main Menu and then write a message asking for access. To get descriptions of the conferences, read the bulletin called CONFER. The conferences serve as message collection points on such topics as sewage sludge, wastewater reclamation, and drinking water quality.

The files are divided into nine directories. Here are some of the highlights:

- Groundwater protection work plans.

- A fact sheet about small-diameter sewers.

- Information about dealing with oil and grease from restaurants.

- Environmental regulations for very small communities.

- Bibliographies and design manuals for constructed wetlands.

- A nonspecialist's guide to technical terms.

- A list of wastewater publications available from the Environmental Protection Agency.

- A wide range of files about drinking water and storm water.

**VITAL STATS**
Data: 404-347-1767
Voice: 404-347-3633
Manual: BBSGUIDE.ZIP (the manual is excellent)
File list: ALLFILES.ZIP (compressed) or ALLFILES.TXT (uncompressed)

- Sludge regulations.
- Information about vacuum sewers.
- Telecommunications, decompression, and anti-virus programs for DOS computers.
- Several dozen utility programs for DOS computers.

## Wastewater Treatment Information Exchange (WTIE)

National Small Flows Clearinghouse
P.O. Box 6064
Morgantown, WV 26506

The Wastewater Treatment Information Exchange (WTIE), which is part of the National Small Flows Clearinghouse, contains hundreds of files about wastewater management and prevention issues. There are more than forty bulletins, which you can access by typing **b** at the Main Menu. They explain the board's features, provide news about grants, list other environmental BBSs, and describe publications.

Callers can use the BBS to request searches of the bibliographic database at the National Small Flows Clearinghouse. The search results are posted on the board, and users can request copies of documents listed in the search.

The board also has conferences on nearly a dozen topics, including wastewater plant operators' problems and solutions, constructed wetlands, regulations affecting small communities, and wasterwater-related software.

The files are divided into sixteen directories and offer the following types of information:

- Descriptions of dozens of publications produced by the National Small Flows Clearinghouse.

- News about new state and federal regulations.

- Hundreds of articles on wastewater issues, including such topics as financing, operation and maintenance, and troubleshooting problems with small wastewater systems.

- News about workshops for small communities.

- Communications, decompression, and anti-virus shareware programs for Macintosh computers.

**VITAL STATS**
Data: 800-544-1936 or 304-293-5969
Voice: 800-624-8301 or 304-293-4191
FedWorld gateway: 37
To access files: At the Main Menu, type **f**

# ETHNIC GROUPS AND MINORITIES

## INDIANnet

Americans for Indian Opportunity
22571 Smoky Ridge Rd.
Rapid City, SD 57702

American Indians and Alaskan natives are the primary audience for INDIANnet. The BBS is sponsored by Americans for Indian Opportunity, a nonprofit advocacy organization that receives funding from the Bureau of Indian Affairs, the Administration on Native Americans, the Environmental Protection Agency, and the Department of Agriculture.

The board is set up differently from most others, but it's relatively easy to use. The board's biggest flaw is that most of the file lists do not provide file descriptions. This makes it virtually impossible to determine what's in a file without downloading it and taking a look.

Here are some highlights of what's available:

**VITAL STATS**
Data: 605-394-6858
Voice: 605-348-7293

- News about various federal government actions affecting Native Americans, including information about the Indian Dams Safety Act, Environmental Protection Agency rules affecting tribal air quality, and the Indian Health Service loan repayment program.

- Data about various Indian tribes extracted from the 1990 U.S. Census.

- More than a dozen publications from the Small Business Administration, including *Minority Businesses, How to Write a Business Plan, Raising Money for Small Businesses, Women Business Ownership,* and *Starting a Home Business.*

- Background information about the Administration for Native Americans, a federal program that promotes social and economic self-sufficiency among Native Americans.

- Hundreds of shareware and freeware programs for Macintosh computers.

## Minority Impact BBS

National Minority Energy Information Clearinghouse
Office of Minority Economic Impact
U.S. Department of Energy
1000 Independence Ave., S.W., Room 5B110
Washington, DC 20585

The Minority Impact BBS contains information about opportunities for minorities through the Department of Energy (DOE). All information on the board is presented in bulletins, which you can access by typing b at the Main Menu. You can read the bulletins online and save them by using your communications software's capture feature. There are no files.

The bulletins present information about various topics:

- DOE's Office of Minority Impact.

- Programs for minorities at DOE's national laboratories and its energy program offices.

- DOE's programs for historically black colleges and universities.

- The Socioeconomic Research and Analysis Program in DOE's Office of Minority Economic Impact, including a list of publications.

- Future energy-related conferences.

**VITAL STATS**

Data: 800-543-1561 or 202-586-1561

Voice: 202-586-7898

FedWorld gateway: 62

Time limit: 60 minutes per call

# GOVERNMENT

# ETHICS, FRAUD, AND WASTE

## Ethics Bulletin Board System

Office of Information Resources Management
U.S. Office of Government Ethics
1201 New York Ave., N.W., Suite 500
Washington, DC 20005-3917

The Ethics Bulletin Board System contains ethics laws, regulations, policies, and opinions affecting the executive branch of the federal government. Information is presented in bulletins that can be read online and files that can be downloaded. The bulletins and files contain nearly identical information, so you may want to go directly to the files.

Downloading files, which are separated into six areas, is a bit of a pain. To download a file, you must be in the area where the file is located. If you want to download files from several areas, you must enter each of the areas. Here are highlights from each area:

**Regulations** Copies of regulations issued by the Office of Government Ethics (OGE) and the section of the Code of Federal Regulations pertaining to the OGE.

**Opinions** Formal advisory opinions, informal letter opinions, and policy memoranda issued by the Office of Government Ethics. They discuss how to interpret and comply with conflict of interest, postemployment, standards of conduct, and financial disclosure requirements in the executive branch. The opinions date from 1979 to the present. A file in this area called INDEX.TXT provides an index to all of the opinions on the board.

**DAEOgrams** Memoranda from the OGE to executive branch ethics officials. They provide guidance on interpreting and complying with ethics rules.

**Education/training** Information about ethics training classes and training materials available from the OGE.

**Public affairs** Copies of proposed and final ethics rules published in the *Federal Register* and an OGE staff directory.

**Miscellaneous** A list of ethics officials at federal agencies and a list of ethics reports that agencies must file, complete with due dates.

---

**VITAL STATS**

Data: 202-523-1186

Voice: 202-523-5757

FedWorld gateway: 91

To access files: At the Main Menu, type **f**

Available: 24 hours a day except from 7 a.m. to 8 a.m. EST

# Federal Deficit Reduction BBS

House Government Operations Committee
Subcommittee on Information, Justice, Transportation, and Agriculture

The Federal Deficit Reduction BBS seeks two kinds of information from federal employees and the public: (1) ideas about how to reduce the federal deficit; and (2) reports about waste, fraud, and abuse in the federal government. Callers can leave messages or upload files to congressional investigators. There are no public files or public messages on the board, which is operated by the Subcommittee on Information, Justice, Transportation, and Agriculture of the House Government Operations Committee.

The investigators seek information about problems involving large amounts of federal money or major instances of wrongdoing. They cannot investigate personal problems of federal workers or constituents.

Callers can use aliases rather than their real names. If you use an alias, however, be sure to remember it so that you can call back later to check for messages from investigators.

The bulletins, which you can access by typing **b** at the Main Menu, describe the board's purpose and explain how to use it. To leave a message, type **c** at the Main Menu and then type the message. To upload a file to investigators, type **f** at the Main Menu and **u** at the File Menu.

**VITAL STATS**

Address: Mail support not provided
Data: 202-225-5527
Voice: Voice support not provided
Time limit: 60 minutes per call

## GAO Watchdog

U.S. General Accounting Office
P.O. Box 1736
Washington, DC 20013

Members of the public can use the GAO Watchdog BBS to report federal government misconduct and wrongdoing to the General Accounting Office (GAO), the investigative arm of Congress. Callers are asked to use their real names, which are kept confidential upon request. People who are uncomfortable using their real names can use aliases. If you use an alias on this board, be sure to remember it so that you can exchange messages with GAO investigators.

The bulletins provide an introduction to the board and hints on reporting problems relating to federal money or programs. Callers can leave a report either by using the e-mail system or by uploading a document.

Users cannot access any files on the board and can exchange messages only with GAO investigators.

**VITAL STATS**
Data: 202-371-2455
Voice: 202-512-7476
FedWorld gateway: 41
Time limit: 60 minutes per day

# OPERATIONS AND MANAGEMENT

## CASUCOM

Cooperative Administrative Support Program
18th and F Sts., N.W.
Room 7007
Washington, DC 20405

The Cooperative Administrative Support (CASU) program is a project in which federal agencies share services in an effort to save money and improve efficiency. It is conducted under the auspices of the President's Council on Management Improvement. The CASUCOM BBS serves agencies involved in the program.

The board has fourteen conferences. They are on such topics as mail management, marketing the CASU program, modems, recycling, and telecommuting.

Files are divided into seventeen library information banks. Some of the most interesting banks are the following:

**Main**  Numerous documents about the National Performance Review, a report about improving the federal government, and a copy of PKUNZIP, the DOS program for decompressing files.

**Articles**  Articles about the Cooperative Administrative Support program.

**CASUnews**  Electronic copies of the program's newsletter.

**Policy**  CASU policy documents.

**Sites**  Profiles of sites that are using the program, along with contact information.

**Tcommute**  Descriptions of various telecommuting projects, a list of telecommuting centers in the Washington, D.C., area, and information about the Washington State Model Telecommuting Project.

> **VITAL STATS**
>
> Data: 202-653-7516 or 202-653-7522
>
> Voice: 202-273-4660
>
> FedWorld gateway: 73
>
> Manual: To access the online manual, type **i** at the Main Menu and **h** at the next prompt. This is a generic manual for the BBS software.
>
> To access files: At the Main Menu, type **l**

## GAO Office of Policy's BBS

Office of Policy
U.S. General Accounting Office
441 G St., N.W., Room 6800
Washington, DC 20548

The GAO Office of Policy's BBS from the General Accounting Office contains several large files listing GAO recommendations that either have or have not been implemented by federal agencies and departments. The board also includes an electronic version of the GAO's telephone book. It does not offer copies of any GAO reports, however.

Unfortunately, the most useful files have been compressed in a self-executing format that makes them unusable on Macintosh computers. The sysop says there are no plans to make the files available in other formats.

**VITAL STATS**
Data: 202-512-4286
Voice: 202-512-6100
FedWorld gateway: 135
To access files: At the Main Menu, type **f**
Time limit: 3 hours per day

# GSA Electronic Management Information (GEMI) BBS

U.S. General Services Administration
Room 3111
18th and F Sts., N.W.
Washington, DC 20405

The GEMI BBS contains information about other General Service Administration (GSA) boards, sub-boards on such topics as computer accommodation for people with disabilities, and copies of the National Performance Review report.

The following list describes areas that you can access from the Main Menu. To reach an area, type the appropriate letter or number:

**D. Directory**  This area contains descriptions of every GSA BBS. You can read the list online and save it by using your communications program's capture feature. There is no version to download.

**C. COCA**  This sub-board is operated by GSA's Clearinghouse on Computer Accommodation (COCA). The Files Menu, which you can reach by typing 1 at the COCA Menu, offers numerous files about federal government electronic information, a list of vendors and producers of access products, and COCA reports. The sub-board also has a forum, a news section that primarily describes new files, and its own e-mail system.

**4. X.400**  This sub-board on interagency X.400 is primarily for federal managers. The board has bulletins that list upcoming meetings and describe GSA's participation in X.400, files about governmentwide e-mail, a directory of X.400 addresses, and its own e-mail system.

**P. PASS (Planning, Quality Assurance, Systems Security Programs)**  This sub-board presents extensive information about GSA's Information Resources Management (IRM) plan, including a copy of the five-year plan. Other files contain directives, IRM reviews and reports, lists of contacts, and system security guidelines. The sub-board also has a forum about PASS issues, news about upcoming meetings, and its own e-mail system.

**F. Files**  This area contains a few general files, including the full text of the National Performance Review report.

**L. Local GEMI functions**  An e-mail system is included in this area, but otherwise all the functions duplicate those in other areas of the board.

**VITAL STATS**
Data: 202-219-0132
Voice: 202-501-3481
FedWorld gateway: 100
Manual: BBSUSER.DOC (a generic manual for the BBS software)

## POLICIES AND REGULATIONS

## ACF BBS

U.S. Administration for Children and Families
Aerospace Building
370 L'Enfant Promenade, S.W.
Washington, DC 20447

The ACF BBS provides information about programs operated by the Administration for Children and Families. Here are some highlights of what you'll find:

- More than two dozen brief fact sheets on ACF programs, including Aid to Families with Dependent Children (AFDC), child support enforcement, Head Start, foster care and adoption assistance, and runaway and homeless youth.

- Information about the Child Support Enforcement Network (CSENET). CSENET is a nationwide communications network that's being developed to link state child support enforcement systems.

- Information about the ACF's Child Support Enforcement program, which monitors state and local child support enforcement efforts.

- Information about the Low Income Heating Energy Assistance Program (LIHEAP).

- Press releases from the ACF.

**VITAL STATS**

Data: 800-627-8886 or 202-401-5800
Voice: 202-401-5682
FedWorld gateway: 108
Manual: BBSUSER.DOC (a generic manual for the BBS software)

## OCA BBS Document Exchange

Office of the Consumer Advocate
U.S. Postal Rate Commission
1333 H St., N.W.
Washington, DC 20268-0001

The OCA BBS Document Exchange contains documents filed in rate cases being considered by the Postal Rate Commission. Most of the documents are filed by major customers and competitors of the U.S. Postal Service. The BBS contains only documents filed electronically; it has no documents filed in paper form.

There are a half-dozen bulletins, which you can access by typing **b** at the Main Menu. Most explain how to use the BBS.

The board also has a newsletter, which you can access by typing **n** at the Main Menu. It contains information about new files and features available on the board.

The files are separated into more than a dozen directories. Although most of the files are comments in rate cases, the files area also contains the following:

- An electronic copy of the Domestic Mail Classification Schedule.

- An electronic copy of the report of the Joint Task Force on Postal Rulemaking.

- An electronic copy of the Postal Rate Commission's Rules of Practice and Procedure.

- Orders and opinions from the Postal Rate Commission.

**VITAL STATS**
Data: 202-789-6891
Voice: 202-789-6838
FedWorld gateway: 99
File list: FILES.TXT
To access files: At the Main Menu, type **f**

# PRESS INFORMATION

## HUD News and Events Bulletin Board

U.S. Department of Housing and Urban Development
Room 10136
451 7th St., S.W.
Washington, DC 20410

The HUD News and Events Bulletin Board contains information from the public affairs office of the Department of Housing and Urban Development (HUD).

The board offers the following information:

- HUD news releases.

- Speeches, statements, and congressional testimony by HUD officials.

- Fact sheets about major HUD programs.

- The public schedule of the HUD secretary.

- Biographies of senior HUD personnel.

- Contact information for HUD field offices.

- Fair market rent data.

- Files from the Interagency Council on the Homeless.

- A survey of mortgage lending activity.

**VITAL STATS**

Data: 202-708-3460 or 202-708-3563
Voice: 202-708-0685, ext. 113
FedWorld gateway: 85

## PR On-Line

Stephen K. Cook and Company, Inc.
Suite 800
1090 Vermont Ave., N.W.
Washington, DC 20005

PR On-Line is a privately operated BBS for journalists. It contains press releases from the White House and four committees in the House of Representatives. In addition, it has press releases from the Brookings Institution and various trade associations.

The BBS is arranged into sub-boards, each of which has its own files. To access the files on a particular sub-board, you must join the sub-board where they're located. To do so, type j at the Main Menu, leave a space, and type the number of the sub-board you want.

You can conduct subject searches within each sub-board. The "Zippy Search" option searches terms in headlines but not within the text.

Several sub-boards provide federal government information:

**VITAL STATS**
Data: 410-363-0834
Voice: 202-347-8918

**News**  White House press releases for the previous week, including texts of the president's radio speeches, statements by the president and cabinet officials, transcripts of White House press conferences and press briefings, selected schedules for the president and cabinet officials, and information about presidential nominations.

**House Committee on Foreign Affairs**  Transcripts of speeches by the committee chairman, press releases from the committee, information on foreign affairs bills passed by the House, and information on selected General Accounting Office reports. The sub-board recently contained information about Haiti, South Africa, Europe, Vietnam, Nicaragua, Bosnia, U.S. nuclear testing, the North American Free Trade Agreement (NAFTA), peacekeeping by the United Nations, and classified information. The committee's jurisdiction includes U.S. relations with foreign nations in general, establishment of boundary lines between the United States and other countries, intervention abroad and declarations of war, and measures to foster business with foreign nations.

**House Committee on Science, Space, and Technology**  Press releases about bills introduced, detailed descriptions of bills, schedules of upcoming committee hearings along with lists of expected witnesses, transcripts of speeches by the committee chairman, and information about science-related bills passed by Congress. The sub-board recently contained information about national competitiveness legislation, U.S. science policy, fire safety, biodiversity, a plea agreement at a nuclear weapons plant, desalination research, protection of Antarctica, space commercialization, and UNESCO reform, among other subjects. The committee's jurisdiction includes astronautical research and development, outer space, the National Aeronautics and Space Administration, the National Science Foundation, science research, federal energy laboratories, and the National Weather Service.

**House Committee on Ways and Means** Information about upcoming hearings and lists of witnesses scheduled to testify, information about bills passed by the committee, and announcements about the filling of committee and staff vacancies. The sub-board recently contained information about unemployment compensation, pension plans, taxes, health care reform, Medicare, NAFTA, and the Customs Service's loss of firearms, among other subjects. The committee's jurisdiction includes revenue bills, customs, reciprocal trade agreements, tax-exempt foundations, Social Security, and work incentive programs.

**House Small Business Committee** Hearing notices along with lists of scheduled witnesses, opening statements by the chairman at hearings, and press statements by committee members. The sub-board recently contained information about NAFTA, economic development, small-business technology, Japanese automobile imports, the franchise industry, credit conditions for small business, venture capital, and health reform and small business. The committee's jurisdiction includes aid to small business, protection of small business, and participation of small businesses in federal procurement and government contracts.

# PROPERTY AND ASSETS

## Client Information Center BBS

U.S. General Services Administration
18th and F Sts., N.W.
Washington, DC 20405

The Client Information Center BBS is aimed at General Services Administration employees who manage federal government buildings. The board's arrangement is different from most other federal BBSs. To access the files, you must join a conference.

To join a conference, type j at the Main Menu, and then type the number of the conference you want. The board has conferences on delegations, energy, leasing, safety, and specifications. The files contain lease information and specifications for cleaning and repairing federal buildings.

**VITAL STATS**

Data: 202-208-1747 or 202-501-2038

Voice: 202-501-4455

To access files: You must first join a conference.

## Federal Real Estate Sales Bulletin Board

U.S. General Services Administration
Room 4242
18th and F Sts., N.W.
Washington, DC 20405

Information about real estate for sale by federal government agencies can be found on the Federal Real Estate Sales Bulletin Board. The board contains general information about federal agencies that sell real estate, listings of specific properties for sale by the General Services Administration, and lists of military base closings nationwide.

To access information on the BBS, type the first letter of the area's name as it appears on the Main Menu:

**VITAL STATS**
Data: 800-776-7872 or 202-501-6510
Voice: 202-501-3273
FedWorld gateway: 126

**[I]ntroduction for public users**  Provides an overview of the BBS and instructions for using its Query Area.

**[C]ontacts**  Lists federal agencies that sell excess, seized, forfeited, or repossessed real estate. The agencies sell individual houses, multifamily units, office buildings, industrial plants, and vacant land. The area describes the kinds of property that each agency sells and provides instructions about where to call or write for further information.

**[Q]uery**  Allows users to examine listings of properties for sale by the General Services Administration. The board normally lists about fifty properties. In the future the sysop hopes to add listings for properties being sold by other federal agencies as well. The listings can be searched by state, GSA region, first three digits of the zip code, agency selling the property, type of property, sale date, and sale type.

**[B]ase closures**  Lists military base closures by state and contacts for each of the military branches.

**[G]SA**  Lists addresses and telephone numbers for GSA Federal Property Resource Service offices nationwide.

## FMS Inside Line

Cash Management Directorate
Financial Management Service
U.S. Department of the Treasury
401 14th St., S.W., 5th Floor, LCB
Washington, DC 20227

The primary focus of FMS Inside Line, which is operated by the Treasury Department's Financial Management Service, is management of federal inventories, assets, and finances. However, the board also has numerous text files and programs for operators of BBSs.

The bulletins, which you can access by typing **b** at the Main Menu, are quite technical. They cover such topics as banking management, asset management support, electronic commerce, and artificial intelligence.

A dozen conferences support individual Financial Management Service programs. The board has conferences about electronic benefits transfer, asset management support, Treasury financial management and policy information, and the Cash Management Improvement Act of 1990, among other subjects. Most conferences have their own bulletins, files, and messages, and some have sub-conferences. You can access the conferences by typing **j** at the Main Menu.

The board has more than two dozen file directories, which you can access by typing **f** at the Main Menu. Here are some highlights of what's available:

- The complete text of the *Treasury Financial Manual*, which provides instructions about fiscal management for federal agencies and departments.

- Extensive information about the distribution of federal funds to states and territories. One table lists each state's ranking, the total funds received, and the funds received per capita.

- A list of financial officers at federal agencies and departments.

- An electronic copy of the final rule to implement the Cash Management Improvement Act.

- Numerous files of population projections to the year 2050.

**VITAL STATS**
Data: 202-874-6817 or
  202-874-6953 or
  202-874-7034
Voice: 202-874-6995
FedWorld gateway: 50
File list: ALLFILES.TXT
To access files: At the Main Menu, type **f**

- Text files for people considering starting a BBS.
- Numerous programs and utilities for BBS operators.
- Lots of utility programs for DOS computers.

## Sales Bulletin Board System

U.S. General Services Administration
33rd Floor
525 Market St.
San Francisco, CA 94105

The Sales Bulletin Board System has information about surplus federal government property available for sale in Alaska, Arizona, California, Hawaii, Idaho, Oregon, Utah, and Washington State.

The BBS is arranged differently from most other federal BBSs, and it's quite cumbersome. After logging in you'll see the Private Mail Sub-board, which is of no use unless you send or receive private mail. Hit the Return key to pass it by.

Next, you'll be told that you can access two sub-boards, Personal Mail and GSA Sales. To reach the GSA Sales sub-board, type **95** at the prompt. When you get another menu, you should type **f** to get a list of the files. The files provide a calendar of upcoming sales and details about the property being sold.

**VITAL STATS**

Data: 415-744-8970

Voice: 415-744-5245

Account code: **gsasales**

Password: **sales**

Note: Set your communications software to emulate a VT100 terminal.

# HEALTH AND MEDICINE

## GENERAL

### Aeromedical Forum

Federal Aviation Administration
Office of Aviation Medicine
800 Independence Ave., S.W.
Washington, DC 20591

The Aeromedical Forum is aimed at FAA aviation medicine employees. Although it is open to the public, only FAA employees can access the files and conferences on aviation medicine.

New users are assigned security level 1. At this level you can examine parts of the board and download some files. The available files consist primarily of utility programs for DOS computers, but most are a couple of years old. FAA employees who wish to access the aviation medicine files and conferences must fill out a questionnaire. To do so, type a at the Main Menu.

**VITAL STATS**
Data: 202-366-7920
Voice: 202-267-3535
Time limit: 75 minutes per call

## Bureau of Health Professions (BHPr) BBS

Room 8809
5600 Fishers Lane
Rockville, MD 20857

The Bureau of Health Professions (BHPr) BBS provides information about students and professionals in the health field, along with a few health-related statistics. Information on the board is divided into bulletins and files. The bulletins, which you can access by typing **b** at the Main Menu, describe Bureau of Health Professions programs, give BHPr telephone numbers, list national professional meetings and international conferences, and provide information about reports and publications.

The files are separated into thirteen directories. Here are some examples of what's available:

- A list of sites that serve the medically underserved. This file has been compressed in a format that will not work on Macintosh computers.
- A list of 200 ways to put your talent to work in the health field.
- Statistics on the number of families living below the poverty level during the years 1973–1990.
- AIDS death rates for 1987–1989.
- Maternal mortality rates for 1970–1989.
- Statistics about patient visits to doctors and dentists.
- Statistics about the enrollment of minorities and women in health education programs.
- A huge book filled with statistics about health professionals. The files have been compressed in a format that will not work on Macintosh computers.
- A book about public health.
- Information about compliance by states with the Radiation Health and Safety Act of 1981.
- A book with extensive information about health occupations.
- A list of geriatric education centers that includes addresses, phone numbers, and fax numbers.

**VITAL STATS**
Data: 301-443-5913
Voice: 301-443-2850
FedWorld gateway: 111
To access files: At the Main Menu, type **f**
Time limit: 60 minutes per call

## CDRH Electronic Docket

Center for Devices and Radiological Health
U.S. Food and Drug Administration
12200 Wilkins Ave., Room 202
Rockville, MD 20852

Documents on the CDRH Electronic Docket advise the medical device industry about how to create products that will meet with approval from the Food and Drug Administration. The board also has announcements about related advisory committee meetings.

The FDA Center for Devices and Radiological Health regulates a wide range of medical devices—everything from patient examination gloves to breast implants to heart valves to X-ray machines. The center is charged with ensuring that the devices are safe and effective.

After you log in, the system presents a list of fifteen file directories:

1. Instructions and indexes
2. Medical device regulations
3. Evaluation guidance
4. Compliance guidance
5. Postmarket surveillance
6. Manufacturer assistance
7. Radiological health guides
8. Speeches and letters
9. Congressional testimony
10. Press releases/talk papers
11. Center periodic publications
12. Committee/panel meeting minutes
13. Product clearance
14. Center personnel information
15. News, events, conferences

**VITAL STATS**

Data: 800-252-1366 or 301-594-2741

Voice: 301-443-6597

FedWorld file: 18

Note: Set your communications software to emulate a VT100 terminal.

Typical document titles are "Office of Device Evaluation's Device Labeling Guidance," "Reviewer Guidance for Computer-controlled Medical Devices," "Draft Guidance for Preparation of FDA Submissions of Silicone Gel-filled Breast Prostheses," "Development of Required Postmarket Surveillance Study Protocols under Section 522(a)(1) of the Federal Food, Drug, and Cosmetic Act," and "Preproduction Quality Assurance Planning Recommendations for Medical Device Manufacturers." The board also has the "FDA Medical Devices Standards Activities Report," a comprehensive list of current national and international voluntary and regulatory standards for medical devices.

## FDA Electronic Bulletin Board

Press Office
Public Health Service
U.S. Food and Drug Administration
5600 Fishers Lane
Rockville, MD 20857

A wide range of information about the Food and Drug Administration's regulation of food, drugs, medical devices, animal feed and drugs, cosmetics, and the blood supply can be found on the FDA Electronic Bulletin Board. The FDA establishes standards, inspects domestic manufacturing facilities, inspects imports, and orders recalls of hazardous products. In recent years, it has done everything from developing food labeling regulations to approving new AIDS drugs to approving a fat substitute for use in foods.

The FDA's BBS is harder to use than many others, but it is also more sophisticated than most other federal government bulletin boards. Best of all, the system allows full-text searching of every document on the BBS.

No master list of files is available because there are no files to download. Instead, you can read all documents on screen and capture them by using your communications software's capture feature.

Documents on the BBS are divided into seventeen topic areas:

**News**   Press releases about FDA actions, including recalls. Sample titles are "Streptomycin Approved for TB," "FDA's Announcement on the Female Condom," "Warning on Hearing Aids," and "Hairspray Warning." Press releases are added to the board as soon as they are released and remain there for one month. Older press releases can be obtained from the press office.

**Enforce**   The weekly *FDA Enforcement Report*, which lists FDA-regulated products being recalled. Each listing includes the product, the manufacturer, who recalled it, the quantity recalled, where the product was distributed, and the reason for the recall. Also listed are seizure orders, injunctions, and prosecutions. A new report appears every Tuesday afternoon.

**Approvals**   The complete text of the *Drug and Device Product Approvals List*, published monthly. The list describes human drugs, veterinary drugs, and medical devices that have been approved for sale.

### VITAL STATS

Data: 800-222-0185 or 301-594-6857

Voice: 301-443-3285 (FDA press office); 301-443-7318 (technical support)

Internet: telnet fdabbs.fda.gov

Manual: MANUAL (must be read online)

**CDRH**   Two bulletins published by the Center for Devices and Radiological Health (CDRH). The *Medical Device Bulletin* and the *Radiological Health Bulletin* are each issued monthly and contain information on recent CDRH developments and meetings.

**Bulletin**   The current issues of two newsletters: *FDA Today* and the *Medical Bulletin. FDA Today* is an employee bulletin, while the *Medical Bulletin* is aimed at physicians. The files are updated when new newsletters are issued.

**AIDS**   Various information about AIDS. The topic is broken into six sub-topics: press releases, policy, articles, fraud, speeches, and meetings.

**Consumer**   The table of contents and selected articles from the current issue of *FDA Consumer,* FDA's official monthly magazine. The table of contents and articles are available on the board for one month. Sample article titles are "Cystic Fibrosis: Tests, Treatments Improve Survival," "The Food Pyramid–Food Label Connection," "Bottled Water: New Trends, New Rules," "FDA Reports on Pesticides in Foods," "Lead Threat Lessens, but Mugs Pose Problem," and "Hair Dye Dilemmas."

**Subj-Reg**   Summaries of all FDA *Federal Register* announcements arranged by subject. Primarily, these announcements are about new rules or upcoming meetings. The summaries are posted on the board as soon as they go on public display at the FDA hearing clerk's office and remain on the board for one week. They contain a short summary of the article and the name of a contact person. The summary also lists where and when public meetings will be held. The topic is divided into nine sub-topics: foods, human drugs, medical devices, biologics, veterinary drugs, cosmetics, radiological health, meetings, and general agency.

**Answers**   Answers to current questions arising as a result of news stories. Material remains on the board for one month. Sample titles are "BST Meeting," "Safety of the Blood Supply," "FDA Proposes to Review Penile Implants," "Women in Clinical Trials," and "AZT Trials."

**Index**   Indexes of press releases and answers issued by the FDA press office from January 1984 to date. Only items issued within the past thirty days are available on the BBS, although older items can be obtained from the press office.

**Date-Reg**   Summaries of all FDA *Federal Register* announcements arranged by publication date. Typically, these announcements are about new rules or upcoming meetings. Each contains a short summary of the article and the name of a contact person. The file also lists where and when public meetings will be held. Summaries appear on the BBS the day before the information is published in the *Federal Register* and remain on the board for one week.

**Congress**   The full text of prepared statements delivered by FDA officials at congressional oversight hearings. Statements are added to the board the same day as the hearing and remain for one month.

**Speech**   The full text of prepared speeches delivered by the FDA commissioner and deputy commissioner at various meetings. Speeches remain on the board for one month.

**Vetnews**   Contains CVM Updates, which are news items issued by the FDA's Center for Veterinary Medicine. All updates are added to the board as soon as they are issued and remain for one month.

**Meetings**   Lists of upcoming meetings of the Ophthalmic Devices Panel of the Medical Devices Advisory Committee, the Fertility and Maternal Health Drugs Advisory Committee, the Science Board to the Food and Drug Administration, the Medical Imaging Drugs Advisory Committee, the Arthritis Advisory Committee, the Cardiovascular and Renal Drugs Advisory Committee, and other FDA panels. Each listing includes the date, time, and place for the meeting, a contact person, and a description of the topics to be discussed.

**Import**   Representative Import Detention Summaries, which are reports about imported items that have been detained because they violate a law. Each detention summary lists the product, quantity, shipper, country of origin, port of entry, date, and reason for detention. The topic is broken into six subtopics: food articles, medical devices, biological articles, cosmetic articles, radiological health, and veterinary medicine. The summaries are posted approximately twice a month.

**Manual**   The user's manual, which is very helpful. All new users should read it before using the board further.

After you log onto the board, a prompt will ask you to enter the topic you want. Alternatively, you can type **topics** to get a list of the seventeen topic areas. When you enter a topic, be sure to type its full name. Many boards allow you to type just the initial letter of a name, but this one does not.

Once you are in a topic area, the prompt will say, "Please enter a BBS command." You have several options at this point, but one of the best is to type **scan**. Doing so will provide you with a list of the documents in the topic area. Note that each document name has a number next to it. If you see a title that you want to read, type **read**, leave a space, and type the document number. For example, type **read 1** if you want to read the first document listed.

If you want to read all the documents in a topic, first do a scan. Then type **read** at the next prompt. The BBS will let you scroll through all the documents in the topic.

If you would prefer to conduct a search, type **search** when prompted to enter a BBS command. You will get another prompt asking you to enter keyword(s). You can enter a single keyword or several keywords separated by *and* or *or*. For example, if you want documents about breast implants, type **breast and implant** at the keyword prompt. If you want documents that specifically mention the Food and Drug Administration, type **Food and Drug or FDA**. After entering the search string, press the Enter key. You will get a message saying the system is searching. The system then will tell you how many "hits" you got. To read the documents, type **read** when asked to enter a BBS command.

The system also allows you to search with wildcards at the beginning or end of a word. For example, if you type the search term **drug\***, you will get documents with any form of the word *drug* in them. Thus you will get documents with the words *drug, druggist, drugs,* or *drugged.*

Unfortunately, you cannot search all documents on the BBS at once. You must search each topic area individually.

Help is always nearby when using the FDA BBS. If you get stuck, type **help** at any prompt and you will get more information.

## FDA Prime Connection

U.S. Food and Drug Administration
HFS-625
200 C St., S.W.
Washington, DC 20204-0001

Although navigating FDA Prime Connection is a bit difficult, it offers a wealth of information about food safety. It focuses primarily on retail food protection, milk safety, and shellfish sanitation and is aimed at federal, state, and local regulatory officials. Most of the files are produced by the Office of Compliance at the Food and Drug Administration's Center for Food Safety and Applied Nutrition.

Information on the board is separated into bulletins and conferences. You can skip the files area because it simply repeats parts of the bulletins area.

The main board has six bulletin areas. To get a list of bulletins, type b at the Main Menu, and at the "Read What Bulletin?" prompt, type the two- or three-letter code for the area you want. Some of the bulletin areas have sub-menus, so the system can get a little confusing. Following are highlights of what you will find in the six bulletin areas:

**FP: Retail food protection**   An electronic copy of the *Program Information Manual* for the Retail Food Protection Program.

**MS: Milk safety**   A list of tolerances of animal drug residues allowed in milk.

**SS: Seafood safety**   A list that includes the market name, scientific name, common name, and regional name for various fish.

**FBP: Foodborne pathogenic microorganisms and natural toxins**   An electronic copy of *Foodborne Pathogenic Microorganisms and Natural Toxins,* a book that has chapters on salmonella, viruses, shellfish toxins, mushroom toxins, and other microorganisms and toxins.

**TR: Other technical references**   Extracts from the weekly *FDA Enforcement Report* related to food recalls, seizures, and other enforcement actions; a telephone directory of FDA personnel and contractors; and regulations about sanitizing solutions.

---

**VITAL STATS**

Data: Number provided after registration

Voice: 202-205-8140

Fax: 202-205-5560

Time limit: 60 minutes per call

Note: New users must call, fax, or write to obtain a password, the data number, and connecting instructions.

**SB: System bulletins**   More than a dozen bulletins about the BBS. Bulletin 12 has an example of a session on the BBS.

All of the bulletins can be read online or downloaded. Some bulletin lists include file names for the bulletins, and you can download the bulletins by using those file names. You can download the bulletins that lack file names by typing the bulletin number. For example, to download Bulletin 6, type **f** at the Main Menu, **d** at the File Menu, and **b6** at the "Download what file?" prompt.

The BBS has nine conferences, which you can access by typing **j** at the Main Menu. All have their own message areas. Each conference also has anywhere from a few to one hundred bulletins, which are separate from the main board bulletins. You can read them online or download them by using basically the same procedure as for the main board bulletins. The only difference is that instead of downloading from the main board's menu, you must download from the menu for the conference in which the bulletin is located. For example, if you want to download a bulletin from the food conference, you must download it from the Main Menu for the food conference. Following are the conferences and sample titles of particularly interesting bulletins:

**FOOD: Retail food protection**   Sample titles are "First Things First: An Essay on Food Inspection Priorities," "NSF International Conducts Tests on Safety of Wood and Plastic Cutting Boards," "Genetically Engineered Foods," "Meeting on Monosodium Glutamate (MSG)," "Bottled Water: New Trends, New Rules," "Senate Testimony on Ground Beef Cooking," and "High-Tech Tools for Food Safety Sleuths."

**CFP: Food protection**   Sample title: *CFP Newsletter.*

**ILL: Foodborne illness reports and information**   Sample titles are "Parasitic Invaders and the Reluctant Human Host," "USDA Report on E. coli Outbreak," "MMWR Preliminary Report on E. coli 0157:H7 Outbreak," "Diseases Transmitted through the Food Supply," and "Foodborne Illness and Long-Term Care Facilities."

**HACCP: HACCP applications in retail food programs**   Sample titles are "Ensuring Food Safety—The HACCP Way," "Educational Foundation's HACCP Reference Book," and "Foodborne Disease Risk Assessment."

**MILK: Milk safety**   Sample titles are "GAO Report on BST: FDA's Response," "BST and Milk Safety," and "Milk Fortification Findings in Scientific Journal."

**FISHNET: Seafood safety and quality**   Sample titles are "Seafood Hotline Publications List," "FDA and Aquaculture," "Kessler's Statement to Congress on Seafood," "Advice on Consumption of Raw Molluscan Shellfish," and "FDA's Seafood Safety Program."

**MARTOX: Marine toxins, including sampling data and alerts**   This conference is supposed to begin posting results from state sampling programs.

**COMPUTE: Computer topics**   Sample titles are "Montana's Virtual Medical Center," "CD ROM—FDA on Disc," "Federal Software Directory," and "Modem Primer" (four bulletins).

**CODEX: Codex alimentarius**   Food regulation topics.

## Grateful Med BBS

MEDLARS Management
National Library of Medicine
National Institutes of Health
Building 38A, 8600 Rockville Pike
Bethesda, MD 20894

The Grateful Med BBS supports users of Grateful Med, a software program that provides a menu-driven interface for MEDLARS. MEDLARS is a collection of more than twenty databases at the National Library of Medicine. Although it costs nothing to access the BBS, both the software and access to MEDLARS cost money.

The Grateful Med software is easier to use than the normal MEDLARS interface. In addition, it can help save on connect charges because all searches are composed offline. Searching MEDLARS usually costs about $18 an hour.

The BBS bulletins, which you can access by typing **b** at the Main Menu, describe how to use the board, provide information about Grateful Med, and contain ordering information for the software. The software costs $29.95 and is available for IBM and compatible and Macintosh computers.

The files offer the following information:

- An application for a MEDLARS account.

- A list of MEDLINE CD-ROM vendors.

- Case studies of Grateful Med searches.

- A list of search publications available from the National Technical Information Service.

- Support files for the IBM and compatible version of Grateful Med.

**VITAL STATS**
Data: 800-525-5756
Voice: 800-638-8480

## NIDR Online

Management Information Systems and Analysis Section
National Institute of Dental Research
National Institutes of Health
Room 707, Westwood Building
Bethesda, MD 20892

The NIDR Online BBS allows users to order free publications from the National Institute of Dental Research (NIDR), search databases that list dental schools and dental libraries, and learn about grants and contracts that are available or that have been awarded.

There are three ways to access this BBS:

**VITAL STATS**

Data: 800-358-2221 (see description)

Voice: 301-594-7645

FedWorld gateway: 69 (you must switch to a half-duplex communications setting when you move from FedWorld)

Internet: telnet wylbur.cu.nih.gov

Manual: Call voice number for free brochure.

Note: Dial-in users will require special communications settings in their software: even parity, 7 data bits, 1 stop bit, and half duplex (or local echo).

1. **Through FedWorld** You must switch to a half-duplex communications setting when you move from FedWorld. If your communications program does not have a half-duplex setting, turn on local echo instead. A message will tell you when to make the change. If you don't change the setting, what you type will be invisible on the screen.

2. **Through the toll-free telephone line** This option requires special communications settings in your software: even parity, 7 data bits, 1 stop bit, and half duplex. If your communications program does not have a half-duplex setting, turn on local echo instead. In addition, you may need to experiment with your terminal setting to see what works. A VT100 setting seems to work well. After you connect, type **,gen1** (the comma is essential) and press the Enter key. You will not be prompted to do this. Next, you will get a prompt asking for initials. Type **kil** and press Enter. Then you'll get a prompt asking for your account. Type **hdt1** (that's hdt and the number 1) and press Enter.

3. **Through the Internet** After you connect, type **,gen1** (the comma is essential). At the "Initials?" prompt, type **kil** and at the "Account?" prompt, type **hdt1** (that's hdt and the number 1).

You can read all the documents on the BBS online and capture them to your computer by using your communications program's capture feature. There are no files to download.

The Main Menu lists five information categories, most of which lead to sub-menus:

1. **Science Information and Transfer**   Seven types of information are available:

    - A description of the National Institute of Dental Research.

    - News releases from the NIDR. Sample titles are "Dental Researchers Report Novel Approach for Treating Arthritis," "NIDR Awards Grants to Develop Minority Oral Health Regional Centers," and "Conference Focuses on Saliva as a Diagnostic Fluid." Press releases also list new publications and describe data files of dental research that are available.

    - Dental librarians' bulletin board, a place for dental librarians to post messages about job opportunities, new publications, and other subjects.

    - Conferences/symposia, which lists upcoming conferences sponsored by the NIDR and other organizations.

    - Films list, which lists films about dental health. Most of the movies are aimed at students or teachers involved in school dental health programs. Each listing describes the film, gives the target audience, and explains how to obtain the film. Some films are free, while others have a rental fee.

    - Publications list, a list of NIDR publications aimed at the general public and health professionals. Single copies of all publications are free and can be ordered online. Many publications are available in both English and Spanish versions. Sample titles are "A Healthy Mouth for You and Your Baby," "Dental Tips for Diabetics," "Detection and Prevention of Periodontal Disease: A Guide for Health Care Providers," "Fever Blisters and Canker Sores," and "Opportunities for Minorities in Research." Other publications report the results of surveys conducted by the NIDR. Sample titles are "Broadening the Scope: Long-range Research Plan for the Nineties," "Survey: Oral Health of United States Adults," and "Survey: National Survey of Dental Caries in U.S. Schoolchildren." The list also includes posters, many of which are aimed at elementary school children.

    - NIH Office of Education Bulletin Board, a board designed for communication among NIH scientists, students, teachers, and other members of the academic and lay communities who are interested in biomedical education. Users can directly access this BBS through NIDR Online. For a full description of this BBS, see NIH EDNET (p. 129).

2. **Grants and Contracts**   The sub-menu offers information about grants and contracts available from or awarded by the NIDR. Documents provide NIH

grant policies and guidelines and list grant availability and grants awarded. By selecting Option 9, you enter a database of active grants. You can search the database by project number; investigator name; institution; city, state, or country; and title words. For each grant, the database lists the project number, investigator name, amount awarded, institution, project title, and dates the grant starts and ends.

3. **Directories**   Three searchable databases are available:

   - NIDR telephone directory, which can be searched by last name or organizational component.

   - Dental school directory, which lists dental schools in the United States and Canada. It can be searched by state, dean's name, or institution name. Each listing includes the dean's name, address, and telephone number.

   - Dental library directory, which lists dental libraries in the United States and Canada. It can be searched by state, librarian name, or institution name. Each listing includes the library director's name, address, and telephone number.

4. **Message to NIDR**   This option allows users to send an electronic message to NIDR.

5. **Clinician Research Scientist Awardees**   This database of scientists in the Clinician Research Scientists program is searchable. The database lists each scientist's name, year of dental degree, institution that granted the degree, grant number and institution, start and end dates, clinical interest, science track, project title, and mentor.

## NIH Information Center

National Institutes of Health
Building 31, Room 2B09
Bethesda, MD 20902

You can find a vast quantity of information about diseases and the National Institutes of Health on the NIH Information Center BBS. After you connect, the board presents you with a list of toll-free NIH information lines about various diseases. It then presents the Bulletin Menu, which you also can access by typing **b** at the Main Menu. The bulletins provide a glossary of communications terms and information about decompressing files, NIH contracts and grants, and medical libraries.

The files are divided into more than a dozen areas. Here are some highlights:

- Dozens of NIH publications on such subjects as adult brain tumors, Hodgkin's disease, Agent Orange, artificial sweeteners, breast cancer, cervical cancer, food additives, skin cancer, AIDS prevention, and handling stress.

- An index of diseases being investigated at NIH, along with contact numbers.

- Publication lists from institutes at NIH (see box).

- Press releases from NIH.

- Dozens of official NIH news stories. Sample titles are "Alcohol and Creativity: No Connection," "Blood Transfusions May Raise Cancer Risk in Older Women," and "Information on Risks Associated with Cholesterol."

- Calendars of NIH events and biomedical meetings.

- Maps of Washington's Metrorail system in GIF and PCX graphics formats.

- Maps of roads and parking lots at NIH and of regional roads surrounding NIH.

- NIH organizational charts.

- A history of NIH.

- Background information about many of the NIH institutes.

> **VITAL STATS**
> Data: 800-644-2271 or 301-480-5144
> Voice: 301-496-6610
> FedWorld gateway: 127
> To access files: At the Main Menu, type **f**

**Participating NIH Institutes**

National Institute on Aging
National Institute on Alcohol Abuse and Alcoholism
National Institute of Allergy and Infectious Diseases
National Institute of Arthritis and Musculoskeletal and Skin Diseases
National Cancer Institute
National Institute of Child Health and Human Development
National Institute on Deafness and Other Communications Disorders
National Institute of Dental Research
National Institute of Diabetes and Digestive and Kidney Diseases
National Institute on Drug Abuse
National Institute of Environmental Health Sciences
National Eye Institute
National Institute of General Medical Sciences
National Heart, Lung, and Blood Institute
National Center for Human Genome Research
National Institute of Mental Health
National Institute of Neurological Disorders and Stroke
National Institute of Nursing Research

- Clinical Alerts for doctors reporting research findings at NIH.
- The full text of the Surgeon General's Report on HIV Infection and AIDS.
- Information about the National Library of Medicine and a list of its publications.
- A list of cancer information sources.
- A list of AIDS-related bulletin boards.

## Nutrient Data Bank Bulletin Board

Human Nutrition Information Service
Nutrition Monitoring Division
U.S. Department of Agriculture
6505 Belcrest Rd., Room 316
Hyattsville, MD 20782

The Nutrient Data Bank Bulletin Board provides limited information about the nutritional content of food. Primarily, the files contain technical information used during national surveys of eating patterns.

Nearly all the files are compressed in a self-extracting format designed for DOS computers. This format makes them unusable on Macintosh computers.

The two main areas on the board are Bulletins and Files. Here are the major bulletins of interest:

**Bulletin 9**   Describes how to use the BBS.

**Bulletin 11**   Describes the files that can be downloaded.

**Bulletin 13**   Lists the names and telephone numbers of specialists in the Human Nutrition Information Service (HNIS).

**Bulletin 14**   Lists HNIS publications and includes ordering information. Some of the publication titles are "Nutrition and Your Health: Dietary Guidelines for Americans," "The Food Guide Pyramid: A Guide to Daily Food Choices," and "Cooking for People with Food Allergies." Numerous publications also detail the nutritional content of various types of foods.

Following are some of the most interesting files available for downloading:

**DAPZ.EXE**   A freeware program that allows you to analyze what you eat over a three-day period. The program analyzes the food for twenty-eight nutrients and food components, including calories, protein, total fat, saturated fatty acids, monounsaturated fatty acids, polyunsaturated fatty acids, carbohydrates, dietary fiber, cholesterol, vitamin A, carotenes, vitamin E, vitamin C, alcohol, thiamin, riboflavin, preformed niacin, vitamin B6, vitamin B12, folacin, calcium, phosphorus, magnesium, iron, potassium, sodium, copper, and zinc. It produces bar graphs showing the percentage of calories from protein, carbohydrate, fat, saturated fatty acids, and alcohol in addition to other data. If you order it from the National Technical Information Service,

---

**VITAL STATS**
Data: 301-436-5078
Voice: 301-436-8491
FedWorld gateway: 31
Manual: BULLETIN 9
File list: BULLETIN 11
To access files: At the Main Menu, type **f**
Time limit: 100 minutes per call

the program costs $60. Downloading it from the BBS is free. The program is available only for DOS computers.

**SUGAR.EXE**  Information on amounts of monosaccharides, disaccharides, other sugars, and total sugar in more than 500 foods.

**HG72.EXE**  Nutrient data expressed in common household units for more than 900 foods.

# OASH BBS

National AIDS Program Office
U.S. Department of Health and Human Services
Hubert Humphrey Building, Room 729-H
200 Independence Ave., S.W.
Washington, DC 20201

A wide range of information about AIDS, including reports from the National Commission on AIDS, bibliographies of materials about AIDS, and the Surgeon General's Report on HIV Infection and AIDS, can be found on the OASH BBS. The board also has a limited number of files on other health subjects.

Although the BBS has lots of useful information, it's cumbersome to use. It starts out badly with a long registration questionnaire that asks everything from your name and address to the location (work, home, school, or public library) from which you are accessing the BBS.

You are then asked to choose which of two BBSs to enter: the Office of the Assistant Secretary for Health (OASH) BBS or the White House HIV/AIDS Policy BBS. This is confusing because the overall system is called the OASH BBS as well. Nonetheless, you must type the number of the BBS you want.

The White House HIV/AIDS Policy BBS offers a limited number of White House documents about AIDS and HIV. These include speeches, proclamations, and press releases. This board also has conferences on community-based organizations, gay men, minorities, pediatrics, people with AIDS, and women, in addition to separate conferences on HIV/AIDS planning at the local, state, territory, national, and international levels.

Most of the useful information, however, is on the OASH BBS. To get a calendar of HIV/AIDS events, type 5 at the Main Menu. To enter the file area, type 2 at the Main Menu. Files are divided into four directories, and you must type the number of the one you want:

1. HIV/AIDS files areas

2. Health related files areas (non-AIDS)

3. PC/Mac utility file areas

4. List help/text files

**VITAL STATS**
Data: 202-690-5423
Voice: 202-690-6248
FedWorld file: 51
Time limits: 90 minutes per call, 3 hours per day

The first two directories are further divided into file areas by topic. Unfortunately, to download a file you must be in the area where the file is located. If, for example, you are in File Area 9 of the HIV/AIDS files directory and remember that you want something in File Area 8, you must return to File Area 8 to download the file. To switch among file areas, type a at the prompt that appears after the file list, leave a space, and type the number of the area you want to switch to. For example, type **a 11** to switch to File Area 11.

Downloading is a pain if you want files from numerous areas, since you have to keep switching around. To make matters worse, there is no master list of files on the BBS.

The only thing that redeems the OASH BBS is the high quality of the information it offers. Here are some examples of what's available:

- Articles from the *Morbidity and Mortality Weekly Report,* which is published by the Centers for Disease Control.

- Daily summaries of articles about AIDS from newspapers, wire services, and magazines. Each listing includes a summary, headline, date published, page number, and author.

- The Surgeon General's Report on HIV Infection and AIDS.

- A list of AIDS-related BBSs.

- The Public Health Service's Strategic Plan to Combat HIV/AIDS.

- Reports from the AIDS Litigation Project.

- Bibliographies of scientific articles, audiovisual materials, and reports about AIDS, which are compiled by the National Library of Medicine. The bibliographies are updated monthly.

- Legal notices about AIDS published by various federal agencies in the *Federal Register.* The notices list upcoming meetings of Food and Drug Administration advisory committees, announce the availability of grants, and announce the receipt of applications to export biological products. The notices are posted weekly.

- Public Health Service press releases announcing clinical trials of new AIDS drugs. Some provide information about how to enroll in the trials.

- Clinical Alerts on AIDS issues, which are aimed at physicians. Most provide the results of new studies.

- Various types of information about immunization, including notices about upcoming meetings and descriptions of grants available for immunization programs.

- The *ORI Newsletter,* published by the Office of Research Integrity at the Public Health Service. The quarterly newsletter has articles about lawsuits, cases, and federal actions involving scientific integrity. It also lists publications and upcoming meetings about scientific misconduct.
- Reports from the National Commission on AIDS, including "Preventing HIV Transmission in Health Care Settings," "The Challenge of HIV/AIDS in Communities of Color," "Living with AIDS, "Failure of U.S. Health Care System to Deal with HIV Epidemic," and "AIDS in Rural America."
- Numerous documents from the Centers for Disease Control's National AIDS Clearinghouse. Sample titles are "CDC Facts about HIV and Its Transmission," "Role of Condoms in Preventing HIV Infection and Other Sexually Transmitted Diseases," "CDC's HIV/AIDS Prevention Activities," "Scope of the HIV/AIDS Epidemic in the U.S.," and "CDC Facts on Women and HIV/AIDS."
- Bibliographies of educational materials about HIV/AIDS and African Americans, Hispanics, adolescents, women, tuberculosis, nutrition, and substance abuse.
- More than a dozen training bulletins on basic AIDS issues prepared for the National AIDS Hotline staff. These have the latest information on such subjects as the use of spermicides and condoms, transfusions and AIDS infection, HIV transmission in health care settings, and AIDS transmission during dental procedures.
- An extensive list of organizations that provide health-related information and have toll-free numbers. Each listing provides the phone number, a brief description of the services provided, and the hours of operation. Subjects covered include adoption, aging, AIDS, alcoholism and drug abuse, Alzheimer's disease, arthritis, cancer, child abuse, diabetes and digestive diseases, eating disorders, fitness, food safety, grief, headaches and head injuries, hearing and speech, hospices, impotence, lung diseases, mental health, paralysis and spinal cord injury, pesticides, pregnancy, rare disorders, urological disorders, vision, and women's health, among others.
- A list of federal government clearinghouses and information centers on a wide range of topics, including aging, AIDS, alcohol and drug information, allergies and infectious diseases, Alzheimer's disease, arthritis, cancer, child abuse and neglect, children's mental health, deafness, diabetes, digestive diseases, disability, drug use, health care policy, homelessness and mental illness, indoor air quality, minority health, nutrition, occupational safety and health, smoking and health, sudden infant death syndrome, and teacher education, among others.

## Quick Facts BBS

Cygnus Corporation
Suite 1275
1400 Eye St., N.W.
Washington, DC 20005

Virtually any statistic you could possibly want about alcohol and alcohol abuse can be found on the Quick Facts BBS. The board is operated by a private contractor for the National Institute on Alcohol Abuse and Alcoholism (NIAAA).
The files contain the following types of information:

- Estimated and projected numbers of alcohol abusers and alcoholics.

- Two dozen NIAAA "Alcohol Alert" publications on alcohol and aging, alcohol withdrawal syndrome, children of alcoholics, alcohol and women, fetal alcohol syndrome, alcohol and AIDS, the genetics of alcoholism, alcohol and cancer, and related subjects.

- Statistics on alcohol consumption for individual states, the United States, and foreign countries.

- Statistics on state tax revenues from alcohol.

- Alcohol advertising expenses for 1975–1991.

- Statistics on hospital admissions for alcohol-related problems.

- A wide range of statistics on alcohol-related deaths from cirrhosis and traffic accidents.

- More than two dozen files containing demographic information about drinking. The files contain information on drinking patterns by whites, African Americans, Mexican Americans, Cuban Americans, Puerto Ricans, high school seniors, and other groups.

**VITAL STATS**
Data: 202-289-4112
Voice: 202-289-4992
FedWorld gateway: 118
Manual: NEWUSER.TXT (a generic manual for the BBS software)
To access files: At the Main Menu, type **f**

# DISABILITIES

## ABLE INFORM BBS

NARIC and ABLEDATA
Suite 935
8455 Colesville Rd.
Silver Spring, MD 20910-3319

ABLE INFORM has hundreds of files and five databases related to disabilities, assistive technology, and rehabilitation. It also has an excellent collection of guides to the Internet. The BBS is operated by a private contractor with funding from the National Institute on Disability and Rehabilitation Research (NIDRR), which is part of the Department of Education.

Information on the board is divided into bulletins, files, databases, and conferences:

### Bulletins

The bulletins, which you can access by typing **b** at the Main Menu, describe how to use the BBS, list publications from the NIDRR, describe how to access disability information on the Internet, and explain the basics of online communications.

### Files

The files are separated into eleven file areas. To help find your way through the files, be sure to download the list of all files on the board (A_INFORM.LST or A_INFORM.ZIP). ABLE INFORM's list is excellent because it contains detailed descriptions of each file, unlike lists on most BBSs that give only a couple of words of description. The file areas have the following information:

1. **Utilities**  Information about other BBSs with disability information, several shareware communications programs for DOS and Macintosh computers, and shareware decompression programs for DOS and Macintosh computers.

2. **ABLEDATA fact sheets**  Fact sheets on van lifts, car seats, bath lifts, reclining bath seats, powered scooters, ramps, stair lifts, patient lifts, wheelchairs, seat cushions, standing aids, modular seating components, and assistive devices for arthritis, in addition to numerous files of thesaurus terms used in the ABLEDATA database.

> **VITAL STATS**
> Data: 301-589-3563
> Voice: 800-227-0216 or 301-588-9284
> FedWorld gateway: 115
> File list: A_INFORM.LST (uncompressed) or A_INFORM.ZIP (compressed)
> To access files: At the Main Menu, type **f**
> Time limit: 60 minutes per day
> Note: If you get garbage characters when you connect, type **2** at the first prompt.

3. **Pre-run ABLEDATA database searches**  Database searches about assistive technology and rehabilitation equipment. Files are available about grab bars, emergency alert systems, modified keyboards, adjustable beds, exercise equipment, and other devices.

4. **NARIC (National Rehabilitation Information Center) publications**  *The Americans with Disabilities Act: A NARIC Resource Guide,* which lists organizations, documents, periodicals, online resources, software, and videos pertaining to Titles 1–4 of the act; *Directory of National Information Sources on Disabilities,* a 555-page book published by the NIDRR; copies of the NARIC newsletter; information about NIDRR-funded projects; and resource guides on spinal cord injury, traumatic brain injury, and stroke.

5. **Pre-run REHABDATA database searches**  Searches of the REHABDATA database, which contains bibliographic records with abstracts of more than 40,000 documents in the NARIC library. Searches are available about funding issues in rehabilitation, costs and cost benefit analysis in rehabilitation, legislation affecting people with disabilities, management issues in rehabilitation, service issues, and social service issues in rehabilitation.

6. **Other publications/files**  Various newsletters and publications on disability issues.

7. **Advocacy, legal rights, ADA**  Extensive information about the Americans with Disabilities Act (ADA), including the full text of the act, a bibliography of ADA resources, information about the ADA from the Department of Justice, ADA guidelines from the Architectural Barriers and Compliance Board, final ADA rules from the Department of Transportation, the *ADA Technical Assistance Manual* from the Equal Employment Opportunity Commission, a list of statutory deadlines for the ADA, and analyses of various sections of the ADA.

8. **Issues of the publication Rehab Brief**  Various articles from this publication.

9. **Resources for/on the Internet**  Copies of many of the best Internet guides, including *The Big Dummy's Guide to the Internet; Special Internet Connections; There's Gold in Them Thar Networks! or Searching for Treasure in All the Wrong Places; NYSERNet New User's Guide to Useful and Unique Resources on the Internet; Using Networked Information Resources: A Bibliography; SURAnet Guide to Selected Internet Resources; Surfing the Internet: An Introduction;* and *Zen and the Art of the Internet.* In addition, this area has information about file compression, details about federal government

information available on the Internet, a list of all files at the Handicap News FTP site, and information about sending electronic mail on various systems.

10. **Electronic Industries Assoc. REC files**  Reports about the needs of people with disabilities prepared by the Rehabilitation Engineering Center at the Electronic Industries Foundation.

11. **Thesaurus terms for ABLEDATA searchers**  A number of thesaurus files to use in searching ABLEDATA.

## Databases

The BBS has five databases, which you can access by typing **dbs** at the Main Menu. There is also a file in this area that explains how to search the databases; you should download it before starting a search. The uncompressed version is called DBS-V2.TXT, and the compressed version is called DBS-V2.ZIP. You will find the following information in the databases:

**REHABDATA**  Bibliographic records with abstracts of more than 40,000 items in the National Rehabilitation Information Center library. The materials include research reports, books, journal articles, and audiovisual items. Photocopies of materials identified through the database are available for five cents per page.

**ABLEDATA**  Detailed descriptions of more than 18,000 assistive technology products, ranging from white canes to voice output programs. Price and company information is provided for each product. In addition, the database has information on noncommercial prototypes, customized and one-of-a-kind products, and do-it-yourself designs.

**NIDRR Program Directory**  Approximately 300 records that describe research, demonstration, and dissemination projects funded by the NIDRR.

**NARIC KnowledgeBase**  A referral directory that lists information sources of local and national scope. The database contains about 3,000 records.

**NARIC Guide to Periodicals**  A directory of newsletters, magazines, and journals about disability and rehabilitation. The database contains about 400 records.

## Conferences

There are three conferences, which you can access by typing **r** at the Main Menu. All three are simply collections of messages and contain no bulletins or files:

**Main board**   A conference on general topics.

**Classified advertisements**   A place to post ads for buying or selling used assistive devices and equipment.

**News watch**   A place to post information about upcoming events, new books and videos, and other topics.

## Americans with Disabilities Electronic BBS

Public Access Section
Civil Rights Division
U.S. Department of Justice
P.O. Box 66738
Washington, DC 20035-6738

You'll find a wealth of information about the rights of people with disabilities on the Americans with Disabilities Electronic BBS. Nearly all the files concern the Americans with Disabilities Act (ADA).

You can access the files by typing l at the Main Menu. Here are some highlights:

- The full text of the ADA.

- ADA regulations developed by federal agencies.

- ADA enforcement status reports from the Justice Department.

- Fact sheets, booklets, and pamphlets about the ADA.

- Information about specific Justice Department enforcement actions under the ADA.

- Citations to private lawsuits filed under the ADA.

- A technical assistance manual for employers who must comply with the ADA.

- Standards for accessible design of new construction and alterations.

- Information about technical assistance grants awarded by the Justice Department under the ADA.

**VITAL STATS**
Data: 202-514-6193
Voice: 202-307-1084 or 202-307-0663 (TDD)
FedWorld gateway: 9
To access files: At the Main Menu, type l
Time limit: 2 hours per call

## Dial-JAN BBS

West Virginia Research and Training Center
5088 Washington St. West
Cross Lanes, WV 25313

Dial-JAN contains information about job accommodations for people with disabilities. The board has files about the Americans with Disabilities Act, the Rehabilitation Act of 1973, and the Randolph-Sheppard Act. The board also has discussion groups on adaptive technology and disability law.

The BBS is a sister board of Project Enable (p. 239), which is much more extensive but does not have a toll-free number. Although Dial-JAN is not operated by a federal agency, it is funded primarily by the President's Committee on Employment of People with Disabilities.

The files are located in three directories:

1. **Rehabilitation Act of 1973** The full text of the law and of the 1992 reauthorization.

2. **Randolph-Sheppard Act** The full text of the law, regulations, and related files.

3. **Americans with Disabilities Act** Nearly 100 files on the act, many of which have been uploaded from the Americans with Disabilities Electronic BBS operated by the Department of Justice (p. 237). The files provide the full text of the ADA, deadlines for compliance, questions and answers about the law, a list of federal agencies and other organizations that can provide assistance in complying, a summary of federal tax credits and deductions that can help businesses complying with the ADA, a description of the law's legislative history, information about related federal disability laws, booklets published by the Equal Employment Opportunity Commission called *The ADA: Your Employment Rights as an Individual with a Disability* and *The ADA: Your Responsibilities as an Employer,* ADA regulations, the ADA Accessibility Guidelines, and news articles about the ADA.

**VITAL STATS**

Data: 800-342-5526
Voice: 800-624-8284 or 304-759-0716
To access files: At the Main Menu, type **f**
Time limit: 45 minutes per call

## Project Enable

West Virginia Research and Training Center
5088 Washington St. West
Suite 200
Cross Lanes, WV 25313

Project Enable has more than 1,000 files on disability topics, searchable databases of disability information, and more than 100 conferences. Many of the conferences, which primarily cover topics related to disability, rehabilitation, employment, and education, are "echoes" from international networks. Project Enable is operated by the West Virginia University Rehabilitation Research and Training Center, with funding from the U.S. Department of Education.

The board is too extensive to describe here fully. However, the major areas are Bulletins, Files, Databases, and Conferences:

### Bulletins

There are more than a dozen bulletins about how to use the BBS, in addition to information about Project Enable. You can access the bulletins by typing **b** at the Main Menu.

### Files

The files are divided into more than three dozen directories. Here are some highlights:

- Software and text files related to visual impairments and blindness, hearing impairments, mobility impairments, education for people with disabilities, and legal issues related to disabilities.

- Regulations under the Family and Medical Leave Act of 1993.

- Dozens of files about the Americans with Disabilities Act. Most of them have been uploaded from the Americans with Disabilities Electronic BBS operated by the U.S. Department of Justice (p. 237).

- Information about the Rehabilitation Act of 1973 and its 1992 reauthorization, the Randolph-Sheppard Act, and the Individuals with Disabilities Education Act.

- The proposed Health Security Act and related documents.

**VITAL STATS**

Data: 304-759-0727

Voice/TDD: 800-624-8284 or 304-759-0716

Manual: PE-QUICK.TXT (short version), P-ENABLE.ZIP (long version in compressed format), P-ENABLE.TXT (long version in uncompressed format)

File list: PCBFILES.ZIP

To access files: At the Main Menu, type **f**

- A list of Internet mailing lists about disabilities.
- Several general guides to the Internet.
- A guide to online disability information.
- A manual about using modems.
- Communications programs, decompression utilities, and offline mail readers for a variety of computers.
- A large collection of Windows 3.1 fonts that are freeware or shareware.
- Guide dog access laws for each state, Canadian province, and some other areas.
- Information about chronic fatigue syndrome (CFS), including a bibliography of articles and a list of BBSs that carry information about CFS.
- Dozens of different newsletters about disabilities.
- Graphics and images related to disabilities.

## Databases

Most of the databases, which you can access by typing **open** at the Main Menu, allow keyword searches of large documents. For example, you can search the Americans with Disabilities Act, the Rehabilitation Act of 1973 and related regulations, and the Randolph-Sheppard Act and related regulations. In addition, one database allows users to check their eligibility for food stamps, Aid to Families with Dependent Children (AFDC), Medicaid, and other federal programs.

## Conferences

The board has more than 100 conferences, many of which are echoes from networks such as FidoNet and QuickLink. Most of the conferences are public, although a few are not. Access to a private conference can be requested by sending a message to its moderator. You can access the conferences by typing j at the Main Menu.

There are conferences on sports for people with disabilities, artists with disabilities, occupational disabilities, disability rights, Alzheimer's disease, arthritis, blindness and other visual impairments, cancer, chronic fatigue syndrome, diabetes, environmental illness, nutrition, rare conditions and diseases, stress management, dealing and coping with terminally ill relatives, working from home, K-12 education (broken down by subject), desktop publishing, home schooling, Native American issues, computer viruses, and writing, among many other subjects.

# RSA BBS

Rehabilitation Services Administration
U.S. Department of Education
330 C St., S.W., Room 3033
Washington, DC 20201

The RSA BBS, operated by the Rehabilitation Services Administration, serves people with disabilities and agencies that provide them with services. The BBS focuses on programs funded under the Rehabilitation Act of 1973 and the Randolph-Sheppard Act, including vocational rehabilitation, independent living, supported employment, and client assistance. Most of the files are technical.

The files area includes the full text of the Rehabilitation Act, information memos from the RSA, chapters from the RSA manual, and numerous RSA policy directives.

> **VITAL STATS**
> Data: 202-205-5574
> Voice: 202-205-8444
> FedWorld gateway: 125
> Manual: BBSMAI.DOC
> To access files: At the Main Menu, type **l**

# JOBS AND EMPLOYMENT

# FEDERAL JOBS

## Automated Vacancy Announcement Distribution System (AVADS) BBS

U.S. Geological Survey
U.S. Department of the Interior
206 National Center
Reston, VA 22092

The Automated Vacancy Announcement Distribution System (AVADS) BBS lists job vacancies at the U.S. Department of the Interior. Vacancies are listed for eleven Interior divisions: Bureau of Indian Affairs, Bureau of Land Management, Bureau of Mines, Bureau of Reclamation, Fish and Wildlife Service, Minerals Management Service, National Biological Survey, National Park Service, Office of the Secretary, Office of Surface Mining, and the U.S. Geological Survey.

Searching the vacancy lists is a tad tricky. New users should type **h** at the Main Menu to access several brief files that explain how to use the BBS.

The job descriptions are very detailed. They include opening and closing dates for the vacancy, a telephone number for further information, a mailing address, information about how to apply, and descriptions of the skills needed and the job duties.

**VITAL STATS**

Data: 800-368-3321 or 703-648-6000
Voice: 703-648-7239
FedWorld gateway: 132

## BUPERS Access

Bureau of Naval Personnel Command
PERS 471C
Federal Building 2
Washington, DC 20370

BUPERS Access is available only to federal government employees and active, reserve, and retired military personnel. It serves primarily as a way for Navy personnel to learn where they will be assigned next. Navy personnel also can send electronic messages in an effort to negotiate their next duty station.

The BBS also has some news and downloadable programs of interest to Navy personnel.

**VITAL STATS**
Data: 703-695-6900
Voice: 703-614-8083
FedWorld gateway: 83

## Census Personnel Board

Personnel Division
Bureau of the Census
U.S. Department of Commerce
Room 1412, FB3
Washington, DC 20233

Job openings at the Bureau of the Census are listed on the Census Personnel Board. Most of the openings are for clerk-typists, statisticians, geographers, mathematical statisticians, and administrative managers.

**VITAL STATS**
Data: 301-763-4574
Voice: 301-763-5800
FedWorld gateway: 8

## Detroit Service Center BBS

Federal Job Information Center
U.S. Office of Personnel Management
477 Michigan Ave., Room 565
Detroit, MI 48226

The Detroit Service Center BBS lists federal job openings around the country. Information on the board is separated into two categories: bulletins and files.

The bulletins, which you can access by typing **b** at the Main Menu, describe how to use the BBS, list addresses for Federal Job Information Centers in the Chicago Region, and describe the Career America Smart and the Presidential Management Intern programs.

The files area has federal job lists issued by Office of Personnel Management offices in Albuquerque, Anchorage, Atlanta, Baltimore, Boston, Chicago, Dallas, Dayton, Denver, Detroit, Honolulu, Huntsville, Kansas City, Los Angeles, Memphis, Norfolk, Orlando, Philadelphia, Raleigh, Sacramento, San Antonio, San Francisco, San Juan, Seattle, St. Louis, Syracuse, Twin Cities (Minneapolis and St. Paul), and Washington, D.C.

The files area also has a list of vacancies in the Senior Executive Service, a list of federal jobs commonly filled by recent college graduates, Merit Promotion listings, a description of federal employee benefits, general information on federal career opportunities, and a description of special programs for veterans, students, and the disabled.

**VITAL STATS**

Data: 313-226-4423

Voice: 313-226-6950 (leave a message on the automated system)

To access files: At the Main Menu, type **f**

Time limit: 5 hours per day

Note: This BBS also can be accessed through the OPM Mainstreet gateway.

## DoDIGNET

U.S. Department of Defense Inspector General
Room 512
400 Army Navy Drive
Arlington, VA 22202

DoDIGNET lists job openings in the Defense Department's Office of the Inspector General. The jobs are located throughout the United States and Europe.

To access the job openings, type f at the Main Menu and l at the File Menu. You'll get a list of the available jobs, and you can download detailed information about any of them. You also can download a compressed file with detailed information about all of the jobs.

**VITAL STATS**

Data: 703-604-5768

Voice: 703-604-9729

To access files: At the Main Menu, type **f**

Time limit: 60 minutes per day

## Federal Job Opportunity Board

Staffing Service Center
U.S. Office of Personnel Management
4685 Log Cabin Dr.
Macon, GA 31298

The Federal Job Opportunity Board provides extensive information about federal employment—everything from lists of federal jobs available nationwide to copies of bills being considered by Congress that affect federal employees. The lists of federal jobs are updated daily, Tuesday through Saturday morning, at 5:30 a.m.

If you are going to use this BBS much, you should read the manual. It is excellent and provides extensive help in using the board.

The following descriptions highlight the major areas that can be accessed from the Main Menu. Each area has numerous sub-menus:

**Opportunities for Federal Employment**   Lists of job openings by region and state, recruitment announcements from various federal agencies, a calendar of upcoming job fairs and career days, and an online system for searching through federal job openings.

**Merit Promotion (Data Entry)**   Restricted to federal personnel offices that issue merit promotion vacancy announcements.

**MDC—Management Development Center**   Information about courses offered at management development centers.

**Policy Operations and Staffing Headquarters—POSH**
More than a dozen conferences, most of which are private. The public conferences include the following:

- *Visiting BBS sysops*   A conference for people who run BBSs.
- *Staffing operations/policy*   An area for personnel officers to share information, policies, and guidelines.
- *Affirmative recruiting*   Recruiting initiatives, job fairs, career days, and other employment opportunities nationwide.

---

**VITAL STATS**

Data: 912-757-3100

Voice: 912-757-3030

Internet: telnet fedjob.mail.opm.gov

Manual: HANDBOOK.EXE (ASCII) or FJOBHAND.EXE (WordPerfect). These files cannot be used on Macintosh computers. Mac users can go to the Info Menu and read online the file called FJOB HANDBOOK.

File list: FJOBFILE.LST (uncompressed) or FJOBFILE.ZIP (compressed)

Available: 24 hours a day except Monday from 2 a.m. to 4 a.m. EST and Tuesday through Saturday from 4:30 a.m. to 6 a.m. EST

Note: This BBS can be accessed through the OPM Mainstreet gateway.

- *RIF conference*   Information on reduction in force (RIF) procedures.
- *VETS conference*   Information on veterans policy issues.

**Utilities and Miscellaneous Files**   Virus utilities for Macintosh and DOS computers; decompression programs for DOS, Macintosh, Apple II, and Commodore Amiga computers; a script to use with ProComm Plus to automate the online Federal Job Opportunity search program; a calendar of upcoming job fairs and career days; addresses for Federal Job Information Centers; addresses for state job service centers; and various programs for reading e-mail offline.

**Bulletins**   Lists of Federal Job Information Centers, other OPM bulletin boards, other bulletin boards with job information, and other federal bulletin boards. There also is information about how to obtain federal job information through the Internet.

**Info: System Information**   Files with information about the BBS. This area has the *FJOB Handbook*, which Macintosh users can read online or capture with their communications software's capture feature.

**HELP! How do I ....**   Extensive help files that explain the board's features.

## Federal Jobline

U.S. Office of Personnel Management
Suite 100A
9650 Flair Dr.
El Monte, CA 91731

Federal Jobline specializes in lists of federal job openings on the West Coast, although it also lists federal job openings nationwide and overseas. In addition, it has some useful files for people with disabilities—especially those living in California.

Information on the board is split into bulletins and files. The bulletins, which you can access by typing **b** at the Main Menu, explain how to use the BBS and list other sources of federal job information. You should particularly note Bulletin 3, which describes the various job files available on the BBS and lists their file names.

The files are separated into two areas: A and G. The A area includes federal job information. The job files are updated on approximately the first and fifteenth of each month. The A area includes the following:

- Lists of federal jobs available worldwide; in Alaska, Hawaii, California, Nevada, Oregon, Washington, and Idaho; in Anchorage, San Francisco, and Seattle; and in the Senior Executive Service.

- Information about the rehiring of air traffic controllers who were fired when they went on strike during President Ronald Reagan's administration.

- A summary of federal employee benefits.

- A list of addresses for Federal Job Information Centers nationwide.

- A flyer explaining opportunities in the federal government for veterans with disabilities.

- A copy of *The Hitchhiker's Guide to the Internet.*

- Information about Internet access to federal job listings.

- A description of the types of federal employment and details about how to apply for various jobs.

**VITAL STATS**

Data: 818-575-6521

Voice: 818-575-6500

To access files: At the Main Menu, type **f**

Time limit: 120 minutes per call

Note: This BBS also can be accessed through the OPM Mainstreet gateway.

- Information about federal job sharing.
- A list of federal salary rates.

The G file area lists organizations that provide services for persons with disabilities or other special needs. Most of the lists include only organizations in California, although some include organizations nationwide. The file area offers the following:

- A list of advocacy groups that provide legal and civil rights assistance.
- Information about assistive technology.
- A list of consulting resources.
- A huge list of service providers.
- A list of independent living centers.
- A list of job placement services.
- Information about the Job Training Partnership Act.
- A list of rehabilitation departments in southern California and southern Nevada.
- A list of support groups.

## OPM FedJobs Philly BBS

U.S. Office of Personnel Management
Room 3200
600 Arch St.
Philadelphia, PA 19106

The OPM FedJobs Philly BBS specializes in federal job listings for the Philadelphia Region, which includes Office of Personnel Management offices in Philadelphia, Baltimore, Boston, Syracuse, and San Juan. It also lists federal job openings nationwide and overseas.

Information on the board is presented in bulletins, files, and doors to online databases:

**Bulletins** The bulletins, which you can access by typing **b** at the Main Menu, list federal jobs in the region served by the board, other BBSs operated by OPM, and white-collar job groupings and trades and labor job groupings. They also provide local street maps for some OPM offices in the Philadelphia Region.

**Files** The files list federal job openings in the Philadelphia Region and across the country, openings in the Senior Executive Service, and upcoming seminars at OPM Management Development Centers. They also offer a guide to federal careers in Washington, D.C., provide information about the civil service retirement system, and discuss OPM reduction in force (RIF) regulations and placement programs. There also are copies of shareware communications programs for DOS and Windows computers, a shareware decompression program for DOS computers, and copies of historic documents such as the Bill of Rights, the Constitution, the Declaration of Independence, the Emancipation Proclamation, and the Magna Carta.

**VITAL STATS**

Data: 215-580-2216

Voice: 215-597-3804

Manual: CALGUIDE.ZIP (excellent manual, though a generic manual for the BBS software)

Time limit: 30 minutes per call

Note: This BBS also can be accessed through the OPM Mainstreet gateway.

**Doors** The doors are gateways to online databases or lengthy documents. You can access each door by typing its name at the Main Menu. The major doors are the following:

- *Best* Provides information about exemplary personnel practices within OPM's Philadelphia Region.

- *Compete*   Allows users to search federal job lists by region. The lists can be searched by job title, location, grade, closing date, and other variables.
- *Courses*   Allows users to search OPM training course calendars throughout the country.
- *Philly*   Allows users to search job lists produced by OPM offices in the Philadelphia Region.
- *Promote*   Allows users to search a database of merit promotion announcements.
- *Quals*   Provides the full text of the *Qualification Standards Handbook for General Schedule Positions,* which lists the qualifications needed for various federal jobs.
- *Series*   Allows users to search the definitions of federal jobs. The database can be searched by keyword or text string.

## OPM Mainstreet

U.S. Office of Personnel Management
AG/OIRM/OSB
Theodore Roosevelt Building
1900 E St., N.W., Room 6H30
Washington, DC 20415-0001

OPM Mainstreet, which is the main BBS operated by the Office of Personnel Management, provides extensive information about federal government job openings and employment policies. You must register to receive full access to the BBS. To register, type **r** at the Main Menu. You'll be asked to answer a few simple questions. After you do so, your access will be upgraded immediately.

Following are descriptions of the major areas available on the board:

**File Areas for Download**   To access the files, type **2** at the Main Menu. The files are separated into more than a dozen areas. Here are some highlights of what's available:

- Lists of federal government job openings nationwide, divided by region.
- Lists of job fairs and career days, federal personnel offices, Office of Personnel Management offices, and personnel offices in the Washington, D.C., area.
- Information about federal policy on hiring people with disabilities.
- Electronic copies of various forms used by federal personnel offices. PCFORMS.DOC is a user's guide for the forms, PCFORMS.LST lists the forms that are available, and PCFORMS.TXT explains the PCFORMS system.
- Shareware anti-virus programs for DOS and Windows computers.
- Information about employment opportunities for veterans.
- Shareware communications and decompression programs for DOS and Macintosh computers.
- Information about federal government locality pay.
- More than a dozen files that explain how to use OPM Mainstreet.

**VITAL STATS**
Data: 202-606-4800
Voice: 202-606-1396
FedWorld gateway: 44
Manual: MS-HELP.LNG
Time limit: 90 minutes per day

**Forums**  You can access the forums by typing **1** at the Main Menu. All of the forums have their own e-mail systems, and most also have files. The board offers forums on quality management, communications and public affairs, personnel records and systems, OPM procurement, retirement, downsizing, work and family, compensation and leave policy, employee and labor relations, the National Performance Review, and other issues.

**OPM Mainstreet information and utilities**  You can access this area by typing **5** at the Main Menu. It contains information about how to use the BBS.

**Internet access**  To enter this area, type **i** at the Main Menu. It's divided into three parts:

- *1. Internet electronic mail*  An e-mail gateway to the Internet. It also has information about how to use the e-mail gateway.

- *2. Newsgroups*  Access to more than three dozen Internet newsgroups, which are collections of e-mail messages on specific topics. Some of the topics covered are the Internet, politics, job openings, and computer hardware and software.

- *3. Files*  Downloaded messages from nearly two dozen Internet mailing lists about various topics, including employment, human resources development, public policy, reinventing government, and training and development.

**Connect to OPM's other BBSs**  This is a gateway to other Office of Personnel Management BBSs in Detroit, Los Angeles, Philadelphia, Washington, D.C., and Macon, Georgia. There is no charge for accessing these systems, and OPM pays for the long-distance call. To reach the gateway, type **c** at the Main Menu.

## Washington Area Service Network (WASNET)

U.S. Office of Personnel Management
Room 1425
1900 E St., N.W.
Washington, DC 20415

The Washington Area Service Network (WASNET) is open to groups, organizations, and government agencies of virtually any kind. It is not open to individuals. Individuals should use OPM Mainstreet (see previous entry) which has virtually the same files as WASNET and a whole lot more.

Groups interested in accessing the board must call the voice number and leave a message giving the name of a contact person, the name of the organization, and a password. Access will be granted within twenty-four hours.

The BBS has a small files area that includes lists of federal job openings arranged by region, information on placement assistance for federal employees, a list of federal personnel offices in the Washington, D.C., area, and information about employment opportunities for veterans.

**VITAL STATS**

Data: 202-606-1113
Voice: 202-606-1848
Manual: WASNET.MAN
To access files: At the Top Menu, type **d**
Note: You must obtain a password before you can access this BBS.

# LABOR LAWS AND REGULATIONS

## Boards of Wage and Service Contract Appeals BBS

Wage Appeals Board
U.S. Department of Labor
200 Constitution Ave., N.W., Room N1651
Washington, DC 20210

The Boards of Wage and Service Contract Appeals BBS contains hundreds of administrative decisions in disputes involving wages paid to employees of federal government contractors and subcontractors. The files are separated into Library Information Banks. To access the files, type f at the opening menu. This option gets you a list of library services. To get a list of all of the libraries, type s?. To get a list of the files in the library you are in, type f.

The libraries contain the following files:

**Main**  A list of all files on the BBS and a list of all files indexed by keyword.

**History**  Numerous files detailing the legislative history of the Davis-Bacon Act. The law, originally passed in 1931, requires the payment of prevailing wages and fringe benefits to laborers and mechanics employed by contractors and subcontractors working on federal construction projects.

**Scadecns**  The text of decisions by the Service Contract Appeals Board from 1987 to the present. The board helps enforce the McNamara-O'Hara Service Contract Act of 1965. The law set wage rates and other labor standards for employees of contractors and subcontractors that provide services to the federal government. The decisions are arranged chronologically and list the company involved. Most involve relatively small companies, although there are a few decisions affecting large firms such as McDonald's.

**WAB-decs**  The text of decisions by the Wage Appeals Board, which helps enforce the Davis-Bacon Act. The library also contains the text of administrative law judge decisions that were incorporated by reference in board decisions. A file called README explains how to interpret codes in the file names.

**VITAL STATS**
Data: 800-735-7396 or 202-219-5286
Voice: 202-219-9039
FedWorld gateway: 90
File list: FILES

# Labor News

Office of Information and Public Affairs
U.S. Department of Labor
200 Constitution Ave., N.W., Room S-1032
Washington, DC 20210

Labor News offers a wide range of economic data, lists of federal job openings, the text of selected regulations from the Occupational Safety and Health Administration (OSHA), information about the employment rights of people with disabilities, descriptions of recent mining accidents, the text of the Family and Medical Leave Act of 1993, and hundreds of other files.

By typing **i** at the opening menu, you will enter the board's Information Center. It contains bulletins and other information about the BBS that you can read online.

The files are separated into more than a dozen Library Information Banks. There are two ways to get a list of all of the files on the BBS:

- Download the file called INDEX. It indexes files by both date and keywords. The index is huge (216,000 bytes, or just over 100 printed pages), however, and a bit cumbersome to use.

- After you enter the Main Library of Files, you will get a prompt. Type **f** for file directory, and the BBS will list on your screen all of the files arranged by library. You can capture this list to your computer by using your communications software's capture feature. This list is much smaller than the index (only about twenty printed pages).

The Library Information Banks contain the following types of files:

**VITAL STATS**
Data: 202-219-4784
Voice: 202-219-8831
FedWorld gateway: 26
Manual: MANUAL.BBS (the manual is excellent)
File list: INDEX
To access files: After the opening menu, type **m**

**MAIN** An index of all files on the BBS, sorted two ways. They are sorted first by date in chronological order and then alphabetically by keywords. For each file, the index lists the keyword, library where it is located, file name, and a brief description. The index is updated daily.

**ARTICLES** Abstracts of articles published in the Bureau of Labor Statistics' *Monthly Labor Review*. Sample article titles are "Employment Effects of the Rise and Fall in Defense Spending," "Education and the Work Histories of

Young Adults," and "Recuperation Time for Work Injuries, 1987–91." Each file also explains how to order the magazine.

**BLMRFACTS**  Two-page fact sheets describing major programs of the Bureau of Labor-Management Relations and Cooperative Programs. Sample fact sheet titles are "Labor-Management Cooperation," "Employee Protection for Transit Workers," and "Airline Deregulation Act Rehire Program."

**BLSFACT**  Background fact sheets about the Bureau of Labor Statistics, which produces a wide range of economic statistics.

**BOSTON**  Press releases issued by the Department of Labor's Northeast regional office, in Boston. The press releases report unemployment rates, the consumer price index, food and energy prices, and fatal work injury numbers for the region and selected states and cities. They also report on regional enforcement actions by the Employment Standards Administration, the Occupational Safety and Health Administration, and the Pension and Welfare Benefits Administration.

**CPIINFO**  Monthly reports of the consumer price index.

**ESAFACT**  Two-page fact sheets prepared by the Employment Standards Administration. The fact sheets discuss the Migrant and Seasonal Agricultural Worker Protection Act, the Employee Polygraph Protection Act, black lung benefits, workers' compensation for federal workers, federal child labor laws, and minimum wage and overtime pay, among other subjects.

**ETAFACT**  Two-page fact sheets about major programs of the Employment and Training Administration. These programs target workers dislocated by economic changes and defense cutbacks, migrant and seasonal farm workers, Native Americans, and others. The library also has a file that describes sources of information about overseas jobs.

**JOBS**  Lists of federal government job openings in the United States and overseas. The jobs are listed by region, and there is a separate list for jobs in Washington, D.C. The library also includes a list of addresses for state job and employment service offices nationwide.

**MISC**  A user's manual, a list of federal government bulletin boards, and software for both DOS and Macintosh computers to decompress files. The library also has a file that lists publications available from the Women's Bureau.

**MISCFACT**  Fact sheets about various Labor Department programs. They describe how to report fraud, waste, and abuse (and include toll-free hotline numbers); detail assistance available to small businesses; and provide an overview of the Department of Labor.

**MSHA** An electronic copy of the Federal Code of Regulations on Mineral Resources (a 770-page book), an electronic copy of the Mine Safety and Health Act of 1977, transcripts of hearings on mining issues, and fact sheets from the Mine Safety and Health Administration that describe injury trends and list major mining accidents.

**OSHAFACT** Fact sheets on a wide range of Occupational Safety and Health Administration (OSHA) programs. The fact sheets discuss such subjects as safety with video display terminals, access to exposure and medical records, employee rights and responsibilities, farm safety, and OSHA help for new businesses.

**OSHAPUBS** A list of addresses and telephone numbers for OSHA regional and area offices nationwide, fact sheets on ergonomic stress in various jobs, fact sheets describing fatal accidents on the job, and electronic copies of pamphlets describing OSHA regulations.

**OSHAREGS** More than thirty files containing the text of selected OSHA regulations on air contaminants, asbestos, bloodborne pathogens, respiratory protection, employee exposure and medical records, and occupational noise exposure, among other subjects.

**PUBS** Electronic versions of a number of Department of Labor publications, including "The Americans with Disabilities Act: Your Employment Rights as an Individual with a Disability," "Job Directions for a Secure Future," "ADA Resource List," "Small Business Handbook: Laws, Regulations, and Technical Assistance Services," "Nontraditional Employment Programs for Women," and "Job Search Guide for Professionals." The library also contains the text of the Family and Medical Leave Act of 1993 and regulations under it.

**PWBAFACT** Fact sheets prepared by the Pension and Welfare Benefits Administration with titles such as "How to Become Eligible for Pension Benefits," "Your 'Right to Know' under the Pension Reform Law," "Filing Claims for Pension and Welfare Benefits," and "Survivor Benefits."

**RELEASES** Press releases issued during the previous sixty days by various agencies in the Department of Labor. The releases report employment and earnings statistics, the results of collective bargaining agreements, college enrollment statistics, consumer price index statistics, producer price index statistics, unemployment statistics, and a wide range of similar information. They also report on enforcement actions taken by Department of Labor agencies.

Users can arrange to have the daily news releases package automatically delivered to their electronic mailbox by sending an e-mail request to the sysop. The package is generally delivered about 3:00 p.m. Individual releases are usually available for downloading from the Releases Library within an hour after they are issued.

**TRENDS** Annual Foreign Labor Trends reports for more than two dozen countries, including Australia, China, France, Germany, Mexico, and Turkey. The reports contain extensive statistics and text descriptions regarding labor trends in the countries. The reports are prepared by American embassies.

**VETSFACT** Fact sheets prepared by the Veterans' Employment and Training Service. They describe the service's programs and list addresses and phone numbers for regional offices.

## PayPerNet

Office of Compensation Policy
U.S. Office of Personnel Management
1900 E St., N.W., Room 7420
Washington, DC 20415

PayPerNet has hundreds of extremely technical files about federal government employment and wages. It provides information about pay and performance management programs, special rates authorized under Title V, standards in position classification, federal pay administration, total quality management (TQM), significant court cases involving labor relations, job opportunities and developments in the Senior Executive Service, pay issues related to the Federal Employees Pay Comparability Act of 1990, and federal personnel records processing and management, among other issues.

You can access the bulletins by typing b at the Main Menu. Several provide useful information:

**BULLETIN 5**  Tips on downloading files.

**BULLETIN 6**  Information about BBSs operated by the Office of Personnel Management around the country.

**BULLETIN 8**  A brief user's guide.

**BULLETIN 9**  Descriptions of the board's commands.

These bulletins can be read online. If you prefer to download them, copies are available in the Utility Conference.

Files on PayPerNet are organized differently from the way files are organized on most other federal BBSs. The main board has no files. Instead, the files are organized under eleven conferences. To join a conference, type j at the Main Menu. You will be presented with a list of the conferences, and you can type the number of the one you want. To download files, you must be in the conference where the file is located. If you want to download files from several conferences, you have to keep switching conferences. This becomes a nuisance rather quickly. Each conference also has its own e-mail function.

Following are brief descriptions of the conferences:

1. SRTIS   Information about the Title V Special Rates program.

2. UTILTY   Shareware utility programs for DOS computers.

**VITAL STATS**

Data: 202-606-2675

Voice: 202-606-2092

FedWorld gateway: 71

Manual: BULLETIN 8 and BULLETIN 9

File list: PCBFILES.LST

To access files: At the Main Menu, type **j** and then choose a conference to join

Time limit: 60 minutes per call

3. QUALNET   Total quality management issues.

4. CLASSIF   New developments in position classification.

5. PAYAD   Information about pay issues and the Family and Medical Leave Act of 1993.

6. PERFMANA   Information about performance management.

7. LABORREL   Information about labor relations.

8. SES   Information about Senior Executive Service job opportunities and development programs.

9. FEBCA   Information about pay issues and initiatives relating to the Federal Employee Pay Comparability Act of 1990.

10. PERSRCDS   Guidance for federal personnel offices.

11. WAGESYS   Information about the federal wage system.

# SCIENCE AND TECHNOLOGY

# EARTH SCIENCE

## Earth Science Data Directory (ESDD)

U.S. Geological Survey
U.S. Department of the Interior
801 National Center, Mail Stop 801
Reston, VA 22092

The Earth Science Data Directory (ESDD) is a collection of more than 2,500 references to earth science and natural resource databases. The databases are maintained by government agencies, academic institutions, and private organizations. The databases cover five subject areas:

- Geology, hydrology, cartography, and biology
- Natural resources protection and management
- Geography, sociology, economics, and demographics
- The Arctic region
- Global change

Each listing typically includes a description of the database; the name of the organization maintaining it; the name, address, and telephone number of a contact; the time period covered by the data; the frequency that the database is updated; the geographic coverage of the database; and the computer type and location.

You can obtain extensive information about using the system and an index of database names by calling the voice number.

**VITAL STATS**

Data: Number provided after registration

Voice: 703-648-7112

Note: Before access is allowed, you must call the voice number to request registration materials and then fill out and return those materials.

## Global Land Information System (GLIS)

EROS Data Center
GLIS User Assistance
U.S. Geological Survey
Sioux Falls, SD 57198

The Global Land Information System (GLIS) contains descriptions of information that can be used in earth science research and global change studies. The system contains detailed references to regional, continental, and global land information. This includes land use, land cover, and soils data; cultural and topographic data; and remotely sensed satellite and aircraft data.

Scientists who find a data set they need can place a request for it online. The producing organization will receive the request and send price and ordering details.

GLIS also serves as a gateway to eight other systems: the National Oceanic and Atmospheric Administration's Earth System Data Directory, the Global Change Master Directory, the Canada Centre for Remote Sensing, the On-Line Earthnet Data Availability, the Earth Observation Center Information System, the University of Rhode Island AVHRR Inventory, the Space Shuttle Earth Observation Program, and the Pilot Land Data System.

**VITAL STATS**

Data: 605-594-6888

Voice: 800-252-4547 or 605-594-6099

Internet: telnet glis.cr.usgs.gov

Note: Dial-in users may need to experiment with the terminal settings in their communications program. A setting of VT100 works well.

## Global Seismology and Geomagnetism On-line Information System

National Earthquake Information Center
U.S. Geological Survey
Mail Stop 967
Box 25046, Denver Federal Center
Denver, CO 80225

You'll find both current and historical information about earthquakes on the Global Seismology and Geomagnetism On-line Information System. There are four ways to access the BBS:

1. **FedWorld**  Because the communications settings for this BBS are different from those of most other boards, you can run into problems trying to access through FedWorld.

2. **Toll-free telephone number**  After you connect, press the Enter key a couple of times until you get a message about unauthorized use of the computer.

3. **Toll telephone number**  After you connect, press the Enter key a couple of times until you get a message asking you to "enter class." Type **c neis** and press the Enter key. You may need to hit Enter a couple of times before you get the opening message about unauthorized use of the computer.

4. **Internet**  When you are asked for your user name, type **qed** and press the Enter key. There may be a rather long pause before you get the opening message about unauthorized use of the computer.

From the Main Menu, you can select one of three options:

**Quick Epicenter Determinations**  Brief, technical descriptions of earthquakes that occurred anywhere in the world during the previous three weeks. For each earthquake, the BBS lists the date, time, latitude, longitude, depth in kilometers, magnitude, body wave magnitude, vertical surface wave magnitude, and the standard deviation from the arithmetic mean of residuals. Some listings provide additional information. You can search the database by date, location, and magnitude. Type **g** to have the entire

---

**VITAL STATS**

Data: 800-358-2663 (1200 baud) or 303-273-8672 (9600 baud)

Voice: 303-273-8500

FedWorld gateway: 38 (but access through FedWorld is not recommended)

Internet: telnet neis.cr.usgs.gov

Note: Your communications software must be set at full duplex, zero parity, 7 data bits, and 1 stop bit.

list scroll on your screen. Type **e** to get an explanation of abbreviations used in the list.

**Earthquake Lists**   Numerous, nontechnical lists of earthquakes. The files list significant earthquakes of the world by year, significant earthquakes in the United States from January 1986 to June 1989, the most destructive earthquakes in the world, world earthquakes since 1900 that caused 1,000 or more deaths, the ten largest earthquakes in the United States, and the number of earthquakes per year since 1900 of magnitude 7 or greater.

A file called Earthquake Facts and Statistics lists the average annual frequency of various magnitudes of earthquakes; the number of earthquakes in the United States since 1900, by magnitude and region; and the number of earthquakes worldwide from 1983 to 1992, by magnitude and year. It also explains the relationship between earthquake magnitude, ground motion, and energy release.

**Geomagnetic Field Values**   A database that provides values of the elements and parameters of the Earth's magnetic field. The values are estimates based on mathematical models. Values of several elements and their rates of change are available: declination, inclination, horizontal intensity, north component, east component, vertical intensity, and total intensity.

## National Earthquake Information Center (NEIC) BBS

Denver Federal Center
U.S. Geological Survey
Box 25046, Mail Stop 967
Denver, CO 80225-0046

The National Earthquake Information Center (NEIC) BBS is a great resource for amateur seismologists, but it has little of interest to the general user.

The largest file directory is AMSEIS, or Amateur Seismology. It contains a file called AMSEIS12.ZIP, which is a program that displays and prints seismograms from data files uploaded regularly to the directory. Seismograms graph the motion of the Earth's surface when waves caused by distant earthquakes pass by. The directory has dozens of data files to use with the program. The file called SEISBULL.TXT lists the data files that are available. The program can be used only with DOS computers.

The PDE file directory contains a file called QEDEVENT.DAT, which lists epicenter information for recent earthquakes. The file is updated daily.

The BBS also has a database called Preliminary Determination of Epicenters, which you can search by date, geographical area, magnitude, and depth. To access it, type **d** at the Main Menu. Then type **1** for the PDE search, and respond to the program's prompts. If you want to download the resulting file of earthquakes, go to the Files System Menu. Once there, type **j** to reach the PDE directory, and then type **d** to download the file called OUT.DAT. The database contains information about 250,000 earthquakes that occurred anywhere in the world from 1900 to the present.

**VITAL STATS**
Data: 303-273-8508
Voice: 303-273-8420
Manual: USERMAN.LZH
To access files: At the Main Menu, type **f**
Time limit: 30 minutes per day

## U.S. Geological Survey Bulletin Board System

U.S. Geological Survey National Center
Mail Stop 803
12201 Sunrise Valley Dr.
Reston, VA 22092

The U.S. Geological Survey Bulletin Board System has a few press releases from the Geological Survey on such topics as flooding and place names. To access the press releases, type **f** at the Main Menu and **5** at the Files Menu.

The primary features of the board, however, are conferences about geology and CD-ROM technology. The conferences contain messages and some files uploaded by users.

First-time callers can look around the board but cannot download files. Your access is upgraded a few days after you fill out a brief registration questionnaire online.

The board has a dozen file areas, which contain more than 100 shareware and freeware programs for DOS and Windows computers. These include communications and word processing programs, various utilities, and files to use with Lotus 1-2-3.

**VITAL STATS**

Data: 703-648-4168

Voice: 703-648-7300

FedWorld gateway: 48

To access files: At the Main Menu, type **f**

Note: You may need to experiment with the terminal setting in your communications software. A setting of VT100 works well.

# SPACE

## EnviroNET

Mail Code 400.1
NASA Goddard Space Flight Center
Greenbelt, MD 20771

EnviroNET provides access to eighteen interactive computer models of the space environment. The models, which you can access by typing **i** at the Main Menu, are aimed primarily at designers of satellites and space shuttle payloads.

Callers use the models online and can save any data generated during the session. You can obtain an extensive user's manual that explains all of the models by calling the voice number.

Logging into the board requires several steps:

- After you connect, press the Return key.
- Type **envnet** at the "Enter number" prompt.
- Press the Return key when the board responds "Call complete."
- Type **envnet** at the "User name" prompt.
- Type **henniker** at the "Password" prompt.

Two handbooks also are available on the board:

- EnviroNET Database—Natural and Induced Environmental Information   This book has information about the space environment and its effects on instruments and spacecraft. The chapters describe the space environment for the space shuttle and the space station, as well as for low-altitude and high-altitude satellites.

- Spacecraft Environmental Anomalies Handbook   This book examines the adverse effects of radiation on electronics.

You can browse through both books online or download individual chapters. To browse, type **b** at the Main Menu. To download chapters, type **d** at the Main Menu.

**VITAL STATS**

Data: 301-286-9000 (2400 baud) or 301-286-4500 (9600 baud)

Voice: 301-286-5690

FedWorld file: 102

Internet: telnet envnet.gsfc.nasa.gov

Manual: Call the voice number to obtain the manual.

Note: Your communications software should be set to emulate a VT100 terminal.

# JPL Info

Public Information Office
Jet Propulsion Laboratory
4800 Oak Grove Dr.
Pasadena, CA 91109

JPL Info, which is operated for the National Aeronautics and Space Administration by the Jet Propulsion Laboratory at the California Institute of Technology, contains images of unmanned spacecraft, images taken by unmanned spacecraft, publications for educators, and text files about spacecraft missions. It also has a few images taken by the Hubble Space Telescope.

The board has more than 500 files. Here are some highlights:

- More than 100 text files that include press releases, status reports, and fact sheets on spacecraft missions. There are files on missions by Galileo, Magellan, the Mars Observer, Ulysses, and Voyager, among others. Other files discuss NASA's budget request, balloon ozone studies, spy plane science, ozone levels, and other topics.

- More than 100 pictures of celestial objects and JPL facilities taken by NASA/JPL spacecraft. The pictures are stored in the GIF format. Pictures are available of the Earth, Saturn, Uranus, Venus, a Jupiter moon, an asteroid, craters on Mars, and various spacecraft and spacecraft launches. A few images are animated. Utility programs that allow users to view the images are available in the software directory.

- Articles from the JPL's in-house newspaper.

- Numerous utility programs, including GIF viewers, decompression programs, an orbital tracking program, and a planetarium program. Programs are available for DOS, Windows, Macintosh, NeXT, Unix, Amiga, and Atari ST computers.

- Teacher materials provided by the JPL's Public Education Office on such topics as comets, convection, impact craters, eclipses, life in the universe, moon phases, the solar system, robotic spacecraft, the space shuttle, and sunspots.

**VITAL STATS**

Data: 818-354-1333

Voice: 818-354-5011

Internet: ftp jplinfo.jpl.nasa.gov *or* http://www.jpl.nasa.gov

Manual: README (the manual is very helpful)

To access files: At the Main Menu, type **I**

Note: If you use FTP to access this site instead of giving your e-mail address as the password, type your city and state (15 characters maximum).

## NASA Spacelink

Mail Code CA21
NASA Marshall Space Flight Center
Huntsville, AL 35812

Although NASA Spacelink is designed for teachers and students, it provides tons of valuable information for anyone interested in space exploration and the National Aeronautics and Space Administration (NASA). It offers more than 4,000 files and computer programs on everything from unidentified flying objects to upcoming space shuttle flights.

If you tried using Spacelink in recent years and gave up because of the board's complexity, try again. NASA has totally redesigned Spacelink, transforming it from an ugly duckling into a beautiful swan. Now, when you call the BBS, you're presented with a clean Internet gopher interface that's extremely easy to use.

When this book was being written, Spacelink's biggest problem was that it lacked a method for searching all the files at once. Spacelink's thousands of files make such a feature essential. NASA is working on the problem, however, and a search feature may be installed by the time you read this.

Without writing a whole book about Spacelink alone, it's impossible to provide a complete description of everything it offers. Suffice it to say that if you're seeking anything about space, it's probably available on Spacelink. Here are some highlights:

- Status reports about current NASA missions.

- NASA news releases.

- Congressional testimony and speeches by NASA officials.

- Extensive historical information about past NASA missions, starting with the beginning of the space program.

- Details about NASA's budget request.

- Information about newsletters, workshops, and other services for educators.

- Lesson plans for classes in science, math, engineering, and technology.

**VITAL STATS**

Data: 205-895-0028

Voice: 205-544-6360

Internet: telnet spacelink.msfc.nasa.gov *or* ftp spacelink.msfc.nasa.gov *or* gopher spacelink.msfc.nasa.gov *or* http://spacelink.msfc.nasa.gov

Login: guest (dial-in and telnet only)

Note: You must set your communications program to emulate a VT100 terminal.

- Images of Earth taken from space.
- Astronomy, aviation, and satellite tracking programs for several kinds of computers.
- Information about NASA's facilities around the country.
- Information about NASA research projects.
- Biographies of all the astronauts.
- Detailed information about every flight of the space shuttle, along with images from some flights.
- Background information about NASA's planetary probes, including images from the missions.
- Information about various satellites.
- Status reports, news releases, and images from the Hubble Space Telescope.
- Information about technology transfer.

## NOAA Environmental Information Services

National Oceanic and Atmospheric Administration
U.S. Department of Commerce
1825 Connecticut Ave., N.W., Room 506
Washington, DC 20235

The NOAA Environmental Information Services system provides three searchable databases that contain information about oceanic, atmospheric, and related earth science data available from the National Oceanic and Atmospheric Administration (NOAA) and other sources. It also has links to dozens of Internet sites that have related information. The system is easy to use because it transfers you into a gopher rather than using a BBS interface.

To learn how to use the system, it's helpful to read the file called "How to Find, Order and Download Data from NOAA." It's item 2 in the main directory.

Following are the three databases that you can search full text by using keywords:

1. **NOAA Environmental Services Data Directory (NOAADIR)**   Describes data sets available from NOAA relating to global change and other earth science studies.

2. **National Environmental Data Referral Service (NEDRES)**   Describes more than 22,200 environmental data sets from federal, state, private, public, and academic organizations.

3. **NOAA Product Information Catalog**   Describes various products available from NOAA, including nautical and aeronautical charts, brochures on severe weather, information about cosmic rays, climate atlases, and other products.

Here are some other highlights:

- A link to a NOAA Internet site that has a personnel locator and vacancy announcements.

- Links to more than two dozen other NOAA Internet sites, including sites with images from satellites.

- Links to other Internet sites that have environmental data.

- Links to more than four dozen Internet sites that have weather information and images.

**VITAL STATS**

Data: 800-722-5511 or 202-606-4653

Voice: 202-606-4548

FedWorld gateway: 66

Internet: telnet gopher.esdim.noaa.gov *or* gopher gopher.esdim.noaa.gov *or* http://www.esdim.noaa.gov

Login: gopher (dial-in and telnet only)

Note: If you use a dial-in number to access this site, type **c esdim1** at the Xyplex prompt and **gopher** at the login prompt.

- Information about how to subscribe to various NOAA periodicals.
- A list of National Oceanographic Data Center publications.

# NODIS

National Space Science Data Center
CRUSO
NASA Goddard Space Flight Center
Greenbelt, MD 20771

NODIS provides access to extremely technical data and other information from the National Space Science Data Center and the Space Physics Data Facility. It has both space and earth science data in such areas as astrophysics, space physics, planetary science, earth science, and life science. The system is designed for access through the Internet, so accessing it through a dial-in connection is a tad tricky.

Here's the login procedure:

- After you connect, slowly press the Enter key several times until the "Enter Number" prompt appears.
- Type **nssdca** at the prompt.
- After a few seconds, the system will respond "Call Complete." Hit the Enter key again.
- Type **nodis** at the "Username" prompt.

Much of the information on the BBS concerns spacecraft, their instruments, and data collected during flights. The board has records for about 4,600 launched spacecraft. Only about 10 percent of these were NASA missions.

A wide variety of information is available about each mission. For example, you can get a description of the mission, an overview of data collected, archiving plans and status, orbit parameters, the status of the Project Data Management Plan, personnel involved, and instrument complements, among other data. The board also offers the following information:

- Sample images from NASA's CD-ROM collections. Viewing software for DOS, Macintosh, SGI-Indigo, and DEC VAX computers is also included.
- Data from NASA's Cosmic Background Explorer project.
- Solar-terrestrial models.
- Research announcements from NASA headquarters.

**VITAL STATS**

Data: 301-286-9000 (2400 baud) or 301-286-4000 (9600 baud)

Voice: 301-286-6695

FedWorld file: 32

Internet: telnet nssdca.gsfc.nasa.gov *or* ftp nssdca.gsfc.nasa.gov

Note: Your communications software must be set to emulate a VT100 terminal, and your parameters should be set at 7 data bits, 1 stop bit, and no parity.

## Space Environment Laboratory

National Oceanic and Atmospheric Administration
U.S. Department of Commerce
325 Broadway
Boulder, CO 80303

The Space Environment Laboratory contains extremely technical data on solar and geomagnetic activities. The data are produced by the Space Environment Service Center, which is operated by the Space Environment Laboratory. The center monitors solar activity in collaboration with the Air Force. It provides advisories and forecasts of solar activity and the resulting effects on the Earth's near space environment.

The BBS does not have files. Instead, you can capture data that scrolls on your screen by using the capture feature in your communications software.

The BBS is being operated on an experimental basis. The result is that when the board goes down, it can be a while before it is back in operation.

**VITAL STATS**
Data: 303-497-5000
Voice: 303-497-5827

# TECHNOLOGY

## Fleet Imaging BBS

Fleet Imaging Center
Building 321
Naval Air Station Oceana
Virginia Beach, VA 23460

The primary focus of the Fleet Imaging BBS is photography and other kinds of visual images. Most of the files are of interest to professionals in the field, although some shareware and freeware programs will be useful for anyone with DOS or Windows computers.

The board has twenty bulletins, which you can access by typing **b** at the Main Menu. Several bulletins contain basic information about how to use BBSs in general.

The files are divided into more than a dozen areas. The photographic areas cover photo lab management, electronic darkrooms, and FAQs (frequently asked questions about photography). The freeware and shareware areas have communications programs, offline mail readers, file archivers, utilities, and similar types of programs. File Area V has a few photos of Navy ships and airplanes.

---

**VITAL STATS**

Data: 804-433-2534

Voice: Telephone support is not provided. If you have a question, leave a message on the board for the sysop.

File list: FICLFILE.TXT (uncompressed) or ALLFILES.ZIP (compressed)

To access files: At the Main Menu, type **f**

# Microcircuit Obsolescence Management (MOM) PC Board

Naval Air Warfare Center
Aircraft Division Code 7010 MS-38
6000 E. 21st St.
Indianapolis, IN 46219-2189

The Microcircuit Obsolescence Management (MOM) PC Board contains extensive information about obsolete microcircuits. People involved with the design, production, and support of electronic equipment who need to know whether a particular microcircuit is obsolete are the primary audience.

The board has two dozen bulletins, which you can access by typing **b** at the Main Menu. The bulletins explain how to use the board, describe how to use BBSs in general, and present news about defense microcircuit obsolescence.

Two databases are among the board's highlights. They allow users to search for obsolescence at the microcircuit level or by the type of equipment affected. You can access the databases by typing **op** at the Main Menu.

**VITAL STATS**

Data: 317-351-4992

Voice: 317-353-3768

Manual: MAN-TXT.EXE (ASCII text format), MAN-WORD.EXE (Microsoft Word format), or BULLETIN 5

Note: The files with EXE extensions are self-extracting and cannot be used on a Macintosh.

## Telephone Time for Computers

U.S. Naval Observatory
3450 Massachusetts Ave., N.W.
Washington, DC 20392-5420

You can call Telephone Time for Computers to get the official time from the Naval Observatory's atomic clock. The service is similar to the National Institute of Standards and Technology's Telephone Time Service (see next entry).

Every second, the Naval Observatory's service provides the updated Universal Time Coordinated, previously known as Greenwich time. It actually is the time in Paris. The first five digits are the modified date under the Julian calendar. The next three digits are the day of the year. The last six digits are the time by hour, minute, and second. There are no files available for downloading.

You can use various shareware programs to call the Naval Observatory and automatically set the clock in your computer. A shareware program for DOS computers called Time Set allows you to call this time service and the one operated by the National Institute of Standards and Technology.

**VITAL STATS**
Data: 202-653-0351
Voice: 202-653-1460

## Telephone Time Service

NIST-ACTS
National Institute of Standards and Technology
U.S. Department of Commerce
325 Broadway, Mail Stop 524
Boulder, CO 80303

The Telephone Time Service provides the official time from the atomic clock at the National Institute of Standards and Technology (NIST). The clock provides the Universal Time Coordinated, which previously was called Greenwich time.

Within six seconds of connecting, type ? to get a one-page description of the service. After you connect, the service will continually update the time. There are no files.

You can buy software that enables you to set your computer's clock by NIST's atomic clock automatically. An official NIST program for DOS computers, which costs $35, can be obtained by ordering Research Material 8101 from NIST. The address is Office of Standard Reference Materials, B311-Chemistry Building, National Institute of Standards and Technology, Gaithersburg, MD, 20899. The telephone number is 301-975-6776. Various shareware programs are also available.

**VITAL STATS**
Data: 303-494-4774
Voice: 303-497-3198

# TRANSPORTATION

## AVIATION

### AEE BBS

Office of Environment and Energy
Federal Aviation Administration
AEE-120
800 Independence Ave., S.W.
Washington, DC 20591

The focus of the AEE BBS is noise and pollution control. The board is basically for internal use, however, and has little of interest to the general user.

The files area contains a few policy and regulatory documents. The board also has eight conferences on such topics as hazardous materials, helicopter noise modeling, and economic costing modeling of air carriers.

**VITAL STATS**
Data: 202-267-9647
Voice: 202-267-3559
FedWorld gateway: 98
Manual: BBGUIDE.TXT
Note: New users must call the sysop to obtain access.

## Air Transport Division BBS

Federal Aviation Administration
Program Management Branch, ASS 260
800 Independence Ave., S.W.
Washington, DC 20591

The Air Transport Division BBS contains technical files that are primarily of interest to airlines and pilots, though it also has a few documents of more general interest. For example, it has a copy of the FAA's interim final rule on aircraft de-icing.

The files, which are available on the BBS for free, are also loaded on the fee-based CompuServe service. The files are of two major types:

**Master minimum equipment list (MMEL)** These lists, available for every type of aircraft, detail what equipment must be operational before an aircraft can fly.

**Flight standardization board (FSB) documents** These documents describe the training that must be completed before a pilot can fly a specific type of aircraft.

With both kinds of documents, the file's name is a type of code. For example, B747R2.EXE means that the MMEL is for a B747 and is the second revision (R2).

Most of the files have an EXE extension, which means they are compressed in a self-extracting format. These files cannot be used on Macintosh computers unless you have a DOS-emulation program such as SoftPC.

**VITAL STATS**
Data: 202-267-5231
Voice: 202-267-3764
FedWorld gateway: 96
Time limit: 30 minutes per call

## Airports BBS

Office of Airport Safety and Standards, AAS 100
Federal Aviation Administration
800 Independence Ave., S.W.
Washington, DC 20591

Even if you don't give a hoot about airports, call the Airports BBS at least long enough to download the user's manual. Besides explaining how to use the board, the manual provides a thorough introduction to BBSs in general. It explains the differences between various file transfer protocols (and tells which is best), explains arcane terms you may come across on various boards, and provides other useful information. It very well may be the best introduction to bulletin boards other than a few telecommunications books that cost $30 to $40.

The board contains hundreds of technical files about airport safety and operations. It is aimed at airport operators and designers, officials in the Federal Aviation Administration's Office of Airports Standards, and others interested in airport issues. The board's primary role is to distribute advisory circulars (ACs), which provide guidance to airport operators.

First-time users are given sixty minutes to look around but cannot download files. If you fill out a brief questionnaire, your access will be upgraded the next day. The upgrade gives you more time and unlimited downloading privileges.

After you log in, the BBS presents a series of news briefs about new files and features. The Bulletin Menu appears next. The bulletins explain how to use the BBS and answer common questions about the FAA. They also list upcoming airport conferences and other aviation-related BBSs. All of the bulletins can be read online or downloaded from the Files Menu.

The files are arranged into more than a dozen directories. Here are some of the highlights:

- Guidance for airport sponsors in selecting and employing architectural, engineering, and planning consultants under the FAA's airport grant programs.

- Guidance for airport operators on conducting airport snow and ice control programs.

**VITAL STATS**
Data: 202-267-5205
Voice: 202-267-7669
FedWorld gateway: 101
Manual: BULLET20.ZIP
File list: AASFILES.ZIP
To access files: At the Main Menu, type **f**
Available: 24 hours a day except from 4 a.m. to 5 a.m. EST

- A list of manufacturers that have obtained qualification approval for their airport equipment.
- Standards for construction of airports. Items covered are earthwork, drainage, paving, turfing, lighting, and incidental construction.
- Computer programs for airport operators.
- A checklist of FAA advisory circulars.
- Forty-eight engineering briefs on airport construction and maintenance issues.

The BBS also has five public conferences and two private conferences for FAA employees. Topics of the public conferences include airport winter operations, airport design and construction, airport maintenance, airport firefighting and rescue, and introductions of BBS members. The two private conferences provide a general conference and a computer forum for FAA employees.

## Aviation Rulemaking Advisory Committee (ARAC) Bulletin Board

Federal Aviation Administration
Room 302
800 Independence Ave., S.W.
Washington, DC 20591

The Aviation Rulemaking Advisory Committee (ARAC) Bulletin Board contains information about rules being developed by the Federal Aviation Administration. The following kinds of information are available:

- Notices of proposed rulemaking that are open for comment.
- Final rules that have been issued recently.
- Information about the Aviation Rulemaking Advisory Committee, its subcommittees, and its working groups. The files list upcoming meetings, describe each group's function, list members of each group, provide the status of recommendations to the FAA, and provide minutes of meetings.

**VITAL STATS**

Data: 800-322-2722 or 202-267-5948

Voice: 202-267-3345

FedWorld gateway: 105

Manual: A.TXT

File list: At the Main Menu, type **e** to get a list of all files

To access files: At the Main Menu, type **e**

## FAA Headquarters BBS

Office of Aviation Policy
APO-120
Federal Aviation Administration
800 Independence Ave., S.W.
Washington, DC 20591

Press releases from the Federal Aviation Administration, a list of other FAA-supported BBSs, and a list of telephone and fax numbers for members of Congress are available on the FAA Headquarters BBS. The board also features more than thirty conferences, several on aviation subjects.

This board is more sophisticated than most, so it takes a little getting used to. Once you have learned your way around, however, it is fairly easy to use.

After displaying opening messages, the board presents the Bulletin Menu. You can read the bulletins online or download them from the Main Menu. The bulletins are divided into nine sub-menus. To select a sub-menu, type its number at the prompt:

**VITAL STATS**
Data: 202-267-5697
Voice: 202-267-3332
FedWorld gateway: 103
Manual: See various bulletins in sub-menu 2

**Sub-menu 1**   The BBS Ten Commandments, privacy and legal considerations, rules and guidelines, BBS etiquette, and registration requirements.

**Sub-menu 2**   Various bulletins explaining how to use the board.

**Sub-menu 3**   Lists of FAA-supported BBSs, transportation-related BBSs, toll-free BBSs, BBSs in the Washington, D.C., area, all files on the board, and all callers to the board.

**Sub-menu 4**   FAA press releases and *FAA Aviation News*.

**Sub-menu 5**   Lists of the most frequently asked questions about the FAA, meetings and events at FAA headquarters, and telephone and fax numbers for members of Congress. In addition, bulletins provide information about the FAA's toll-free consumer hotline, the FAA's toll-free safety hotline, and the Transportation Department's Gay, Lesbian, or Bisexual Employees Organization (GLOBE).

**Sub-menu 6**   Lists of job openings at FAA headquarters, FAA personnel offices across the country, and overseas job openings at the International Civil Aviation Organization.

**Sub-menu 7**  Statistics on use of the BBS.

**Sub-menu 8**  Fact sheets about the proposed U.S. Air Traffic Services Corporation.

**Sub-menu 9**  Information about FAA efforts to streamline.

If this is your first call, you will be presented with a New User Questionnaire after you leave the Bulletin Menu. You must fill out the questionnaire to get your status upgraded and gain greater access to the board.

Next, you will see the Main Menu, which is slightly different from those on most BBSs. The FAA Headquarters BBS is actually four different boards, and files are separated into file areas on each one. The default board—and the one with the most files—is the Bulletin and Public Affairs Files Board. To switch among its file areas, type c at the Main Menu and then type the number of the file area you want. If you want to switch to another board, type c at the Main Menu and at the next prompt type c again. Then type the number of the file area you want. This procedure sounds complicated, but it's not once you try it.

The Bulletin and Public Affairs Files Board is divided into nine file areas:

1. **Bulletins, etc., files area**  All of the bulletins and a file that explains how to use the Qwik Mail Door feature on the BBS.

2. **Civil penalty files area**  Electronic copies of FAA decisions in cases where airlines, pilots, mechanics, or passengers appealed civil penalties assessed against them by administrative law judges for violating FAA rules. Most of the decisions contain detailed descriptions of the event that precipitated the penalty. Many of the cases involve passengers who tried to get guns through security checkpoints. A few involve firms that improperly shipped hazardous chemicals on passenger aircraft.

3. **Legal interpretation files area**  Legal opinions issued by the FAA counsel on a variety of aviation issues. Each file contains numerous opinions.

4. **FAA news release files area**  News releases from the Federal Aviation Administration. Some sample titles are "FAA Forecasts Moderate Growth in Airline Industry," "FAA Proposes Regulation on Pairing of Inexperienced Flight Crews," "FAA Releases 'Age 60' Study, Sets Public Meeting," and "FAA Acts on Problem of Buildup of Ice on Aircraft." These are the same news releases that appear on several commercial services, including CompuServe. The sysop tries to upload the news items within twenty-four hours of their release.

5. **DOT news release files area**  News releases on aviation issues from the Department of Transportation. Some sample titles are "Airline Complaints

Drop to Record Low in November, DOT Reports," "DOT Approves Air Canada/Air Partners Investment in Continental Airlines," "DOT Approves United Complaint against Japan," and "U.S. to Seek New Aviation Pact with British."

6. **FAA administrator speeches files area**   Speeches by various FAA administrators.

7. **FAA Aviation News**   Electronic copies of the bimonthly publication *FAA Aviation News*. Some sample article titles are "Staying Alert in the Cockpit," "Last Leg Syndrome," "Pilot Decision Making, Part 1," "Crew Coordination Problems," and "Corporate Flying." The publication sometimes includes case studies of accidents. The electronic version is free; subscriptions to the paper version cost $8 annually.

8. **Miscellaneous FAA bulletins, notices, files, etc.**   A selection of various documents.

9. **Advisory Circular Checklist file area**   Files relating to the Advisory Circular Checklist.

The other three boards also have file areas, although some of the file areas contain old files or none at all. The boards contain the following information:

**General Interest Files Board**   Lots of utility programs (mostly for DOS computers) and lists of BBSs in the Washington, D.C., area, aviation-related BBSs, medical-related BBSs, and BBSs with toll-free numbers.

**FAA Related Files Board**   Electronic versions of the federal budget and the FAA's strategic plan, a directory of FAA acronyms, old civil penalty files, and a few notices of proposed rulemakings.

**Total Quality Management Files Board**   Currently contains no files.

The BBS also has numerous conferences, some of which are "echoes" from other BBSs around the world. A few of the conferences are on aviation subjects. To access the conferences, type a at the Main Menu and c at the next prompt. Then type the number of the conference area you want to join.

## FAA New England

Federal Aviation Administration
FSDO-05
2 Al McKay Ave.
Portland, ME 04102

The FAA New England BBS contains master minimum equipment lists (MMELs) for dozens of types of aircraft and FAR Part 135 certification information. The MMELs list the equipment that must be operational on an aircraft before it can fly. Several other Federal Aviation Administration BBSs also have these lists, but usually they are in a self-executing format that makes them unusable on Macintosh computers. This board offers the files in both uncompressed and self-executing formats.

**VITAL STATS**

Data: 207-780-3297

Voice: 207-780-3263

Manual: DUALINST.HLP (a generic manual for the BBS software)

To access files: At the Main Menu, type **f**

Time limit: 3 hours per call

## FAA Pilot Examiner Section BBS

Federal Aviation Administration
Box 25082
AFS634
Oklahoma City, OK 73125

The FAA Pilot Examiner Section BBS is intended primarily for pilot examiners and written test examiners, although aviation safety inspectors, certified flight instructors, and others interested in aviation safety are welcome to use it.

Most callers can skip the bulletins because they simply duplicate the files. The files provide the following kinds of information:

- Updates for the *Pilot Examiners Handbook*.
- A list of aviation-related BBSs.
- Details about ordering FAA publications.
- A list of computer testing centers.
- Electronic copies of the *Examiner's Update Newsletter*.
- Electronic copies of *FAA Aviation News*.
- A list of phone numbers for FAA offices in Oklahoma City.

The board also has three conferences:

- Pilot examiners forum.
- WTE forum.
- Q&A to FAA on rules and regulations.

**VITAL STATS**

Data: 800-858-2107 or 405-954-4530

Voice: 405-954-4753 or 405-954-6448

To access files: At the Main Menu, type **f**

Time limit: 90 minutes per day

Note: You may need to experiment with the terminal setting in your communications software to access this board. A VT100 terminal emulation works fairly well.

## FAA Safety Data Exchange

Federal Aviation Administration
ACE-103
601 E. 12th St.
Kansas City, MO 64106

The FAA Safety Data Exchange, which is operated by the Federal Aviation Administration's Small Airplane Directorate, features safety-related information about ultralight aircraft and other planes built by amateurs. The board's major function is to allow owners and pilots of amateur-built aircraft to learn about problems experienced by others and to report their own problems.

The BBS has seven areas, although there are no files to download. All information is displayed on your screen. You can capture it by using your communications software's capture feature. The three most important areas are the following:

2. Reports of aircraft problems filed by owner/pilots. All of the reports are filed anonymously, and they are not confirmed or verified by the FAA. The reports database can be searched by aircraft model or by system such as airframe, engine, or propeller.

4. Information about sources of metric hardware, a BBS for sport aircraft builders, free aircraft-related software, and questions and answers about specific aircraft models.

6. A list of approved aircraft kits, manufacturers' responses to reports, safety alerts, and technical articles. The list of approved aircraft kits lists manufacturers' addresses.

**VITAL STATS**

Data: 800-426-3814

Voice: 816-426-3580

FedWorld gateway: 58

Password: safety

Note: Your communications software must be set to emulate a VT100 or ANSI terminal. Your modem speed must be set at 9600 baud or less because the BBS's modem does not recognize higher speeds.

## Flight Standards BBS

North Florida Flight Standards District Office FSDO-15
Federal Aviation Administration
9677 Tradeport Dr., Suite 100
Orlando, FL 32827-5397

The Flight Standards BBS contains information about accident prevention, flight planning programs, and master minimum equipment lists (MMELs) for commercial aircraft.

The files are divided into two areas, although there is a lot of overlap between the areas. By typing b at the Main Menu, you get a menu of files that can be read online. By typing c at the Main Menu, you get a menu of files that can be downloaded.

Here are some examples of what you will find in Area B:

- A list of meetings within the district.

- A list of local and national airshows.

- Lists of designated flight examiners, written test examiners, accident prevention counselors, designated pilot examiners, and FAA-certified medical examiners in the North Florida region.

- Several dozen news items from the FAA on such topics as pilot certification, accident prevention, hot refueling, instrument flying, defensive flying, severe weather, icing, thunderstorm hazards, and thin air accidents. Some of these provide useful leads for reporters. For example, one news item discusses mix-ups in altitude instructions at 10,000 and 11,000 feet that have caused some near accidents. Many of the news items are reprinted from *ASRS Direction,* a publication that addresses safety issues reported by pilots.

- A list of phone numbers and contacts for the Flight Standards District Office in Orlando.

- A list of phone numbers for the FAA's Mike Monroney Aeronautical Center in Oklahoma City.

- A list other aviation-related BBSs.

Here are a few examples of the nearly 2,000 files available for downloading from Area C:

**VITAL STATS**
Data: 800-645-3736 or
407-648-6309
Voice: 407-648-6840

- Dozens of FAA advisory circulars and accident prevention pamphlets. Some sample titles are "Water in Aviation Fuels," "Certification and Operation of Amateur-Built Aircraft," "Role of Preflight Preparation," "Airplane De-Ice and Anti-Ice Systems," "Tips on Winter Flying," "Human Behavior: The No. 1 Cause of Accidents," "Balloon Safety Tips," and "How to Avoid a Midair Collision."

- Lists of local and national airshows.

- Information about the Freedom of Information Act.

- Updates of FAA rules.

- Copies of speeches by the FAA administrator.

- Information about FAA pilot tests, including practice exams.

- Numerous flight planning programs.

- A list of toll-free numbers for airlines.

- A list of aviation-related BBSs.

- Descriptions of different helicopters.

- Electronic copies of *FAA Aviation News*.

- Master minimum equipment lists for commercial aircraft. MMELs list the equipment the aircraft must have before it can fly. The files are compressed in a format that makes them unusable on Macintosh computers.

- Hundreds of utility programs for IBM and compatible computers, including numerous communications programs.

## ICAP BBS

Interagency Committee for Aviation Policy
GSA Aircraft Management Division (FBA)
CM Building 4, Room 815
Washington, DC 20406

The ICAP BBS is operated by the Interagency Committee for Aviation Policy. Its members include federal departments and agencies that own, lease, or procure aircraft or aircraft services. The panel's goal is to coordinate improvements in government use of aircraft.

Most of the bulletins and files duplicate each other. You can read the bulletins online, and the files can be downloaded. Following are some examples of what is available:

- A list of excess aircraft available for sale.
- A small list of job openings in the aviation field.
- Agendas and minutes from ICAP meetings.
- Information about training opportunities.
- An ICAP membership list.
- A list of ICAP projects.

**VITAL STATS**

Data: 703-305-6204

Voice: 703-305-6263

To access files: At the Main Menu, type **f**

Time limit: 60 minutes per call

# HIGHWAYS

## Federal Highway Administration Electronic Bulletin Board System (FEBBS)

IRM Team (HMS-40)
Federal Highway Administration
400 7th St., S.W.
Washington, DC 20590

Anyone trying to navigate through the Federal Highway Administration's BBS could use a road map. FEBBS is huge and complex—levels frequently run five deep—but it has tons of information about the federal highway and motor carrier programs. As you navigate through the levels, remember two commands: type + to return to the previous menu and − to return to the Main Menu.

Here are examples of what you will find:

- An electronic version of 23 CFR, the section of the Code of Federal Regulations pertaining to highways.

- An electronic copy of the Federal Highway Administration's Federal Aid Policy Guide.

- Extensive information about transportation of people with disabilities under the Americans with Disabilities Act.

- A list of state fuel tax rates.

- Notices of proposed rulemaking.

- Traffic fatality summaries arranged by state.

- Detailed information about the Intermodal Surface Transportation Efficiency Act, including a copy of the law.

- Copies of Federal Highway Administration orders, notices, and technical advisories.

- Requests for proposals (RFPs).

- Lists of job openings in the Federal Highway Administration.

- A headquarters telephone directory for the Federal Highway Administration.

**VITAL STATS**

Data: 800-337-3492 or 202-366-3764
Voice: 202-366-1120
FedWorld gateway: 20
Manual: UFEBBS01.TXT (ASCII text format) or UFEBBS01.WP5 (WordPerfect 5.0 format)
Note: See instructions in the description for downloading the manual. If you want to read the manual online, type **i** at the Main Menu and read it as a series of bulletins.
To access files: At the Main Menu, type **c**

After you connect, the BBS presents a series of announcements and then the Main Menu appears. New users have limited access to the BBS until they register and have their access upgraded. To register, type **r** at the Main Menu and then answer the questions. If you just want to take a look at the board, don't bother registering.

Most of the information on FEBBS is organized by conferences, many of which represent the various program areas of the Federal Highway Administration. There also are conferences covering topics of interest to FHWA field offices and computer issues. Only registered users have access to all the public conferences.

Most conferences include three areas:

**Bulletins**  Text files containing general information.

**Message board**  An e-mail system that allows users to send public and private messages.

**Download file area**  Files containing specialized information relevant to the conference. Unfortunately, many of the files are compressed in a self-extracting format that makes them unusable on Macintosh computers.

The board has a dozen major conference areas. To reach a conference, type **c** at the Main Menu. At the next prompt, type the letter of the conference you want:

T. Federal Transit Administration conference

C. Office of Chief Counsel: 23 U.S. Code, CFR

P. Policy

R. Research and development

D. Program development

S. Safety and system applications

M. Motor carrier safety

A. Administration

K. Contracts and procurement

O. Other FHWA program areas and newsletters

L. LAN: local area networks

H. Hardware, software, communications, forms, and other topics

The board can quickly become confusing because many of the conferences serve mainly as gateways to yet more conferences. Here are two examples:

- The program development conference is a gateway to five conferences: environment and planning; metrics; general engineering; right-of-way; and pavement design, management, and rehabilitation.

- The safety and system applications conference is a gateway to four conferences: Office of Traffic Operations, Office of Highway Safety, traffic software users group, and experimental projects program.

For an example of how cumbersome this procedure becomes, you must go through several steps to download the user's manual:

- At the Main Menu, type **c** to get the Conferences Menu.

- At the Conferences Menu, type **h** to get the hardware, software, communications, forms, and other topics conference.

- At the hardware conference, type **a** to get the Ask Dr. DOS conference.

- Type **d** to get a list of files in the conference.

- Type **d** to download the manual and then follow the prompts to set the transfer protocol.

# WATERWAYS

## Marine Data Computer Bulletin Board

National Oceanic and Atmospheric Administration/National Ocean Service
U.S. Coast and Geodetic Survey
1315 East-West Highway, Station 4746
Silver Spring, MD 20910

Databases available through the Marine Data Computer Bulletin Board list charts of U.S. coastal waterways that are prepared by the National Oceanic and Atmospheric Administration (NOAA). The BBS also contains databases that list some sample airport charts and photos. The actual charts and photos are not available on the BBS.

You can reach the databases by typing **d** at the Main Menu. One of the most interesting databases lists shipwrecks and obstructions in coastal waterways. It supplies the latitude and longitude of each wreck and obstruction. Another database lists NOAA chart sales agents. You can search it by zip code or state.

The board also has a few files, which list NOAA products and services, NOAA contacts, marine pilots organizations, and other marine-related BBSs. You can access them by typing **f** at the Main Menu.

**VITAL STATS**
Data: 301-713-4573
Voice: 301-713-2653
FedWorld gateway: 112
Time limit: 60 minutes per call
Note: Your communications software must be set to emulate a VT100 terminal.

## MARlinspike BBS

Maritime Administration
U.S. Department of Transportation
400 7th St., S.W.
Washington, DC 20590

The primary audience for the MARlinspike BBS is the U.S.-flagged shipping community. New users must register before they can access the board. To do so, type r at the Main Menu and fill out the questionnaire.

The board offers the following kinds of information:

- Press releases from the Maritime Administration.

- Detailed explanations of bills pending before Congress and passed by Congress that affect the shipping industry.

- A calendar of industry events.

- A glossary of shipping terms.

- Lists of contacts at the Maritime Administration.

- Information about cargo preference laws.

- Bulletins and schedules from U.S.-flagged shipping companies.

**VITAL STATS**
Data: 202-366-8505
Voice: 202-366-5807
FedWorld gateway: 72

# Navigation Information Network (NAVINFONET)

Defense Mapping Agency
Hydrographic/Topographic Center
Attn: MCN/NAVINFONET
U.S. Department of Defense
Washington, DC 20315-0030

General users will find little of interest on the Navigation Information Network (NAVINFONET). Its purpose is to provide professional mariners with technical navigation information.

NAVINFONET contains the data used to produce the weekly *Notice to Mariners,* in addition to other information useful to mariners. The BBS includes chart corrections, broadcast warnings, MARAD advisories, the Defense Mapping Agency (DMA) list of lights, anti-shipping activity messages, mobile offshore drilling unit locations, corrections to DMA hydrographic product catalogs, the U.S. Coast Guard lists of lights, and Global Positioning System data.

Selection 54, the General Report on Current Active Anti-Shipping Areas, is interesting because it contains brief reports on pirate attacks against shipping around the world. It also lists ports where ships are particularly at jeopardy. For example, the Brazilian ports of Rio de Janeiro and Santos are among the most dangerous in the world. The report is updated weekly.

You cannot download files from the board. Instead, you can save the information in a capture file as it scrolls on the screen.

> **VITAL STATS**
>
> Data: 301-227-4360
>
> Voice: 301-227-3296
>
> Manual: NAVINFONET MANUAL (Selection 11), USERS MANUAL CHANGES (Selection 12). These files are located in the System Mailbox/Utilities sub-menu.
>
> To access files: At the System Menu, type the number of the sub-menu you want. Type **97** to display a list of all sub-menus and their files.
>
> Note: After dialing the data number and getting a connect message, press the Return key. Then type **login anms** and press Return again. Type **pc 55** when asked for your user ID.

TRANSPORTATION

## U.S. Coast Guard Navigation Information Service (NIS) Bulletin Board

U.S. Coast Guard ONSCEN
7323 Telegraph Rd.
Alexandria, VA 22310-3998

Information useful to recreational boaters, trucking companies, surveyors, and others can be found on the U.S. Coast Guard Navigation Information Service Bulletin Board. The board offers two major types of information:

1. **Information from and about the NAVSTAR Global Positioning System (GPS)** GPS is a satellite radionavigation system that provides position, velocity, and time information. The Department of Defense originally developed the system for military use only, but it has been made available for public use as well. The following information is provided about NAVSTAR:

   - *Notice Advisories to NAVSTAR Users (NANU)* Real-time operational status reports about the satellites. NANU messages notify users about recent, current, or future satellite outages and system adjustments.

   - *Almanacs* Data describing the orbit, health, and clock for each satellite in the system.

   - *Precise emphemeris* Descriptions of the orbit of each satellite, as reported by numerous ground stations.

   - *Status messages* Condensed information about satellite planes, clocks, and current or recent NANUs. The messages are updated daily.

   - *Information about other radionavigation systems* Information on all radionavigation systems involving the Coast Guard, including Omega, Loran-C, GPS, and DGPS.

2. **Notices to mariners** These weekly notices alert boaters to navigation hazards such as burned-out buoys and lights, shipwrecks, and sailboat races.

   There are two ways to access information from the Main Menu:

   - Select a topic sub-menu (General radionavigation, GPS, Differential GPS, Loran-C, Omega, Local notices to mariners, Marine communications library, and Recreational boating safety).

**VITAL STATS**
Data: 703-313-5910
Voice: 703-313-5900
FedWorld file: 54

- Type **f** to enter the Forums. These contain the same information as the topic sub-menus. There are more than two dozen forums, and each one contains both files and messages.

# GLOSSARY

**ANSI graphics**   A set of codes that control various features on a computer terminal. When you log into a BBS, you're frequently asked whether your terminal supports ANSI graphics. If you're not sure, answer "no" to the question.

**ASCII**   A "plain vanilla" text format that includes no coding. Many files on federal BBSs are in ASCII format because virtually every word processing program can read ASCII text.

**Baud**   A rate that indicates how fast a modem can transfer information. In practical terms, a modem transmits characters at about 10 percent of its baud rate. For example, a 2400-baud modem can transmit about 240 characters per second, while a 14,400-baud modem can transmit about 1,440 characters per second.

**BBS**   *See* Bulletin board system.

**Bulletin**   A text file on a BBS that typically provides information about how to use the board or other news. Many boards display the Bulletin Menu when you log in, and you can reach it on other boards by typing **b** at the Main Menu. You can read bulletins online, and some BBSs allow you to download them to your own computer.

**Bulletin board system (BBS)**   A computerized system that users can access by calling with a modem attached to a computer. BBSs usually have text files and/or computer programs that can be downloaded. Most also have e-mail systems that allow users to send messages to each other and conferences where users can exchange messages on specific topics.

**Capture feature**   A feature in most communications software programs that allows you to "capture" in a text file the information that scrolls on your screen from a BBS. After logging off the BBS, you can review the file with your word processing program.

**Communications software**   A software program that allows your computer to "talk" with a BBS.

**Compressed file**   A file that has been made smaller than its original size. Files are compressed so that they will download more quickly and take up less space. To use them, you must decompress them back to their original size after downloading them. Usually, this operation requires a decompression program. However, some files are "self-executing," meaning that you don't need a special program to decompress them. These files have an EXE extension at the end of their names. For example, a self-executing file might be called BBSGUIDE.EXE. Self-executing files cannot be used on Macintosh computers.

**Conference**   An area on a BBS containing messages about a specific topic. BBSs frequently have many conferences. On a few boards, conferences also have files. Some boards use other terms for conferences, such as forum or special interest group (SIG).

**Decompressed file**   *See* Compressed file.

**Door**   An area on a BBS containing a computer program that you can use while connected. On federal BBSs, doors usually lead to searchable databases.

**Download**   To move a file from a BBS to your computer.

**Echo**   The reposting of electronic messages written by users of one BBS on a second BBS. By "echoing" the messages from other boards, a BBS allows its users to exchange messages with users of other BBSs across the nation or around the world.

**E-mail**   Electronic messages written by one BBS user to another. E-mail is basically private, although sysops can (and do) read messages to ensure that the board is being used properly. On most federal BBSs you can exchange messages only with other users of that board. However, a few federal boards also have "echoes" that allow you to exchange messages with users of other BBSs.

**Emulate**   A setting in your communications software that makes your computer act as if it is another type of computer. It is common to make your computer emulate a VT100 terminal when you are BBSing.

**Extension**   A three-letter code at the end of a file name that usually indicates what software program was used to create the file. The extension is separated from the rest of the file name by a period. For example, on a file called BBSGUIDE.W51 the extension W51 indicates that the file was created using WordPerfect 5.1. Sometimes the extension indicates which program was used to compress the file. For example, a file called BBSGUIDE.ZIP was compressed with the PKZIP compression program.

**File**   A text document, graphic image, or computer program. You can download files from a BBS to your own computer. On most BBSs, you type **f** at the Main Menu to reach the files area.

**File transfer protocol (FTP)**   An Internet protocol used to transfer files from one computer to another. Most publicly accessible FTP sites on the Internet allow you to access them by using "anonymous FTP." To use anonymous FTP, type **anonymous** when asked for a login, and type your e-mail address when asked for a password. This procedure allows you to access selected files on the computer without being a registered user.

**Forum**   *See* Conference.

**Freeware**   A software program that you can use free of charge. Some federal BBSs have freeware programs that you can download.

**FTP**   *See* File transfer protocol.

**Garbage**   Nonsensical characters that appear on your computer screen when you connect to a BBS. The characters are caused by noise on the telephone line or incorrect settings in your communications software.

**Gateway**   A connection that allows you to move from the BBS you are logged onto to another computer system. A few federal BBSs have gateways to other federal boards or to the Internet.

**GIF**   *See* Graphics interchange format.

**Gopher**   An Internet program that organizes files into hierarchical menus. The interface is extremely easy to use, making gopher a popular way to access the Internet.

**Graphics interchange format (GIF)**   A popular format for compressing and storing graphic files such as photographs. You need a viewer program to decompress and open the files.

**Hacker**   In common usage, a person who accesses a computer without authorization. Usually, a hacker improperly acquires passwords for a computer network and uses those passwords to break into the network. Some computer insiders define *hacker* as a person who loves to explore the internal workings of computers and computer networks and use the term *cracker* for those who illegally break into computers.

**ID**   The name you use to identify yourself when logging into a BBS. Most federal BBSs require that you use your real name as your user ID.

**Internet**   A vast international network of computer networks. Some federal BBSs can be accessed through the Internet, and a few offer Internet e-mail.

**Login**   A word or words that you must type to access a BBS after connecting to it with your modem.

**Menu**   A list of options that outline how you can proceed on the BBS. The Main Menu is the heart of any BBS. It usually leads to other menus such as the File Menu, the Bulletin Menu, and the Message Menu.

**Modem**   A piece of hardware that transforms data into electronic signals that computers can exchange over ordinary telephone lines.

**Password**  A private code that allows you to gain access to a BBS. You usually choose your own password, although a few boards assign you a password and a few have universal passwords used by everyone. Various boards have different rules about how long your password can be and what characters you can use. When choosing a password, you should avoid anything obvious like your name or the city where you live. Otherwise, a hacker may be able to guess your password and use it to access a BBS. For added security, some people choose passwords containing a combination of letters and numbers.

**Prompt**  A message from the BBS asking what you want to do next. Many prompts present you with a list of options from which you can choose.

**Protocol**  The "rules" two computers must follow to exchange messages or files. For downloading files from a BBS, some of the most common protocols are Zmodem, Ymodem, and Xmodem. For the transfer to work, the BBS and your communications software must both use the same protocol. On the Internet two common protocols are file transfer protocol (FTP) and telnet.

**Shareware**  A computer program you can try for free. If you decide to keep it, you must send the shareware fee to the program's author. Some federal BBSs have shareware programs that you can download.

**SIG (special interest group)**  *See* Conference.

**Sub-board**  A second BBS that is a subsystem of the main board and that can be accessed from it.

**Sysop**  The person who runs the BBS. *Sysop* is short for system operator.

**Telnet**  An Internet protocol that allows you to connect to another computer and use it as if it were sitting on your desk. For example, you can use telnet to access electronic card catalogs at libraries around the world.

**Upload**  To transfer a file from your computer to another computer.

**User**  A person who calls and uses a BBS.

**Userid**  *See* ID.

**Wildcard**  A search capability available on some BBSs that's helpful if you don't know the full name of the file you're seeking. You can type a partial file name with wildcard symbols such as *, and the BBS will search for all files containing the partial name.

**World Wide Web (WWW)**  A hypertext-based interface to the Internet. Hypertext files have links to other, related files embedded within them. To access the related file, you click on the link.

**Zipped**  *See* Compressed file.

# INDEX

Abduction, 24
ABLEDATA database, 233-236
ABLE INFORM BBS, 233-236
Abrasives, 85
*Access EPA,* 161
Access to federal bulletin boards, 20-22
Access to Internet. *See* Internet
Accounting machines, 60
Acetone, 90
ACF BBS, 198
Acid rain, 156
Acquired immune deficiency syndrome (AIDS)
  alcoholism and, 232
  AIDS Litigation Project, 230
  comprehensive information, 215, 225, 229-231
  consumer information, 27
  FDA drug approval, 214
  HIV testing requirements abroad, 24
  National AIDS Clearinghouse, 231
  National AIDS Hotline, 231
  National AIDS Program Office, 229
  1987-1989 mortality rate, 211
  population loss and, 58
  Surgeon General's report, 226, 229, 230
ADA. *See* Americans with Disabilities Act
*ADA, The: Your Employment Rights as an Individual with a Disability* (EEOC), 238
*ADA, The: Your Responsibilities as an Employer* (EEOC), 238
Ada programming language, 100-102, 121
  Ada Information Clearinghouse Bulletin Board, 100-101
  *Ada Information Clearinghouse Newsletter,* 100
  *Ada Language Reference Manual,* 100
  *Ada Technical Assistance Manual* (EEOC), 234
  Ada Technical Support Bulletin Board, 102
Administration for Children and Families, 198
Administration on Native Americans, 188
Adobe Acrobat Reader, 95
Adolescents. *See* Children and families
Adoption assistance, 23-24, 198, 231
Advertising, 232, 236

Advisory Committee on Advanced Television Service, 88
Advisory Council on the NII, 31
AEE BBS, 286
Aeromedical Forum, 210
Aerometric Information Retrieval System, 156
Aeronautics and aerospace. *See* Space science and exploration
Africa, 24
African Americans, 126-128, 231, 232
Agency for International Development, 127
Agent Orange, 225
Aggregates, 85
Aging, 43, 211, 231
AGRICOLA database, 40-43
*Agricultural History Newsletter,* 42
Agricultural Library Forum (ALF), 40
Agricultural Research Service, 49
Agricultural Trade and Marketing Information Center, 42
Agriculture, 39-49
  biological controls, 46-47
  biotechnology, 40, 41, 43, 48
  bulletin board lists, 169
  census data, 58, 59
  comprehensive information, 40-43, 181
  economic and statistical data, 44, 66, 68, 69
  farm safety, 261
  foreign trade, 40, 42, 43, 44, 65
  hay locator service, 45
  Internet sites, 33
  migrant and seasonal workers, 260
  nonpoint source pollution, 181, 182
  technology transfer, 40, 49
Agriculture Department, 40-44, 46-49, 65, 126, 188, 227
AIDS. *See* Acquired immune deficiency syndrome
Aid to Families with Dependent Children, 198, 240
Aircraft. *See* Aviation and airports
Air Force, 126, 127, 279
Air Force CALS Test Bed BBS, 103
Air pollution
  agricultural effects, 43
  comprehensive information, 156-160

indoor air quality, 167, 231
industrial, 60
modeling, 157-158, 171, 176, 177
OSHA regulations, 261
tribal air quality, 188
Air Pollution Training Institute, 157
Airports. *See* Aviation and airports
Airport Safety and Standards, Office of, 288
Airports BBS, 10, 288-289
Air Quality Planning and Standards, Office of, 156
Air traffic controllers, 251
Air Traffic Services Corporation, 292
Air Transport Division BBS, 287
Alabama, 154
Alaska, 167, 207, 251
Alaskan natives, 188
Alcohol abuse and alcoholism, 225
comprehensive statistics, 232
drunk driving/traffic accidents, 123, 232
health-related information, 231
substance abuse bibliographies, 43, 231
substance abuse database, 119
Alcoholic beverages, 71
*ALCTS Network News,* 34
Algebraic calculator program, 113
Alias names permitted, 6, 193, 194
Allergies, 43, 227, 231
Alternative agriculture, 40, 41, 43, 46, 181
*Alternative Agriculture News,* 46
Alternative Farming Systems Information Center, 41, 42
Alternative Treatment Technology Information Center (ATTIC), 168-169
Aluminum industry, 59, 85
Alzheimer's disease, 231, 240
Ambient Monitoring Technology Information Center, 156
Americans for Indian Opportunity, 188
Americans with Disabilities Act (ADA), 27, 34, 234, 237-240, 261, 300
*Americans with Disabilities Act, The: A NARIC Resource Guide,* 234
Americans with Disabilities Electronic BBS, 237, 238, 239
America Online, 4, 9
*AMTIC News,* 156
Anatomy programs, 132

Animal and Plant Health Inspection Service (APHIS), 46-47
Animals, livestock, and wildlife
environmental issues, 154
livestock handling, 43, 44
livestock prices, 68
threatened and endangered species, 167
veterinary medicine, 214-217
welfare concerns, 40, 41, 43, 49
Animal Welfare Information Center, 41
*Annual Report to Congress,* 149
Anorexia nervosa, 43
Antarctica, 83, 202
Antimony, 85
Aphis BC, 47
Applied Modeling Research Branch (AMRB) BBS, 176
Aquaculture, 40, 42
Aquaculture Information Center, 42
Architectural Barriers and Compliance Board, 234
Archives and records management, 34, 36, 121
Arctic science, 83, 266
Arizona, 207
Arkansas, 67
Army (U.S.), 36, 104
Army Corps of Engineers, 75
Arsenic, 85
Arthritis, 223, 231, 233, 240
Arthritis Advisory Committee, 216
Artificial intelligence, 33, 34, 205
Artificial sweeteners, 225
Artists, 240
Asbestos, 158, 261
Asia, 24
*ASRS Direction,* 297
Assistive devices, 233-236, 252
Association for Library Collections and Technical Services, 34
*Association of Applied Insect Ecologists News,* 46
*Association of Natural Bio-control Producers Newsletter,* 46
Asteroids, 273
Astronauts, 275
Astronomy, 21, 83, 132, 273-275
Astrophysics, 278
Atmospheric science, 276-277

Atrazine, 181
Audubon BBS, 171
Australia, 262
Automated Index of Criminal Justice Information Systems, 123
Automated information management, 36
Automated Library Information Exchange (ALIX), 33-35
Automated Vacancy Announcement Distribution System (AVADS) BBS, 244
Automobiles. *See* Motor vehicles
Aviation and airports, 286-299
    aircraft and engine manufacturing, 59
    aircraft de-icing, 287, 292
    airlines toll-free numbers, 298
    airport charts, 303
    air traffic controllers, 251
    amateur-built aircraft, 296, 298
    aviation medicine, 210
    conferences and programs, 121, 275, 291, 293
    emergency management, 139
    FAA rulemaking, 290
    government aircraft use policy, 299
    labor relations, 260
    master minimum equipment lists, 287, 294, 297, 298
    noise and pollution control, 286
    pilot training, 287, 295, 297-298
    policy and legal considerations, 291-293
    safety and operations, 288-289, 295-298
Aviation Medicine, Office, of, 210
Aviation Policy, Office of, 291
Aviation Rulemaking Advisory Committee (ARAC) Bulletin Board, 290
Awards. *See* Government contracts; Government grants
AZT trials, 215

Backup programs, 113
Banking sector, 63, 66-69, 205
Base closures (military), 52-53, 204
Bauxite, 85
BBSs. *See* Bulletin board systems
Beer, 71
Behavior and nutrition, 43
Benefits, employee. *See* Employment issues
Benzene, 90, 156

Best Available Control Technology/Lowest Achievable Emissions Rates Information System (BLIS), 157
Bible, 113
Bibliographic Retrieval System (BRS), 142-143, 151
*Big Dummy's Guide to the Internet, The*, 234
Bill of Rights, 253
*Biocontrol Flash*, 46
Biodiversity, 202
Biofuels, 43
Biological controls, 43, 46-47, 49
Biologic articles, 215, 216
Biology, 21, 46, 160, 266
Biomedicine, 79-80, 130, 223
Bioremediation, 170
Biotechnology/Genetic engineering, 40, 41, 43, 48, 49, 166, 219
Bismuth, 85
BITNET, 42, 80
Black lung benefits, 260
Blindness, 239, 240
Bloodborne pathogens, 261
Blood supply, 214, 215
Blood transfusions, 225, 231
Boards of Wage and Service Contract Appeals BBS, 258
Boating and navigation, 303-307
Bond insurance, 93
Bond rates, 63
Bosnia, 201
Bottled water, 215, 219
Boulder Public Library, 113
Bovine somatotropin (BST), 215, 219
Brain injury, 234
Brain tumors, 225
Brazil, 305
"Break" keys, 12
Breast cancer, 37, 225
Breast implants, 212, 213
Breast lumps, 27
Brookings Institution, 201
Budget. *See* Federal budget
Building and Fire Research Bulletin Board System (BFRBBS), 134
Building and Fire Research Laboratory, 134
Buildings and construction
    access for people with disabilities, 237
    federal buildings management, 203

federal criteria and specifications, 75
federal property sales, 204
industry statistics, 64, 66, 70
Bulimia, 43
Bulletin board systems (BBBs)
connecting, 5
hardware and software, 3-4
help, 9-10
Internet connections, 14
menus, 7-9
problems and solutions, 10-12
registering, 6-7
warning messages, 5-6
BUPERS Access, 245
Bureau of. *See* specific bureau name
Business Analysis, Bureau of, 63
Business Analysis, Office of, 59, 61-64
Business and industry
census and economic data, 58-60, 63-65
client tracking programs, 113
emergency management, 139
patents and trademarks, 54
*See also* Small business; specific sectors
Business Information Service for the Newly Independent States, 65

Cabinet officials, 201
Cadmium, 85
Calendars of events. *See* specific agencies, bulletin boards, and topics
California, 75, 207, 251, 252
California Institute of Technology, 273
Call-ERS/NASS, 44
Call waiting, 5
CALS (Continuous Acquisition and Lifecycle Support), 103
CAMEONet, 135
Canada, 71, 72, 224, 240
Canada Centre for Remote Sensing, 267
Cancer
alcoholism and, 232
blood transfusions and, 225
diet and, 40, 43
information, 27, 37, 225, 226, 231, 240
Canker sores, 223
"Capture" feature, 5
Cardiovascular and Renal Drugs Advisory Committee, 216
Cardiovascular disease, 43

Career America Smart program, 247
Caribbean area, 24
Carpets and rugs, 59-60
Cartography, 266
Cash Management Directorate, 205
Cash Management Improvement Act of 1990, 205
CASUCOM, 195
*Cataloging Newsline*, 33
*Catalog of Resources for Education in Ada and Software Engineering*, 100, 101
Catfish farming, 40, 43
CDRH Electronic Docket, 212-213
CD-ROM conferences, 34, 139, 271
CEAM BBS, 177
Cement, 85
*Census and You*, 56
Census-BEA Electronic Forum, 58-60
Census Bureau, 56, 58-64, 246
Census Economic SIG, 58
Census Personnel Board, 246
Center for Devices and Radiological Health (CDRH), 212, 215
Center for Exposure Assessment Modeling (CEAM), 177, 180
Center for Food Safety and Applied Nutrition, 218
Centers for Disease Control, 230, 231
Central America, 24, 119
Cervical cancer, 225
*CFP Newsletter*, 219
Chambers of commerce, 56
Cheese making, 41
Chemical Abstract Service, 90, 162
Chemical Hazard Response Information System, 164
Chemical industry, 60, 90
Chemicals
document databases, 161, 164, 165
emergency response, 135, 164, 167
index and class lists, 90, 162-163, 171
Chemistry
computer programs, 132
document database, 160
patent licensing, 21
periodic table, 132, 166
Cherry blossoms, 138
Children and families
abduction, 24

adolescent pregnancy, 43
adoption, 23-24, 198, 231
alcoholism, 232
child abuse and neglect, 231
consumer information, 27
dental health, 223
federal assistance programs, 198
food and nutrition, 43
HIV/AIDS education, 231
juvenile justice, 118-120
labor laws, 260
low-weight births, 59
mental health, 231
work issues, 256
Child Support Enforcement Network, 198
China, 24, 25, 71, 262
Cholesterol, 225
Chromium, 85
Chronic fatigue syndrome, 27, 240
Cirrhosis, 232
Citizens band frequencies, 139
Citizens Emergency Center, 23
Citizenship, 23
Civil Air Patrol, 139
Civilian Radioactive Waste Management, Office of (OCRWM), 173-174
Civilian Radioactive Waste Management Information Center, 173
Civil preparedness, 139
Civil service. *See* employment entries
Civil War timeline, 132
Classified advertisements, 236
Classified information, 201
Clean Air Act, 52, 176
Clean Air Act amendments of 1990, 156, 157
Clean Coal Technology program, 147
Clean Lakes Program, 180, 183
Cleanup Information Bulletin Board (CLU-IN), 170-171
Cleanup Standards Outreach (CSO) BBS, 172
Clean Water Act, 52, 181
Clearinghouse for Inventories and Emission Factors (CHIEF), 157
Clearinghouse on Computer Accommodation, 197
Client Information Center BBS, 203
Client tracking programs, 113

Climate. *See* Weather and climate
Clinician Research Scientists program, 224
Clipper programming, 95
CNSP/CNAP Bulletin Board, 110
Coal industry, 85, 86, 146, 147
Coastal areas, 154, 183
Coastal Nonpoint Pollution Control Programs, 183
Coastal waterways, 303
Coastal Zone Act Reauthorization Amendments of 1990, 183
Coast and Geodetic Survey, 303
Coast Guard, 164, 305, 306
Coast Guard Navigation Information Service (NIS) Bulletin Board, 306-307
Cobalt, 85
Code of Federal Regulations, 30, 156, 165, 171, 192, 261, 300
Codex alimentarius, 220
Coins and paper money, 69
Collective bargaining agreements, 261
Colleges and universities. *See* Education and training
Colorado, 75, 113
Colorado Alliance of Research Libraries, 113
Coloring books, 113
*Commander's Handbook for Military/Civil Law*, 121
*Commerce Business Daily*, 84, 147, 170
Commerce Department
  building and fire research, 134
  computer security, 106
  economic data, 52-53, 58, 61, 62
  electronic telephone directories, 21, 32
  environmental information, 276
  freeware and shareware, 113
  job listings, 246
  minority programs, 127
  patents and trademarks, 54
  space environment, 279
  telecommunications systems and policies, 31-32, 108
  telephone time service, 283
  trade information, 65, 74
Commercial fishing, 91
Commission Issuance Posting System (CIPS), 144-145
Commodity prices, 64

Commodity specialists, 85
Communications sector. *See* Telecommunications
Communications software, 240
　DOS, Windows, and IBM-compatible, 42, 59, 112, 115, 116, 121, 134, 185, 233, 253, 255, 271, 280, 298
　information and purchase advice, 3, 4, 134, 136
　Macintosh, 186, 233, 255
Community-based electronic networks, 167
Community Reinvestment Act, 68
Compensation Policy, Office of, 263
COMPLIance Information (COMPLI), 158
Compression and extraction programs, 115
CompuServe, 4, 9, 23, 35, 287
Computer-aided Acquisitions and Logistic Support (CALS), 21, 22
Computer-aided design (CAD) programs, 116
Computer-Aided Management of Emergency Operations (CAMEO), 135
Computers, 99-109
　accommodation for disabled persons, 197
　Ada programming language, 100-102
　Army data distribution systems, 104
　general information, 95, 256
　government acquisitions, 81
　industry data, 60
　integrated services digital network, 109
　list of agency systems, 123
　standards, 103, 105, 108
　time services, 282, 283
　viruses and other security issues, 13, 95, 106-107, 110, 113, 115, 116, 132, 171, 180, 185, 186, 240, 250, 255
Computer Security Act of 1987, 107
Congress
　committees. *See* specific committees and subcommittees
　list of confirmed presidential appointments, 30
　lists of members, 21, 27, 56, 154, 291
Congressional Budget Office, 63
Congressional testimony, 181, 216
Connecticut, 70
Constitution, U.S., 112, 132, 253

Construction. *See* Buildings and construction
Consular Affairs Bulletin Board (CABB), 23-25
Consumer Advocate, Office of the, 199
Consumer affairs
　credit and finance, 27, 63, 69
　information publications, 26-28, 215
　postal rates, 199
Consumer Information Center (CIC) BBS, 26-28
Consumer price index, 63, 67, 260, 261
Consumer prices, 68
*Consumer's Resource Handbook*, 26
Contact lenses, 27
Contraceptives, 27, 214, 231
Control Technology Center, 157
Cooking programs, 132
Cooperative Administrative Support System, 195
Cooperatives, agricultural, 43
Coordinating Committee for Russian Wheat Aphid Biology, 46
Copper, 85
Copyright, 38
Corporate income tax, 70, 97
Corps of Engineers, 75
Cosmetics, 214-216
Cosmic Background Explorer project, 278
Cosmic rays, 276
Counterfeit detection, 69
Credit, 27, 44, 63, 69, 202
Credit cards, 27
Credit unions, 92
Crime and security
　computer viruses and other security issues, 13, 95, 106-107, 110, 113, 115, 116, 132, 171, 180, 185, 186, 240, 250, 255
　criminal justice, 118-120, 122-124
　emergency management, 139
　military justice, 121
　overseas travel, 23-25
　rural America, 40, 43
Crisis relocation, 139
Criteria Bulletin Board System (CBBS), 75
Crop prices, 44, 68
Crosstalk communications software, 49
Crushed stone, 85-86
Cuba, 64

Cuban Americans, 232
currency conversion rates, 71, 73
Customs Electronic Bulletin Board (CEBB), 71-72
Customs Service, 71, 202
Cutting boards, 219
Cygnus Corporation, 232
Cystic fibrosis, 215

Dairy products, 68, 218, 219
Dam safety, 139, 144
Database managers, 115
Data Distribution System, 104
Davis-Bacon Act, 258
Deafness, 231
Death statistics, 211, 232, 300
Declaration of Independence, 253
Decompression software
　DOS, Windows, and IBM-compatible, 28, 33, 42, 59, 100, 116, 134, 171, 180, 185, 195, 233, 250, 253, 255, 260, 273
　information and purchase advice, 4
　Macintosh, 100, 171, 180, 186, 233, 250, 255, 260, 273
　other or unspecified systems, 240, 250, 273
Defense Base Closure and Realignment Act of 1990, 52
Defense Commercial Communications Office Communications Center, 76
Defense Communications Agency Acquisition Bulletin Board System (DABBS), 76
Defense conversion, 52-53, 65, 260
Defense Department (DOD)
　Ada programming language, 100-102, 121
　export licenses, 74
　Inspector General office, job listings, 248
　military base closures, 52-53, 204
　Outplacement Referral Service, 21
　private boards, 20
　radioactive sites cleanup, 172
　telecommunications contracts, 76
Defense Mapping Agency, 305
Defense spending, 59
Defense Technology Security Administration, 74
Demographic information, 266
　alcohol consumption, 232
　comprehensive data, 58-60
　Indian tribes, 188
Dental health, 43, 222-224
Dental procedures, and AIDS transmission, 231
Department of. *See* specific department name
Depression, 27
Desalination, 202
Desktop publishing, 240
Determinations Index, 158
Detroit Service Center BBS, 247
Diabetes, 43, 223, 231, 240
Dial-JAN BBS, 238
DIALOG database, 174
Diet and nutrition, 27, 40, 43, 49, 231, 240
Digestive disorders, 231
*Digest of Education Statistics*, 131
Dinosaurs, 113
Diplomatic license plates, 115
*Directory of National Information Sources on Disabilities* (NIDRR), 234
Disabilities, persons with
　access and computer accommodation, 34, 197
　Americans with Disabilities Act text and information, 27, 34, 234, 237-240, 261
　assistive technology and rehabilitation, 233-236, 239-241, 252
　census data, 59
　employment rights, 238, 259, 261
　federal hiring programs, 247, 251, 252, 255
　health and nutrition, 43, 231
　Library of Congress services, 38
　transportation services, 233, 300
　veterans, 251
Disaster assistance. *See* Emergency response
*Disaster Research News*, 139
Diseases, 225-226
Dislocated workers, 260
Divorce rates, 58
DoDIGNET, 248
Dogs, 43, 240
Downsizing and reductions in force, 21, 250, 253, 256
Drawing and painting programs, 113
Drinking water, 43, 167, 180, 184

*Drug and Device Product Approvals List* (FDA), 214
Drugs and drug abuse
   health-related information, 231
   statistics, 123, 132
   substance abuse bibliographies, 43, 231
   substance abuse database, 119
Drugs and medical devices, 212-217
Drunk driving. *See* Alcohol abuse and alcoholism
Durable goods orders, 63
DynaComm, 134

E. coli outbreaks, 219
Earnings statistics, 64, 261
Earth Charter, 180
Earth Observation Center Information System, 267
Earth pictures, 273, 275
Earthquakes, 139, 268-270
Earth science, 266-271, 276-278
Earth Science Data Directory (ESDD), 266
Earth System Data Directory, 267
Eastern Europe, 24, 44, 65
Eating disorders, 43, 231
ECOLINK.ZIP, 170
Ecology, 160
Economic Affairs, Office of the Under Secretary, 59, 62, 64
Economic Analysis, Bureau of, 58, 59, 61-64, 70
Economic Bulletin Board (EBB), 58, 61-65
Economic Conversion Information, Office of, 52-53
Economic data, 58-70
   agriculture, 44
   banking, economic, and financial data, 66-69
   census information, 56, 58-60
   comprehensive information, 61-65, 202
   defense conversion, 52-53
   earth science, 266
   energy, 146
   international, 67
   New England, 70
Economic Development Administration, 52
Economic Research Institute, 44

Economics and Statistics Administration, 61
ED Board, 77
*Educational Programs That Work*, 131
Educational Research Improvement, Office of (OERI), 131-132
Education and training
   Ada and software engineering, 101
   agriculture, 40, 41, 43, 46, 181
   aircraft pilots, 287
   air pollution abatement, 157
   astronomy and space, teacher materials, 273-275
   aviation training, 299
   biomedicine, 223
   comprehensive offerings, 131-132, 240
   consumer information, 27
   correspondence courses, 43
   criminal justice, 123
   dental health, 222-224
   disabled persons, 239
   economics and finance, 69
   emergency management, 139
   environment, 167
   ethics, 192
   federal employment programs for students, 247
   financial assistance. *See* Government grants
   hazardous materials response, 136-137
   hazardous waste treatment, 169
   health and biomedicine, 129-130
   HIV/AIDS, 231
   home schooling, 240
   library management, 33
   minority colleges, 126-128, 189
   National Science Foundation documents, 83
   statistical data, 58, 59, 131-132, 261
   student issue conferences, 121
   teacher education, 231
   water pollution, 182, 183
Education Department, 77, 131, 233, 239, 241
Education Office (NIH), 223
Elderly people, 24, 43, 211, 231
Electrical equipment, 87-88
Electric power, 144, 146, 159
Electronic equipment, 281

Electronic Filing System (EFS) Bulletin Board, 94
Electronic Industries Foundation, 235
Electronic Information Dissemination Services, Office of, 39
Electronic networks, community-based, 167
Electrotechnology, 21
Emancipation Proclamation, 253
Embassies and consulates, U.S., 24, 62
*EmergencyNet NEWS*, 139
Emergency response
　credit union functions, 92
　fire research, 134
　hazardous materials, 135-138, 160, 164, 167
　natural disasters, 139-140
　small business disaster assistance, 57
　U.S. citizens abroad, 23-25
Emission Measurement Technical Information Center, 158
Employee Polygraph Protection Act, 260
Employment and Training Administration, 260
Employment issues
　defense conversion, 52-53, 260
　disabled persons, accommodation, 238
　federal employee benefits, 21, 23, 247, 251
　federal job sharing, 252
　foreign labor trends, 262
　health professions, 211
　labor relations, 256
　labor standards and regulations, 258-264
　occupational safety, 231, 259-261
　unemployment compensation, 202
　work incentive programs, 202
Employment lists
　aviation field, 299
　Census Bureau, 246
　criminal justice, 122, 123
　Defense Dept. Inspector General's office, 248
　Federal Aviation Administration, 291
　federal jobs, 20-22, 34, 55, 115, 179, 247, 249-257, 259, 260, 263
　Federal Highway Administration, 300
　Interior Dept., 244
　libraries, 33

Library of Congress, 38
　military assignments, 245
　National Institutes of Health, 130
　National Oceanic and Atmospheric Administration, 276
　National Science Foundation, 82
　overseas jobs, 260, 291
　science and technology careers, 37, 46
　Small Business Administration, 55
Employment Standards Administration, 260
Employment statistics
　census and economic data, 58, 59, 63, 64, 67, 261
　defense conversion, 52
　foreign countries, 262
　health professions, 211
　historical data, 67
　New England, 70
　unemployment, 63, 66-68, 260, 261
Encryption, 106
Endangered species, 167
Endangered Species Act, 52
Energy
　comprehensive statistics, 64, 146
　federal buildings, 203
　federal laboratories, 202
　fossil fuels, 147-148
　nuclear. *See* Nuclear power
　oil and gas exploration, 66, 149-150
　prices, 260
　public utilities regulation, 144-145
Energy Department, 61
　education links, 126, 127
　energy information, 146, 147
　hazardous incident response, 137
　minority opportunities, 189
　radioactivity cleanup, 172, 173
Energy Information Administration, 64, 146
Energy Information Administration Electronic Publishing System (EPUB), 146
English language use, 59
Entomology, 46
*Entomophagus, The* (Mexico), 46
EnviroNET, 272
Environment
　air pollution, 43, 60, 156-159
　bibliographic databases, 160-161, 165

INDEX　　　321

bulletin board lists, 21, 42, 169, 171, 180
civil enforcement, 164
consumer information, 27
earth science, 266-271, 276-278
Gulf of Mexico, 154-155
hazardous materials. See Hazardous materials and waste
microbial products, 48, 166
models, 157-158, 171, 176-178
nuclear power plants impact, 142
pesticides, 162-163
publications catalog, 20
Region 10 information, 167
water. See water entries
weather. See Weather and climate
Environmental Health Center, 135
Environmental Information Resources Bulletins, 168
*Environmental Law Deskbook*, 121
Environmental Monitoring and Assessment Program, 166
Environmental Policy and Compliance, Office of, 138
Environmental Protection Agency (EPA), 137, 188. See also Environment
Environmental Research Foundation, 164
Environment and Energy, Office of, 286
Equal Employment Opportunity Commission (EEOC), 234, 238
Ergonomic stress, 261
ERIC Clearinghouse on Reading and Communication Skills, 131
ERIC Digests, 131
EROS Data Center, 267
Ethical and moral issues
　animal welfare, 43
　government misconduct and waste, 192-194, 260
　scientific integrity, 231
Ethics Bulletin Board System, 192
Ethnic groups. See Minority groups; specific minorities
Europe, 24, 201
European Union, 91
Euthanasia, 43
*Evidentiary Foundations*, 121
*Examiner's Update Newsletter*, 295
Exchange rates, 59, 63, 67, 71, 72
EXE extension, 4

Eximbank Bulletin Board, 73
Expert systems, 33, 34, 166, 171
Export Administration, Bureau of, 61
Export-Import Bank of the United States, 73
Export License Information Status Advisor (ELISA), 74
Exports. See Trade and marketing
*ExSel Newsletter*, 46

*FAA Aviation News*, 291, 293, 295, 298
FAA Headquarters BBS, 291
FAA New England, 294
FAA Pilot Examiner Section BBS, 295
FAA Safety Data Exchange, 296
Fabrics and textiles, 60, 64, 71
Fair Credit Reporting Act, 27
Family and Medical Leave Act of 1993, 239, 259, 261, 264
Family issues. See Children and families
Farming. See Agriculture
Fats and oils, 60, 214
*FBI Law Enforcement Bulletin*, 122
*FCC Daily Digest*, 89
FCC Public Access Link (PAL), 87-88
FCC-State Link, 89
*FDA Consumer*, 215
FDA Electronic Bulletin Board, 214-217
*FDA Enforcement Report*, 214, 218
FDA Prime Connection, 218-220
*FDA Today*, 215
Federal Aid Policy Guide, 300
Federal Aviation Administration (FAA), 126, 127. See also Aviation and airports
Federal budget
　congressional jurisdiction, 202
　deficit reduction, 193
　documents, 21, 293
Federal Bulletin Board, 29
Federal bulletin boards, 3
　access guidelines, 5-9, 13-15
　access hardware and software, 3-4
　help and troubleshooting, 9-12
　Internet access, 14
Federal Communications Act, 32
Federal Communications Commission (FCC), 87-89
Federal courts, 3
Federal debt, 67

Federal Deficit Reduction BBS, 193
Federal Emergency Management Agency (FEMA), 136-137, 139-140
Federal Employees Pay Comparability Act of 1990, 263, 264
Federal employment. *See* employment entries
Federal Energy Regulatory Commission, 144-145
Federal government. *See* government entries
Federal Highway Administration (FHWA), 300-302
Federal Highway Administration Electronic Bulletin Board System (FEBBS), 300-302
Federal Information Center, 27
Federal Information Exchange, 126
Federal Job Information Centers, 247, 250, 251
Federal Jobline, 251-252
Federal Job Opportunity Board, 249-250
*Federal Offshore Statistics,* 149
Federal Oil and Gas Royalty Management Act, 149
Federal Property Resource Service, 204
Federal Real Estate Sales Bulletin Board, 204
*Federal Register,* 30, 71, 81, 158, 170, 174, 175, 192, 215, 230
Federal Register, Office of, 30
Federal Register Electronic News Delivery (FREND), 30
Federal Reserve Bank of Boston, 70
Federal Reserve Bank of Dallas, 66
Federal Reserve Bank of Minneapolis, 68
Federal Reserve Bank of St. Louis, 67
Federal Reserve Board, 61, 63
Federal Reserve Economic Data (F.R.E.D.), 67
Federal Reserve System, 68-69
Federal Rules of Civil Procedure, 112
Federal Rules of Evidence, 112
Federal Transit Administration, 301
FED FLASH!, 66
*FedGazette,* 69
FEDIX, 126-128
FEDLINK, 33-35
*FEDLINK TechNotes,* 33, 34

FedWorld, 14, 20-22, 29, 79, 222, 268
Feeds, 44, 214
Feldspar, 86
Fellowships. *See* Government grants
Fertility and Maternal Health Drugs Advisory Committee, 216
Fertilizers, 60
Fetal alcohol syndrome, 232
Fever blisters, 223
FidoNet, 95, 123, 240
File archive software, 280
File transfer protocols, 6-7, 10, 14, 288
File translation software, 4
Financial management, 113, 205
Financial Management Service, 205
Financing information
  environmental programs, 160
  *See also* Government grants
Firearms, 202
FIREDOC, 134
Firefighting, 137, 139
Fire research and safety, 134, 137, 139, 202, 289
Fire Research Information Service, 134
Fiscal policy, 63
Fish and seafood
  Alaskan processors, 167
  catfish farming, 40, 43
  consumption of contaminated fish, 181
  industry statistics, 91
  National Marine Fisheries Service—NW Region
  sanitation, 218, 219
Fish and Wildlife Service, 244
Five-Year Information and Resources Management program plan, 84
Fleet Imaging BBS, 280
Fleet Imaging Center, 280
Flight Standards BBS, 297-298
Floods, 139, 271
Florida, 139, 154, 297
Flour milling, 60
Flowers, 41, 43
FMS Inside Line, 205-206
"Fog indexes," 180
Food
  additives, 26, 27, 225
  allergies, 43, 227
  biotechnology, 40, 41, 43, 48, 166

diet, disease, and nutrition concerns, 27, 40, 43, 49, 231, 240
FDA regulation, 214-217
irradiation, 40, 43
marketing and trade information, 42
nutritional content, 227-228
patent licensing, 21
prices, 260
restaurant oil and grease, 184
safety, 218-220, 231
Food and Drug Administration (FDA), 20, 48, 212-220, 230
*Foodborne Pathogenic Microorganisms and Natural Toxins*, 218
Food crops. *See* Agriculture
Food pyramid, 215, 227
Food stamps, 240
Footwear, 60
Forecast of Nationwide Contracting Opportunities, 84
Foreign Affairs Committee, House, 201
Foreign Agricultural Service, 61
Foreign Assets Control, Office of, 64
Foreign investment, in energy sector, 146
Foreign trade. *See* Trade and marketing
Foreign travel, 23-25, 71-73
Forestry, 43, 167
Forms
   forms generator software, 113
   personnel office forms, 255
   tax forms and instructions, 95, 98
Fossil Energy Communications, Office of, 147
Fossil Energy Telenews, 147-148
Fossil fuels, 147-148. *See also* Oil and gas sector
Foster care, 198
Fractal drawing program, 113
France, 67, 262
Franchise industry, 202
Fraud and waste, 192-194, 260
Freedom of Information Act, 26, 32, 36, 298
Freeware. *See* Shareware and freeware
Fuel Economy Guide, 156, 158
Fuel prices, 146
Fuel tax rates, 300
Funerals, 27

Galileo spacecraft mission, 273
Gallium, 85, 86
Games, 28, 90, 112, 113, 132, 140
GAO Office of Policy's BBS, 196
GAO Watchdog, 194
Gardening, 41
Gas mileage guide, 27
Gasoline prices, 146
Gay, Lesbian, or Bisexual Employees Organization (GLOBE), 291
General Accounting Office (GAO), 34, 40, 42, 194, 196, 201
General Services Administration (GSA), 26, 81, 197, 203, 204, 207
Genetic engineering/Biotechnology, 40, 41, 43, 48, 49, 166, 219
Genetics, and alcoholism, 232
Geography, 132, 266
Geological Survey, 180, 244, 266-270
Geological Survey Bulletin Board System, 271
Geological Survey National Center, 271
Geology, 266, 271
Geomagnetic field values, 269
Geriatrics education, 211
Germanium, 85
Germany, 67, 262
GIF viewers, 273
Glass industry, 60
Global change, 83, 266, 267, 276
Global Land Information System (GLIS), 267
Global Positioning System, 305, 306
Global Seismology and Geomagnetism Online Information System, 268-269
Global warming, 113, 181
Goddard Space Flight Center, 272, 278
Gold, 86
*Goods and Services Manual*, 54
Governmental Affairs Committee, Senate, 29
Government contracts, 256
   aircraft services, 299
   barred companies, 81
   construction criteria, 75
   dental research, 222, 223
   education, 77, 126-128
   energy, 147
   hazardous waste cleanup, 170

labor standards, 258
next generation computer standards, 105
small businesses, 57, 78, 202
telecommunications, 76, 81
Veterans Affairs Dept., 84
Government employment. *See* employment entries
Government Ethics, Office of, 192
Government grants
　AIDS research, 230
　Americans with Disabilities Act technical assistance, 237
　biomedical research, 79-80
　dental research, 222, 223
　education, 77, 126, 127
　scientific research, 82-83
　wastewater management, 186
Government operations, 191-207
　aircraft services leasing, 299
　citizen suggestions, 56
　ethics, fraud, and waste, 192-194, 260
　management, 195-197
　policies and regulations, 198-199
　press information, 200-202
　property and assets, 27, 52, 126, 203-207
Government Operations Committee, House, 193
Government Printing Office, 29, 30
Government publications, 23-30
"Governor's Guide to Economic Conversion," 53
Gradebook and attendance programs, 132
Graduate Record Examination scores, 132
Grants. *See* Government grants
Graphics programs, 4, 112, 115, 138
Graphics standards, 103
Grateful Med BBS, 221
Gravel and sand, 86
Great Lakes, 156
Great Lakes Human Health Effects Research and Information Exchange Network, 181
Greenhouse gases, 146
Greenhouses, 41
Grief, 231
Grocery shopping programs, 140
Gross national product (GNP), 63, 67, 68
Gross state products, 64, 70

Groundwater, 179, 180, 184
GSA Electronic Management Information (GEMI) BBS, 197
Gulfline BBS, 154-155
Gulf of Mexico Program Office, 154
Gypsum, 86

Habitat degradation, 154
HACCP (Hazard Analysis Critical Control Point) methodology, 219
Hackers, 6, 107
Hague Convention on the Civil Aspects of International Child Abduction, 24
Hair dye, 215
Hairspray, 214
Haiti, 64, 201
Handwriting analysis, 122
Hard disks, 121
Hawaii, 207, 251
Hay Locator Service, 45
Hazardous Materials and Information Exchange (HMIX), 136-137
Hazardous materials and waste, 122
　air transport, 286, 292
　bibliographic database, 160
　emergency response, 135-139, 164, 167
　instructional materials, 137
　livestock waste, 43
　management, 164, 165
　municipal solid waste, 166, 169
　radioactive waste cleanup, 172-175
　sites lists, 59, 167, 170
　treatment, 168-171
Hazardous Materials Initiatives and Training, Office of, 136
Headaches, 231
Head injuries, 231
Head Start, 198
Health and Human Services Department, 229
Health and safety
　consumer information, 27
　disease information, 225-226
　education links, 129-130
　health professions, 211
　health-related statistics, 211
　occupational safety, 231, 260, 261
　public health issues, 154, 211
　rural issues, 41, 43, 167

U.S. citizens abroad, 23-25
*See also* specific diseases and topics
Health care
  census data, 59
  nuclear materials use, 142
  policy issues, 231
  reform, 21, 22, 27, 202
  small businesses, 202
Health Effects Research Laboratory, 158
Health Professions (BHPr), Bureau of, BBS, 211
Hearing aids, 214
Hearing impairments, 231, 239
Heart valves, 212
Herbs, 43
Helicopters, 286, 298
Help function, troubleshooting, and advice, 9-15. *See also* specific bulletin boards
Higher Education Opportunities for Minorities and Women (HERO), 127
Highways, 138, 139, 300-302
Hispanics, 126-128, 231
Historic documents, 253
History programs, 132
*Hitchhiker's Guide to the Internet, The,* 107, 251
HIV/AIDS. *See* Acquired immune deficiency syndrome
Hodgkin's disease, 225
Home applications programs, 113
Homeless persons, 200, 231
Home offices, 240
Home schooling, 240
Hospices, 231
Household appliances, 60
House of Representatives committees, 193, 201-202
Housing
  census and economic data, 59, 63, 68
  consumer information, 26, 27
  federal property sales, 204
  New England, 70
Housing and Urban Development Department (HUD), 127, 200
Housing Office Management System (HOMES), 104
*How to Write a Business Plan* (SBA), 188
HSETC BBS, 111
Hubble Space Telescope, 20, 21, 273, 275

HUD News and Events Bulletin Board, 200
Human Nutrition Information Service, 227
Hurricane Andrew, 139
Hurricane Emily, 139
Hurricanes, 21, 139
Hydroelectric dams, 144
Hydrogeologic unit conversion programs, 165, 171
Hydrology, 266
Hypertext and hypermedia software, 33

ICAP BBS, 299
Idaho, 167, 207, 251
IIT Research Institute, 100
Illinois, 67
IMA (Information Mission Area) BBS, 36
Immigration, 58
Imports. *See* Trade and marketing
Impotence, 231
*IMPROVE* newsletter, 156
Incinerators, 164
Income statistics, 58, 59, 63, 64, 68, 70, 97, 211
Independent living centers, 252
Indiana, 67
Indian Affairs, Bureau of, 188, 244
Indian Dams Safety Act, 188
INDIANet, 188
Indian Health Service, 188
Indians. *See* Native Americans
Indium, 86
Individuals with Disabilities Education Act, 239
Industrial hygiene, 137
Industrial plants, 204
Industry SIG, 58
Infectious diseases, 231
INFOLINK, 173-174
Information and Public Affairs, Office of, 259
Information Infrastructure Task Force Bulletin Board, 31
Information, Justice, Transportation, and Agriculture Subcommittee, House, 193
Information management, 36
Information Mission Area (IMA) BBS, 36
Information policy, 21, 31-32
Information Reporting Program (IRP), 96

Information Resources Management, Office of, 192
Information Resources Management (IRM) plan, 197
Information Resources Management Services, 81
Information returns, 96
Information Systems Support BBS, 95
Inorganic chemicals, 60
Inspector General, Office of (DOD), 248
Instruments, patent licensing, 21
Integrated Facilities System Mini-micro (IFS-M), 104
Integrated pest management, 46
Integrated Services Digital Network (ISDN), 109
Intellectual property rights, 21, 38, 49, 54, 56, 72
Interagency Committee for Aviation Policy, 299
Interagency Council on the Homeless, 200
Interest rates, 63, 67
Interior Department, 85, 138, 149, 244, 266
Interior Dept., Office of the Secretary, 244
Intermodal Surface Transportation Efficiency Act, 138, 300
Internal Revenue Service, 56, 94-98
*International Bioherbicide Group News*, 46
International Civil Aviation Organization, 291
International Marketing Insight (IMI) reports, 64
International Trade Administration, 61
International Trade Commission (ITC), 90
Internet
   access and resources, 14, 20, 33, 40, 107, 167, 171, 234, 240, 251, 256
   Ada programming language, 100
   agriculture, 42
   criminal justice, 122-124
   dental health and research, 222
   disability information, 233, 240
   earth science, 268, 278
   economic data, 61
   electronic mail address registry, 35
   environmental information, 42, 177, 276
   federal job information, 250, 251
   glossary, 35
   health education, 129

Library of Congress resources, 37
   National Institutes of Health biomedical research grants, 79, 80
   National Science Foundation research grants, 82, 83
   small business, 56, 57
   Supreme Court opinions, 29
*Internet-Accessible Library Catalogs and Databases* (St. George), 33
Internships, 130
Interstate migration, 58
Invertebrate pathology, 46
Iran, 64
Iran-contra report, 29
Iraq, 64
Iron and steel, 86
IRP-BBS, 96
IRS Statistics of Income Division Bulletin Board, 97
ITC Chemicals BBS, 90

JAGNET Information Center, 112
Japanese auto imports, 202
Jet Propulsion Laboratory, 273
Job issues. *See* employment entries
Job Training Partnership Act, 252
Joint Task Force on Postal Rulemaking, 199
Joint venture opportunities, 20
JPL Info, 273
Judge Advocate General's Information Network (JAGNET), 112
Jupiter moons, 273
Justice. *See* Law and justice
Justice Assistance, Bureau of, 118, 119
Justice Department, 118, 122, 234, 237
Justice Statistics, Bureau of, 118, 119, 123
Juvenile Justice and Delinquency Prevention, Office of, 118, 119
Juvenile Justice Clearinghouse, 119

Kentucky, 67
KIMBERELY, 68-69

Labor Department, 119, 258-262
Labor issues. *See* employment entries
Labor-Management Relations and Cooperative Programs, Bureau of, 260
Labor News, 259

Labor Statistics, Bureau of, 59, 61-64, 259, 260
*Ladybeetle Flyer, The,* 46
Land Management, Bureau of, 244
Land resources, 267
Lakes and streams. *See* water entries
Lake trout, 181
Landfills, 157-158, 164
Land grant colleges, 40
Land sales, 204
Laser printers, 121
Law and justice
　general interest, 112
　legal spelling dictionary, 122
　military justice, 112, 121
　Supreme Court opinions, 29, 122
Law enforcement. *See* Crime and security
Lawn care, 180
Law of Naval Operations, Annotated Supplement to, 112
Laws and regulations
　FREND access, 30
　silly regulations conference, 22
　*See also* specific statutes, agencies, and topics
Lead, 86
Lead poisoning, 180, 215
Leave policy, 256
Leasing, 203
Leslie Davies-Hilliard, 162
Libraries
　card catalog software, 132
　Colorado online catalogs, 113
　dental, 222-224
　digital, 83
　Environmental Protection Agency, 156, 157, 160-161, 164, 179
　library management, 33-36
　patent and trademark depositories, 54
　public library statistics, 131
　rural and small, 43
Library of Congress, 33, 37-38
*Library of Congress Cataloging Newsletter,* 34
Library of Congress News Service, 37-38
Libya, 64
License plates, 115
Licensing
　export licenses, 74

　of inventions, 21, 49
Life science, 278
Lime, 86
Liquefied Gaseous Fuels Spill Test Facility, 147
Livestock, 43, 44, 68
Local Emergency Planning Committee contacts, 137
"Log" feature, 5
Logging off, 7, 13-14
Logging on, 9, 14
Lotus 1-2-3 software, 33, 44, 68, 70, 90, 95, 271
Louisiana, 66, 154
Low Income Heating Energy Assistance Program, 198
Lung diseases, 231

McDonald's Co., 258
Macintosh computers, 121
McKinney Act, 52
McNamara-O'Hara Service Contract Act, 258
Magellan spacecraft mission, 273
Magna Carta, 253
Magnesium, 86
Magnetic Media Bulletin Board System, 98
Mailinfo, 28
Mail readers, offline, 240, 280
Mail service, 27, 28, 113, 199
Maine, 70
Malmstrom Air Force Base, 116
Management and Budget, Office of (OMB), 21, 34, 62
Management Development Centers, 249, 253
Manganese, 86
*Manual of Patent Examining Procedure,* 54
Marine Data Computer Bulletin Board, 303
Maritime Administration, 304
Maritime issues, 303-307
Marketing. *See* Trade and marketing
MARlinspike BBS, 304
Marriage, 23, 58
Mars, 273
Marshall Space Flight Center, 274
Mars Observer mission, 273
MASC Library RBBS-PC, 7-8, 113-114

Massachusetts, 70
Maternal mortality rates, 211
Math programs and games, 115, 132
Meal planning, 27, 140
Meat industry, 43
Mechanical devices and equipment, 21-22
Medicaid, 240
*Medical Bulletin*, 215
*Medical Device Bulletin*, 215
Medical devices, 212-216
Medical Devices Advisory Committee, 216
Medical Imaging Drugs Advisory Committee, 216
Medical information and services
  consumer information, 27
  emergency response, 137, 139
  medical waste, 37
  medicinal plants, 43
  medicines database, 221
  patent licensing, 21
  U.S. citizens overseas, 24
Medicare, 202
MEDLARS Management, 221
Mental health, 231
Mental illness, 231
Menu and editor programs, 121
Mercury contamination of fish, 181
Metallurgy, 22
Methanol, 159
MetroLink, 121
Mexican Americans, 232
Mexico, 24, 42, 72, 136, 262
Michigan, 68
Microcircuit Obsolescence Management (MOM) PC Board, 281
Middle East, 24
Midwest U.S., 68-69, 139
Migrant and Seasonal Agricultural Worker Protection Act, 260
Mike Monroney Aeronautical Center, 297
Military
  base closures, 52-53, 204
  justice and other topics, 121
  Navy personnel assignments, 245
Military Echo Conference Network (MILECHO), 121
Milk safety, 218, 219
Minerals Management Service, 149, 150, 244

Mines, Bureau of, 85, 244
  Bulletin Board Network (BOM-BBN), 85
Mine Safety and Health Act, 261
Mine Safety and Health Administration, 261
Mines and minerals, 85-86, 138, 259, 261
Minimum wage, 260
Minnesota, 68
*Minority Businesses* (SBA), 188
Minority College and University Capability Information (MOLIS), 126-128
Minority Economic Impact, Office of, 189
Minority groups
  alcohol consumption patterns, 232
  dental health, 223
  education, 126-128, 132
  Energy Dept. opportunities, 189
  health education professionals, 211
  HIV/AIDS and health issues, 231
  human resource development, 83
  small business, 57, 188
  *See also* specific minorities
Minority Impact BBS, 189
Mississippi, 67, 154
Missouri, 67
Mobile Sources, Office of, 158
Modeling systems
  air carriers economic costing, 286
  earth environment, 157-158, 171, 176-178, 183
  helicopter noise, 286
  solar-terrestrial models, 278
  space environment, 272
Modems, 3-4, 95, 139, 195, 220, 240
MOLIS, 126-128
Molybdenum, 86
Monetary policy, 63
Money facts, 69
Money market rates, 68
Money supply, 68
Monosodium glutamate, 219
Montana, 68, 220
Montgomery Blair High School Magnet Junior/Senior Science Project, 130
*Monthly Labor Review*, 259
*Morbidity and Mortality Weekly Report*, 230
Mortality statistics, 211, 230, 232, 300
Mortgage data, 27, 68, 200

INDEX   329

Most-favored-nation status, 71
Motor Carrier Safety Program, 137
Motor vehicles
    acidic pollution effects on car finishes, 156
    air pollution, 158-159
    assistive devices, 233
    drunk driving, 123, 232
    fatality statistics, 59, 300
    fuel economy guide, 156, 158
    gas mileage guide, 27
    gasoline prices, 146
    highways, 138, 300-302
    Japanese imports, 202
    oil recycling, 180
Multiple Award Schedule Program, 81
Municipal solid waste, 166, 169
Mushroom toxins, 218

NAFTA, 21, 41, 64, 71, 72, 136, 201, 202
NASA SBIR/STTR Bulletin Board, 78
NASA Spacelink, 274-275
National Aeronautics and Space Administration (NASA), 78, 126, 127, 202, 273-275
National Agricultural Library, 40, 181
National Agricultural Statistics Service, 44
National AIDS Clearinghouse, 231
National AIDS Hotline, 231
National AIDS Program Office, 229
National Air Toxics Information Clearinghouse, 158
National Archives and Records Administration, 30
National Asbestos Registry System, 158
National Biological Control Institute, 46
National Biological Impact Assessment Program (NBIAP), 48
National Biological Survey, 244
National Cancer Institute, 226
National Center for Environmental Publications and Information, 161
National Center for Human Genome Research, 226
National Commission on AIDS, 229, 231
National competitiveness, 202
National Computer Systems Laboratory, 108, 109
National Consortium for Justice Information and Statistics, 122

National Credit Union Administration, 92
National Criminal Justice Reference Service (NCJRS), 118
National Earthquake Information Center, 268, 270
National Ecology Research Center (NERC) Bulletin Board System, 178
National Energy Information Center, 146
National Environmental Data Referral Service, 276
National Environmental Policy Act, 52
National Export Strategy report, 29
National Eye Institute, 226
National Health Security Act, 22, 29, 57, 239
National Heart, Lung, and Blood Institute, 226
National Historic Preservation Act, 52
National Information Infrastructure (NII), 21, 31, 32, 56
National Institute of Allergy and Infectious Diseases, 226
National Institute of Arthritis and Musculoskeletal and Skin Diseases, 226
National Institute of Child Health and Human Development, 226
National Institute of Dental Research, 222-224, 226
National Institute of Diabetes and Digestive and Kidney Diseases, 226
National Institute of Environmental Health Sciences, 226
National Institute of General Medical Sciences, 226
National Institute of Justice, 118, 119, 122
National Institute of Mental Health, 226
National Institute of Neurological Disorders and Stroke, 226
National Institute of Nursing Research, 226
National Institute of Standards and Technology (NIST), 13, 106, 108, 109, 134, 283
National Institute on Aging, 226
National Institute on Alcohol Abuse and Alcoholism, 226, 232
National Institute on Deafness and Other Communications disorders, 226
National Institute on Disability and Rehabilitation Research, 233
National Institute on Drug Abuse, 226

National Institutes of Health (NIH), 79, 129-130, 221, 222, 225, 226
National Library Network Program, 160
National Library of Medicine, 221, 226, 230
National Marine Fisheries Service—NW Region, 91
National Minority Energy Information Clearinghouse, 189
National Oceanic and Atmospheric Administration (NOAA), 91, 154, 155, 267, 276-277, 279, 303
National Oceanographic Data Center, 277
National Ocean Service, 303
National parks, 27, 138
National Park Service, 244
National Performance Review, 21, 27, 29, 34, 56, 167, 195, 197, 256
National Rehabilitation Information Center (NARIC), 233-236
National Safety Council, 135
National Science Board, 82
National Science Foundation (NSF), 82, 127, 202
*National Science Foundation Bulletin,* 82
National Small Flows Clearinghouse, 186
National Space Science Data Center, 278
National Task Force on Hazardous Materials Emergency Preparedness, 137
National Technical Information Service (NTIS), 20-22, 160, 165, 174, 221, 227
National Telecommunications and Information Administration (NTIA), 31, 32
National Trade Data Bank, 70
National Vehicle and Fuels Emissions Laboratory, 158
National Weather Service, 202
Native Americans, 188, 240, 260
*Natural Enemy News,* 46
Natural gas. *See* Oil and gas sector
Natural resources. *See* Environment
Nautical charts, 276
Naval Air Station Oceana, 280
Naval Air Warfare Center, 281
Naval Health Science Education and Training Command, 111
Naval Justice School, 121
Naval Observatory, 282
Naval Personnel Command, Bureau of, 245

Naval Petroleum and Oil Shale Reserves, 147
Naval Research, Office of, 126, 127
Navigation and shipping, 303-307
Navigation Information Network (NAVINFONE), 305
NAVSTAR Global Positioning System, 305, 306
Navy (U.S.), 110, 112, 105, 110, 112, 245, 280
NBCI BBS, 46
NCUA BBS, 92
Nematology, 46
*Networks and Community* newsletter, 167
Nevada, 75, 251, 252
New England, 294
New England Electronic Economic Data Center, 70
New Hampshire, 70
New Jersey Department of Health, 164
Newly independent states and Russia, 65
New Mexico, 66
*Newsletter on Biological Control in Greenhouses,* 46
New Source Review, 158
*New Source Review Prevention of Deterioration and Nonattainment Area Guidance Notebook,* 158
Next Generation Computer Resources (NGCR) standards, 105
NGCR BBS, 105
Nicaragua, 201
Nickel, 86
NIDR Online, 222-224
NIH EDNET, 129, 223
NIH Grant Line, 79-80
*NIH Guide for Grants and Contracts,* 80
NIH Information Center, 225-226
*NIJ Journal,* 119
1987 Census of Agriculture, 59
1990 Census SIG, 58
1992 Economic Census SIG, 58
NIST Computer Security BBS, 13, 106
NIST/NCSL Data Management Information Exchange (DMIE), 108
NIU-Forum Bulletin Board, 109
NJS BBS, 121
*NJS Civil Law Study Guide,* 121
*NJS Criminal Law Study Guide,* 121

*NJS Evidence Study Guide,* 121
*NJS Military Justice Study Guide,* 121
*NJS Procedure Study Guide,* 121
NOAA Environmental Information Service, 276-277
NODIS, 278
Noise control, 286
Noise exposure, 261
Nonpoint Source Program Electronic Bulletin Board, 10, 179-183
North Africa, 24
North American Free Trade Agreement (NAFTA), 21, 41, 64, 71, 72, 136, 201, 202
North Dakota, 68
North Florida Flight Standards District Office, 297
North Korea, 64
Northwest U.S., 91, 167
*Notice to Mariners,* 305
*NPS News-Notes Newsletter,* 183
*NSF Guide to Programs,* 82
NTIA Bulletin Board, 32
Nuclear power
  bibliographic database, 142-143
  decommissioning of power plants, 175
  emergency response, 139
  energy statistics, 146
  operation of power plants, 151
  patent licensing, 22
  radioactive waste cleanup, 172-174
Nuclear Reactor Regulation, Office of, 151
Nuclear Regulatory Commission (NRC), 142-143, 151, 172, 175
Nuclear weapons, 201, 202
NUDOCS records system, 142
NUnet, 80
Nursing homes, 26, 27
Nutrient Data Bank Bulletin Board, 227-228
Nutrition, 49, 231, 240
  diet and disease concerns, 27, 40, 43
  nutritional content of food, 227-228
*NYSERNet Net User's Guide to Useful and Unique Resources on the Internet,* 234

OAQPS Technology Transfer Network, 156
OASH BBS, 229-231
OCA BBS Document Exchange, 199

Occupational safety and health, 231, 259-261
Occupational Safety and Health Administration (OSHA), 137, 259, 261
Ocean science, 276-277
*OCLC Bits and Pieces,* 34
*OCLC Reference News,* 34
*OCRWM Bulletin,* 174
OEPC BBS, 138
*OERI Bulletin,* 132
OERI Bulletin Board System, 131-132
*OERR Infoline Newsletter,* 171
Office buildings, 204
Office equipment, 60
Office of. *See* specific office name
*Official Gazette of the United States Patent and Trademark Office,* 54
Oil and gas sector
  federal regulation, 144
  offshore exploration, 149-150
  oil spills management, 138, 170
  research and development, 147-148
  statistics, 64, 66, 146
  strategic reserves, 147
Oklahoma, 139
On-Line Earthnet Data Availability, 267
Online Library System (OLS), 160-161, 165
On-Line Schedules System (OSS), 81
Ontario, 71
Open Forum, 58
Ophthalmic Devices Panel, 216
OPM FedJobs Philly BBS, 253-254
OPM Mainstreet, 255
Optics and lasers, 22
Oregon, 91, 167, 207, 251
Organic farming, 41, 46
*ORI Newsletter,* 231
OS/2, 95
Outer continental shelf, 149
Outer Continental Shelf Lands Act, 149
Overseas Citizens Services, 23-25
Overseas Security Advisory Council Electronic Bulletin Board, 24, 25
Overtime pay, 260
Ozone depletion, 113, 158

Painting and drawing programs, 113
Paint stripping, 27
Paralysis, 231

Pascal programming, 121
Passports, 23
Passwords, 6, 7, 14
Patent and Trademark Office, 54, 56
Patents and trademarks, 21, 54, 56
Patient examination gloves, 212
PayPerNet, 263-264
Payroll programs, 113
PC-SIG CD-ROM, 110
*PC-SIG Encyclopedia of Shareware: A Comprehensive Guide to Low Cost Software for IBM and Compatibles,* 113
Penile implants, 215
Pension and Welfare Benefits Administration, 260, 261
Pensions and retirement
  civil service, 253, 256
  congressional jurisdiction, 202
  consumer information, 27, 261
  pension funds regulation, 92
  retirement planning program, 113
Pentagon PC User Group—Research, Development, and Acquisition Management Information System (PPCUG-RDAMIS), 115
Periodic table of elements, 132, 166
Personal information managers, 113, 140
Personnel Management, Office of (OPM)
  job lists, 21, 22, 34, 247, 249-257
  labor regulations, 263-264
Pest control
  biological controls, 46-47, 49
Pesticide Information Network (PIN), 162-163
Pesticides
  chemical index, 162
  in drinking water, 180
  in food, 215
  information and monitoring projects, 162-163, 167, 181, 231
  treatability database, 171
*Pesticides Coordinator Report,* 46
Petroleum. *See* Oil and gas sector
Phosphate rock, 86
Photograph preservation, 34
Photography, 121, 280
Physical fitness, 231
*Pilot Examiners Handbook,* 295
Pilot Land Data System, 267

Pirates, 305
PKUNZIP software, 4, 113, 134, 195
PKZIP software, 4, 28, 100
Planetarium simulators, 132, 273
Planetary science, 273, 275, 278
Planning Abstract Listing Service (PALS), 123
Planning, Quality Assurance, Systems Security (PASS) programs, 197
Plant Genome Research Program, 42
*Plant Protection News,* 46
Plants, 40, 42, 43, 46
Plastic cutting boards, 219
Platinum, 86
Police equipment, 119
Policy Operations and Staffing Headquarters (POSH), 249
Pollution. *See* Environment
Polly, Jean Armour, 33
Polypropylene, 90
Population data, 58-60, 64, 67, 205
Postal Rate Commission, 199
Postal Service, 27, 28, 113
Poultry, 44, 68
Poverty statistics, 58, 59, 211
PPCUG-RDAMIS, 115
PRC Inc. 110
Pregnancy, 43, 231
Preservation, 34
President, 21, 201
Presidential Management Intern program, 247
Presidential nominations, 30, 201
President's Committee on Employment of People with Disabilities, 238
President's Council on Management Improvement, 195
Press releases. *See* specific agencies, bulletin boards, and topics
Prices
  commodities, 64
  consumer, 68
  consumer price index, 63, 67, 260, 261
  crops, 44, 68
  energy, 260
  export-import price index, 63
  food, 260
  fuel, 146
  livestock, 68

producer, 68
producer price index, 63, 261
Printer utilities, 115
PRIVACY Forum Digest, 107
Privacy issues, 36, 107
ProComm, 4, 134, 136
ProComm Plus, 4, 250
Procurement. *See* Government contracts
Producer price index, 63, 261
Producer prices, 68
*Program Information Manual* (FDA), 218
Project Enable, 238, 239
Project management programs, 113, 115
PR On-Line, 201-202
PTO Bulletin Board System, 54
Public affairs forum, 256
Public Affairs Office, 37
Public domain programs. *See* Shareware and freeware
Public health, 154, 211
Public Health Service, 79-80, 214, 230, 231
Public Law numbers, 30
Public utility companies, 144-145
Puerto Ricans, 232
Purdue University, 45

*Qualification Standards Handbook for General Schedule Positions,* 254
Quality Education for Minorities Network, 127
Quality management, 256
Quattro, 70
Quick Facts BBS, 232
QuickLink, 240

*Rachel's Hazardous Waste News,* 164
Radiation and Indoor Air, Office of, 159
Radiation experiments, 175
Radiation Health and Safety Act, 211
Radioactive waste, 172-175
Radio communications
  emergency response, 139
  FCC regulation, 87-88
  military affiliate system, 36
Radiological health, 212, 215, 216
*Radiological Health Bulletin,* 215
*Raising Money for Small Businesses* (SBA), 188
Randolph-Sheppard Act, 238-241

Real estate
  federal buildings management, 203
  federal property and equipment sales, 27, 52, 126, 204, 207
  Federal Property Resource Service, 204
  Federal Real Estate Sales Bulletin Board, 204
  industry statistics, 64
Reasonably Achievable Control Technology (RACT)/Best Available Control Technology (BACT)/Lowest Achievable Emission Rate (LAER) Clearinghouse, 157
Reclamation, Bureau of, 244
Records and archives management, 34, 36, 121
Recycling, 195
Reductions in force (RIFs) and downsizing, 21, 250, 253, 256
Registration process, 6-7
Regulations and Government Subcommittee, Senate, 29
Regulations and laws
  FREND access, 30
  silly regulations conference, 22
  *See also* specific statutes, agencies, and topics
Rehabilitation. *See* Disabilities, persons with
Rehabilitation Act of 1973, 238-241
Rehabilitation Services Administration, 241
RelayNet International Message Exchange, 139
Remote Access Chemical Hazards Electronic Library (RACHEL), 164
Remote sensing, 267
Renewable energy, 146
Research and Development, Office of (ORD), 165, 177, 182
Research and Development Electronic Bulletin Board, 165
Research grants. *See* Government grants
Research Integrity, Office of, 231
Resource Conservation and Recovery Act, 52
Respiratory protection, 261
Restaurants, 184
Retail Food Protection Program, 218
Retail food safety, 218-220

Retail sales, 66, 68, 70
Retirement. *See* Pensions and retirement
Rhode Island, 70
Rio de Janeiro
　earth summit, 180
　port hazards, 305
Risk assessment, 177
Risk Reduction Engineering Laboratory (RREL) Treatability database, 168, 171
RISKS-Forum Digest, 107
Rivers. *See* water entries
Romanian adoptions, 23-24
RSA BBS, 241
Rural development and health, 40, 41, 43, 44, 167, 231
Rural Health Research Center, 43
Rural Information Center, 43
Russia, 24, 65, 73
Russian wheat aphid, 46, 47

Safety. *See* Crime and security; Health and safety; specific diseases and topics
St. George, Art, 33
Sales Bulletin Board Service, 207
Salmonella, 218
Sand and gravel, 86
Saturn, 273
SAT verbal prep programs, 132
Savings bonds, 27
Savings deposits, 67, 68
Satellite design, 272
Satellite images, 21, 267, 275
SBA Online, 55-57
Scholarships. *See* Government grants
Schools and students. *See* Education and training
Science and Engineering Alliance Inc., 127
Science and technology
　applications software, 113, 115
　career opportunities, 37, 83
　congressional jurisdiction, 201-202
　documents database, 160
　educational opportunities, 126-128
　NSF funding, 82-83
　policy issues, 202
　science fair projects, 37
　scientific integrity, 231
　technology transfer, 40, 49, 78, 86, 184-185, 275
　telephone time services, 282, 283
　*See also* specific sciences and technologies
Science and Technology Information System (STIS), 82-83
Science and Technology Policy, Office of, 48
Science Board, FDA, 216
Science, Space, and Technology Committee, House, 201-202
Scientific Research, Office of, 126, 127
SDC, 168
Seafood and shellfish, 91, 167, 218, 219
Search and rescue, 139
SEARCH-BBS, 3, 29, 122-124
Seasonal farm workers, 260
Seeds, 43
Seismology, 268-270
Senate committees, 29
Senior Executive Service, 247, 251, 253, 263, 264
Service Contract Appeals Board, 258
Service Corps of Retired Executives (SCORE), 56, 57
Sewage sludge, 184, 185
Sewers, 184, 185
Sexually transmitted diseases, 27, 231. *See also* Acquired immune deficiency syndrome
Shareware and freeware
　anti-virus utilities, 13, 115, 116, 171, 186, 255
　communication programs, 4, 42, 59, 70, 112, 115, 116, 121, 134, 233, 253, 255, 271
　comprehensive offerings, 110-116, 121, 154, 166, 188, 263, 271
　decompression utilities, 4, 42, 59, 116, 171, 233, 253, 255
　echo conferences on, 121
　education, 131-132
　emergency management, 139
　games, 112, 113
　graphics, 112, 115
　libraries management, 33, 35
　nutritional content of food, 227
　photography, 280
　small aircraft, 296
　small business, 57
　tax return preparation, 95
　time services, 282, 283

Windows fonts, 240
word processing, 112, 113, 115, 271
Shipping and navigation, 303-307
Shipwrecks, 303
Silicon, 86
Silver, 86
Skin cancer, 225
Small Airplane Directorate, 296
Small business
   comprehensive information, 55-57, 202
   congressional jurisdiction, 202
   handbook and other publications, 27, 188, 261
   innovation research programs, 57, 78
   rural entrepreneurship, 43
   technology transfer programs, 78
   SBA Online, 55-57
Small Business Administration (SBA), 55-57, 188
*Small Business Advocate,* 56
Small Business Committee, House, 202
Small Business Development Centers, 56, 57
Small Business Innovation Research (SBIR) programs, 78
Small Business Technology Transfer (SBTT) programs, 78
Small Computer Support Center, 116
*Small-Scale Ag Today,* 41
SmartComm, 136
Smoking, 27, 231
Social Security, 59, 202
Social Security Administration, 96
Socioeconomic Research and Analysis Program, 189
Sociology, 266
Soda ash, 86
Soil, 177, 267
Solar activities, 279
Solid waste, 166, 169, 170
Solid Waste and Emergency Response, Office of, 160, 170
South Africa, 201
South America, 24
South Asia, 24
South Dakota, 68
*Southeastern Biological Control Working Group,* 46
Southwestern U.S., 66

Soviet Union countries, 44, 65
Spacecraft Environmental Anomalies Handbook, 272
Space Environment Laboratory, 279
Space Physics Data Facility, 278
Space science and exploration
   aeronautical charts, 276
   aerospace industry, 59
   educational materials, 273, 274
   modeling software, 272
   pictures and images, 21, 273, 275, 278
   small business innovation research, 78
   solar and geomagnetic activity, 279
   space commercialization, 202
   spacecraft missions, 273-275, 278
   technology transfer, 78, 275
Space Shuttle Earth Observation Program, 267
Spanish language publications, 27, 119, 180, 223
Special interest groups (SIGs), 58, 181-182
*Special Internet Connections* (Yanoff), 33, 234
Speech problems, 231
Spelling programs, 132
Spinal cord injury, 231, 234
Sports, 43, 240
Spreadsheets, 113, 115
SQL validation test service, 108
*SSA/IRS Reporter,* 96
*Staff Judge Advocate's Deskbook,* 121
*Staff Judge Advocate's Handbook,* 121
*Starting a Home Business* (SBA), 188
Star Trek conferences, 121
State and Local Emergency Management Data Users Group (SALEMDUG) BBS, 139-140
State Department, 23-25
State police radio frequencies, 139
*Statistical Abstract of the United States,* 59
Statistical information. *See* specific topics
Statistician job openings, 256
Statistics and Information, Office of (OSI) BBS, 149
Steel industry, 60, 86
Stephen K. Cook and Co., Inc., 201
*STING,* 46
Storm water, 184
Strategic Petroleum Reserve, 147

Straw and hay, 45
Streams and lakes. *See* water entries
Stress, 27, 225, 240
Strokes, 234
Students. *See* Education and training
StuffIt decompression utility, 4
Subsaharan Africa, 24
Submerged Lands Act, 150
Substance abuse. *See* Alcohol abuse and alcoholism; Drugs and drug abuse
Sudden infant death syndrome, 231
Sulfur, 86
SuperCalc, 33
Superfund, 52, 167, 170-172
Superfund Innovative Technology Evaluation (SITE) Emerging Technology Bulletins, 168
*Supervisory Committee Manual,* 92
Support Center for Regulatory Air Models, 158
Supreme Court opinions, 3, 29, 122
*SURANet Guide to Selected Internet Resources,* 33, 234
Surety BBS, 93
Surety guarantees, 57, 93
Surface Mining, Office of, 244
Surface Water Treatment Rule, 165
*Surfing the Internet: An Introduction* (Polly), 33, 234
Surveying and navigation, 306
Survey of Income and Program Participation, 58
Sustainable agriculture, 41, 43, 46, 47, 181
Sustainable development, 167
SWAMI software, 165
Sweet potato whitefly, 47
Synthetic organic chemicals, 90

*Tachinid Times,* 46
Taxation
    Americans with Disabilities Act compliance, tax credits, 238
    congressional jurisdiction, 202
    electronic filing, 94
    income statistics, 97
    information returns, 96
    New England, 70
    rates, 58
    tax forms and instructions, 95, 98
    tax return help programs, 113
Tax-exempt organizations, 97, 202
Teachers. *See* Education and training
Technology. *See* Science and technology; specific technologies
Technology Assessment, Office of (OTA), 21
Technology Innovation Office, 170
Technology transfer, 40, 49, 78, 86, 184-185, 275
Technology Transfer, Office of, 49
Technology Transfer BBS, 10, 184-185
Tech Specs Plus BBS, 151
TEKTRAN (Technology Transfer Automated Retrieval System), 49
Telecommunications
    emergency response, 139-140
    equipment, FCC authorization, 87-88
    forums, 256
    government contracts, 76, 81
    information management, 36
    military conferences, 121
    standards and policies, 31-32, 108, 109
Telecommuting, 34, 195
Telemarketing, 27
Telephone communications, 89, 139
Telephone directories. *See* specific agencies, bulletin boards, and topics
Telephone Time for Computers, 282
Telephone Time Service, 283
Television, 88, 139
Tennessee, 67
Terminally ill relatives, 240
Terrorist groups, 25
Test writing programs, 132
Texas, 66, 139, 154
Textiles and fabrics, 60, 64, 71
Text standards, 103
Thallium, 86
*There's Gold in Them Thar Networks! or Searching for Treasure in All the Wrong Places,* 234
Threatened and endangered species, 167
TIGER (Topologically Integrated Geographic Encoding Reference), 58
Time services, 282, 283
Tin, 86
Titanium, 86
Titanium dioxide, 60

Tobacco, 44
Topography, 267
Total Coliform Rule, 165
Total quality management, 263, 264, 293
Toxic materials. *See* Chemicals; Hazardous materials and waste
Toxic Release Inventory, 135, 156, 158
Trade and marketing
　agricultural, 40, 42, 43, 44, 65
　biological exports, 230
　census and economic data, 59, 63-65
　congressional jurisdiction, 202
　Customs information, 71-72
　energy imports, 146
　export financing, 73
　export-import price index, 63
　export licensing, 74
　FDA import detention summaries, 216
　fish and seafood, 91
　promotional information, 62
　Russia and newly independent states, 65
　small business, 57
Trade Information Center, 74
*Trademark Manual of Examining Procedure,* 54
Trademarks, 54
Trade Opportunity Program, 64
Trade Representative Office, 61, 64
Training. *See* Education and training
Transfer protocols, 6-7, 10, 14, 288
Transportation
　aircraft. *See* Aviation and aircraft
　automobiles. *See* Motor vehicles
　disabled persons, 233, 300
　emergency response, 139
　hazardous materials, 136, 137
　highways, 138, 300-302
　labor relations, 260
　urban transit, 138
　waterways, 303-307
Transportation Department (DOT), 136, 137, 234, 304, 291, 292
Transportation equipment industry, 60, 64
Travel, 23-25, 64
Treasury bills, bonds, and notes, 63, 93
Treasury Department, 61, 63, 64, 93, 205
*Treasury Financial Manual,* 205
Treatment Alternative to Street Crime (TASC) programs, 119

Trout, 181
Trucking industry, 60, 306
Truth in Savings Act, 92
Tuberculosis, 214, 231
Tungsten, 86
Turbokeys, 7
Turkey, 262
2000 Census SIG, 58
Typing tutors, 113, 132

Ulysses spacecraft mission, 273
Underground storage tanks, 170
Unemployment compensation, 202
Unemployment statistics, 63, 66-68, 260, 261
UNESCO, 202
Unidentified flying objects (UFOs), 37, 274
United Nations, 201
United Parcel Service, 113
Universal Time Coordinated, 282, 283
Universities and colleges. *See* Education and training
University of Maine, 70
University of Michigan, 61
University of Rhode Island AVHRR Inventory, 267
Unix, 95
Uranium, 146
Uranus, 273
Urban transportation, 138
Urological disorders, 231
U.S. and Foreign Commercial Service, 62, 64
U.S. Code, 138
U.S. EPA Region 10 BBS, 167
U.S. Information Center, 119
Usenet Newsgroups, 124
User manuals, 9-10, 179, 180, 184, 288. *See also* specific bulletin boards
*Using Networked Information Resources: A Bibliography,* 234
Utah, 75, 207
Utility companies, 144-145
Utility software
　DOS and IBM-compatible, 28, 34, 90, 104, 111, 113, 115, 121, 122, 140, 166, 167, 169, 178, 185, 206, 210, 263, 271, 293, 298
　modem checking, 139

other or unspecified systems, 90, 105, 121, 140, 169, 271, 273, 280
See also specific utilities

Vacation planners, 113
Vacuum sewers, 185
Vanadium, 86
VA Vendor BBS, 84
Vegetables, 44
Vegetarian nutrition, 43
Venture capital, 202
Venus, 273
Vermont, 70
Veterans
 echo conferences, 121
 employment, 247, 250, 251, 255, 257, 262
 small business assistance, 57
Veterans Affairs Department, 84
Veterans Employment and Training Service, 262
Veterinary medicine, 214-216
Vice president, 21
Video display terminals, 261
Vietnam, 64, 201
Virginia Polytechnic Institute and State University, 48
Viruses, biological, 218
Viruses, computer, 13
 anti-virus software, 113, 115, 116, 132, 171, 180, 185, 186, 250, 255
 conferences and bulletins, 95, 106-107, 110, 240
VIRUS-L Digest, 107
Visa information, 24
Vision disorders, 231, 239, 240
Vocabulary games, 132
Vocational rehabilitation, 241
Volunteer projects, 182
Voyager spacecraft mission, 273
VSterm communications software, 49

Wage Appeals Board, 258
Wages and salaries, 64, 132, 252, 256, 258, 263-264
Warning messages, 5-6
Washington, 167, 195, 207, 251
Washington Area Service Network (WASNET), 257

Washington, D.C., information, 138, 195, 225
 jobs list, 257, 260
Waste management. See Hazardous materials and waste
Wastewater management, 184-186
Wastewater Treatment Information Exchange (WTIE), 186
Water, Office of, 166
Water pollution
 bibliographic database, 160
 nonpoint source, 179-183
 software models, 177
 wastewater management, 184-186
Water quality, 40, 41, 43, 167, 184
Water resources
 drinking water, 43, 167, 180, 184
 general information, 138
 regulatory agenda, 166
 software models, 178
 watershed management, 183
Watershed Restoration SIG, 181, 182
*WaterTalk* newsletter, 167
Waterways transportation, 303-307
Ways and Means Committee, House, 202
Weather and climate
 general information, 37, 135, 276-277
 global change, 83, 266, 267, 276
 global warming, 113, 181
 disaster assistance, 139
 research, 182
 satellite images, 21
Weeds, 43, 46-47
Weight control, 43, 113
West Coast, federal job openings, 251
West Virginia Research and Training Center, 238, 239
Wetlands, 43, 167, 179, 180, 184, 186
Wetlands, Oceans, and Watersheds, Office of, 183
Wheelchairs, 233
White House
 documents, 20, 21, 29, 56, 57
 press releases, 179, 201
White House HIV/AIDS Policy BBS, 229
Wholesale businesses, 139
Wildflowers, 43
Windows software, 95, 110, 240
Wisconsin, 68

Women
  adolescent pregnancy, 43
  in agriculture, 43
  AIDS, 231
  alcoholism, 232
  in clinical trials, 215
  consumer information, 27
  education, 127
  employment, 260, 261
  health education professionals, 211
  health issues, 231
  in science, 37, 83
  small business, 57, 188
  wife abuse, 27
*Women Business Ownership* (SBA), 188
Women's Bureau, 260
Wood cutting boards, 219
Woodstoves, 158
WordPerfect utilities, 121, 180
Word processing programs, 4, 112, 113, 115, 132, 271

Workers' compensation, 260
Work issues. *See* employment entries
World Criminal Justice Library Network, 119
World Wide Web, 20
Writing, 240

Xmodem protocol, 7
X-ray machines, 212

Yanoff, Scott, 33
Ymodem protocol, 7
Yogurt making, 41
Youth. *See* Children and families

*Zen and the Art of the Internet,* 33, 234
Zinc, 86
ZIP extension, 4
Zmodem protocol, 7
Zterm communications program, 4

# How to Access the Federal Government on the Internet
## Washington Online

By Bruce Maxwell

**COMING SOON! Internet Access to Government Information**

A wealth of federal government information is available to the public for free on the Internet. This new book provides detailed descriptions of more than 250 Internet sites, mailing lists, databases, and other resources.

*The book describes how to access:*

- Text files that offer speeches by President Clinton, the proposed federal budget, the full text of bills being considered by Congress
- Lists of holdings at the National Archives
- State Department travel advisories
- Census data
- Lists of federal job openings nationwide and overseas
- A wide range of information about AIDS
- Economic data
- Federal income tax forms
- Hundreds of thousands of images from NASA, the Library of Congress, and other agencies
- Electronic card catalogs at numerous federal libraries, including the Library of Congress and the National Library of Medicine, and the Environmental Protection Agency's library
- Mailing lists that automatically deliver news to your Internet account from NASA, the Census Bureau, the Centers for Disease Control, and other agencies
- Searchable databases that track bills as they proceed through Congress, list all publications produced by the Government Printing Office, offer the full text of the CIA World Factbook, and provide access to hundreds of White House documents

Some of this information is available on expensive commercial databases. But on the Internet, the information is free. *How to Access the Federal Government on the Internet* is written in easy-to-understand language that makes it useful to Internet newcomers and experienced pros alike. A glossary offers simple definitions of the language of the Internet, and an extensive index helps you quickly zero in on the information you're seeking.

## Order Today!

☐ Yes! Send me ____ copies of *How to Access the Federal Government on the Internet: Washington Online* at $19.95 each as soon as the book is available in May 1995. (Paperback. Approx. 250 pages. ISBN 1-56802-034-1.)

☐ Check enclosed for $_____, payable to Congressional Quarterly (Free shipping in continental U.S. if you include payment)

☐ Charge my (circle one) VISA  MasterCard  in the amount of $_____ (Free shipping in continental U.S.)

Acct.# _____ Exp.Date _____

Signature _____

DC addressees add 5.75% sales tax; NJ addressees add 6%.
Prices subject to change

Name _____

Phone (required) _____

Organization _____

Street address (required) _____

City _____ State ____ Zip _____

Mail to:  **Congressional Quarterly Books**
Dept. U82
1414 22nd St., N.W.
Washington, D.C. 20037

Or call toll-free to order **1-800-638-1710** • In Metropolitan D.C. call **202-822-1475** • Fax order to **202-887-6706**

**CQ  Congressional Quarterly Books**
Washington, D.C.